High Risk Clients

Evidence-based Assessment & Clinical Tools to Recognize and Effectively Respond to Mental Health Crises

Paul Brasler, MA, MSW, LCSW

Copyright © 2019 Paul Brasler

Published by
PESI Publishing & Media
PESI, Inc.
3839 White Ave
Eau Claire, WI 54703

Cover Design: Amy Rubenzer
Layout: Bookmasters & Amy Rubenzer

Proudly printed in the United States of America

ISBN: 9781683731986

PESI
Publishing
& Media
pesipublishing.com

About the Author

 **Paul Brasler**, MA, MSW, LCSW, has worked in community mental health settings, hospital settings (inpatient behavioral health and an emergency department), juvenile drug court, private practice, foster care, and adolescent residential treatment throughout his career. Paul is the head of behavioral health for Daily Planet Health Services, a nonprofit community health center serving the Greater Richmond area. Paul is president of Providence Consulting & Education, LLC, through which he provides clinical supervision and professional education services. He regularly conducts a variety of trainings for his community and across the country. Paul is also a highly regarded adjunct faculty member in the Graduate Social Work program at Virginia Commonwealth University. He teaches advanced clinical courses on serious mental illness and a course on substance abuse interventions.

Paul and his wife, Claire, a licensed professional counselor and pediatric trauma nurse, proudly call Richmond home and are busy raising three energetic boys and one apathetic dog. In his free time, Paul enjoys running, trying new craft beers, anything outdoors, and playing electric bass.

Paul is available for questions or follow for information updates: facebook.com/paulbbrasler or email him at paulbrasler.author@gmail.com.

For Claire, who taught me the most important thing.

For this is all a dream we dreamed
One afternoon long ago.

—Phil Lesh and Robert Hunter, *Box of Rain*

Table of Contents

Acknowledgements

There are many individuals and organizations that have shaped my life and have made this book possible.

To the three greatest teachers in my life, my sons, Sam, Ben, and Eli: I am humbled and amazed as I watch you grow into young men. You have each taught me more about living and loving than you will ever know. You keep me humble and make me laugh and always remind me what is truly important in life. Thanks for sacrificing some of our time together so I could write this.

To my father, Mark Brasler: Thank you for instilling in me a sense of justice and fairness and the value of hard work. To my mother, Keitha Brasler: Thank you for teaching me that people (every person) matters no matter what they have been through. To my stepparents, Mary and Mary-Ann: Thank you for your unconditional love and encouragement. To my brothers, Kevin and Greg: Thank you for your kindness and for being the awesome fathers you are. To my sisters, Jenn and Michelle: Thanks for all the good talks we've had and more to come. To my mother-in-law, Cecil: Thank you for showing such great patience with the many ways the boys and I try to imitate your British accent.

To Sharon Saunders, the first (and greatest) social worker I ever met: Thank you for inspiring me to accept the challenges of helping people and taking the risks that are a part of being a clinical social worker.

To Mr. Wilson from Waggener High School, who convinced me I could write.

To the organizations for which I have worked: The opportunities and challenges you provided me have shaped this book. This includes Camp Alkulana, County Line Baptist Church, United Methodist Family Services, Chesterfield County Mental Health Support Services, Medical and Counseling Associates, Bon Secours, Virginia Commonwealth University, and Daily Planet Health Services. I want to especially recognize the staff of Richmond Community Hospital's emergency department—you do so much for so many people with very few resources. I also want to thank my team at Daily Planet Health Services for their support and encouragement.

To Dr. Bruce Stevens: Thanks for your friendship, passion for psychiatry, and strong, unwavering ethics and commitment to people impacted by mental illness. To Dr. Robin Whelpley: Thank you for your fascination with all things chemical and your patience in helping me understand the basics of pharmacology. To Dr. Lucas English: Thanks for your friendship and dedication to people that most of society would just as soon overlook.

To Dr. Stacy Williams: Thank you for never taking no for an answer and for caring deeply about your coworkers and patients.

To the great folks at PESI: Claire Zelasko—for coming up with the idea for a training on mental health emergencies and taking a chance on me. To Hillary Jenness—for your hard work and encouragement with this book. To Kate Sample—for the title.

To the amazing Priscilla Witwer—for your willingness to edit this book, pointing things out to me that I needed to see and taking me to task when I needed that, as well as reminding me to keep the big picture in mind.

To my friends at Seal Team Physical Training, Inc.: Hoo-Yah (they understand).

To Kevin, Manda, Lucy, and Peter: The only people with whom we could vacation on a regular basis (even when I blow the commanding cornhole lead—sorry, Kevin). Thanks for being on "standby" for our boys.

To my other friends who have encouraged me and supported me along the way. To Marc, who'd lie down in traffic for me and me for him.

To the Grateful Dead, the soundtrack for this book.

Finally, to the love of my life: my wonderful wife, Claire. Thank you for loving me unconditionally despite my many flaws. Thank you for encouraging me to write this book and providing me the time to do so. Thank you for journeying through life with me. It has been, and continues to be, an awesome, amazing adventure. You are as beautiful today as when we were married.

Preface

I have found that there is not a lot of training or education about clients in crisis—people I refer to as *high-risk clients*—particularly for newer clinicians. Despite the need for clinicians to be able to recognize and intervene in crisis situations, many counseling education programs and schools of social work provide little of this training. Thus, even experienced counselors may feel poorly equipped to help people in crisis (Sawyer, Peters, & Willis, 2013).

This text was developed from courses I have taught for PESI since 2016: *Mental Health Emergencies* and *High-Risk Clients*. It is built around the stories of real people I have encountered in my clinical practice (and some in my personal life as well). My hope is that you will find new ways to recognize and engage people who are experiencing a mental health emergency and that the materials in this book will assist you in helping those who are struggling with high-risk situations.

I obviously do not know every clinician's environment or client population. As I say at the beginning of my PESI talks, you know your clients and your environment best. If you do something that works better for you, keep doing it. You must follow the legal and ethical guidelines of your profession as well as the accepted guidelines of your practice and/or agency. I've found that a heavy dose of plain common sense is helpful as well.

CHAPTER 1

What Is a Crisis?

Go through and place an X beside each of the following situations that you believe constitutes a crisis:

____ Lost car keys   ____ Heroin overdose

____ Death of a dog or cat   ____ Retirement

____ Death of a parent   ____ Loss of religious faith

____ Fired from your job   ____ Birth of a child

____ Friend's suicide   ____ One of your parents is an alcoholic

____ Diagnosis of cancer   ____ You see a snake

____ Graduation from college   ____ Confronted by a person wielding a knife

____ Failing out of school   ____ Dropped cell phone into the toilet

____ Broken engagement   ____ Positive pregnancy test

____ Turning 30 (or 40, 50, etc.)

Which of the above can be considered a crisis?

All of them.

Crisis Defined and Crisis Formation

Crisis is a subjective term. What one person considers a crisis is in fact a crisis, even if others do not perceive the situation the same way. We could all agree that a person who is experiencing suicidal ideation is in crisis, but what about the person who just dropped their cell phone in the toilet, losing all their valuable information? In what ways could that be a crisis? Or what about the nurse who has a phobia of bedbugs who gets assigned to a patient with bedbugs? How would that be a crisis for him?

     If we agree that many situations can be considered crises, we next need to define the term *crisis*. Let's start with a broad definition of the word, provided by the "father of modern crisis intervention," Gerald Caplan (1961): "An obstacle that is, for a time, insurmountable by the use of customary methods of problem solving. A period of disorganization ensues, a period of upset, during which many abortive attempts at a solution are made" (James & Gilliland, 2013, p. 18). Caplan makes it clear that a crisis develops through a distinct process that can happen quickly or over an extended period. While we can sometimes determine the source or reason for the crisis, this is not always the case. What is clear, however, is that a crisis involves a series of steps, which Kanel (2012) describes as the trilogy definition of the process of crisis formation.

Use the case study below as an example to take a closer look at this process:

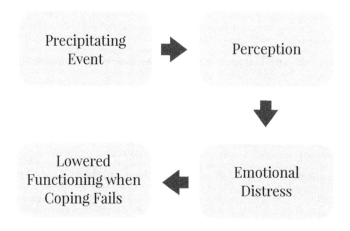

CASE STUDY–ANA

IDENTIFYING A CRISIS

Ana was a new client and was sitting in the waiting room of my clinic.

"I came here because I went to the emergency room last night after I'd had a panic attack. The doctor said I should come here today," she explained. Ana said that she had been diagnosed with bipolar disorder in the past. Her speech was pressured, and her thoughts seemed to wander. She described having made three previous suicide attempts, two of which required hospitalization.

As the interview progressed, Ana gradually opened up, but she required a lot of redirection from me. Ana admitted to current heroin and "bath salts" use. A former counselor, whom Ana trusted, had been able to get Ana to talk about the sexual abuse by her stepfather when she was a child.

"I also sometimes think I can hear things that no one else can," she continued. "And I'm afraid," she shuddered as she whispered. "He's out there, and he's coming for me." Ana started to cry loudly and got up to leave the room.

Precipitating Event. This is when a new or existing situation elicits a response from an individual or community. Ana reported having had a panic attack the night before, so that could have been the precipitating event, or it may have been something about which she and the clinician are unaware.

Perception. This is an individual's understanding of the precipitating event based on facts or beliefs and the meaning derived from these facts or beliefs. Ana's situation was confusing, as we are not sure of her thought process. She appeared to be in a manic or hypomanic state. Was she experiencing delusions, obsessions, or intrusive thoughts? She appeared to have experienced trauma, as she was fearful that she would be harmed by "him." If Ana's thought process and content are compromised by mental illness, her perception of a crisis event (or any event for that matter) could be skewed.

Emotional Distress. This occurs when how we perceive the intensity of an event leads to a negative emotional response. Instead of considering the precipitating event from a cognitive perspective, the individual's emotions are engaged and cause an increased negative perception about their situation. The two processes of emerging emotions and perceptions are reflective and supportive of each other, which increases the person's reaction.

Ana was clearly emotionally distressed, even if we are not certain of what her thought process was. Her emotional distress, combined with what appears to be a mental health disorder, fed into her crisis process to the point that she was trying to leave the initial assessment appointment. As we can see, once the cognitive brain is unable to immediately resolve questions, the emotional brain takes over, and the perception of the precipitating events is magnified into a crisis.

Lowered Functioning as Coping Fails. As the person's negative perception and emotional distress increase, their ability to cope fails, at which point their ability to function decreases, often markedly. For Ana, this process triggered her fight-or-flight response. While the initial impact of a crisis can be negative, if the person is able to rebound from it, there can be both positive and negative outcomes from the experience. Thus, a crisis has a variety of (sometimes contradictory yet still valid) characteristics (Kanel, 2012).

Characteristics of a Crisis

Presence of Both Danger and Opportunity, as Well as Seeds for Change and Growth.
A crisis can be overtly dangerous, such as in situations when someone is being violent toward themselves or others. A crisis can also highlight a hidden danger, such as when a person is confused and has slurred speech, indicating a possible stroke. Furthermore, a crisis with apparent and/or hidden risks can be an opportunity for growth, particularly once the person has emerged from the immediate dangers of the crisis.

Complicated Symptomology. Even the most seemingly "simple" or "basic" emergency is complicated because it is often a "big deal" for the person experiencing it. Ana presents with pressured speech and requires a lot of redirection from the clinician. This could be caused by any number of substances of misuse and/or mental illness and/or trauma: the presenting situation is complicated. Even in situations outside of a clinical setting, seemingly "simple" situations can be more than they appear. While waiting to board a flight last year, a passenger behind me realized he had lost his phone, which had his boarding pass on it. He started to panic. On the surface, this was something as basic as a lost phone, but imagine all the implications there could be for that individual.

No Panaceas or Quick Fixes. While a crisis can occur rapidly, the solutions to the crisis usually take time to implement, and the person often needs time to adjust to a new reality after the crisis. In our fast-paced society, many people seek simple, one-step solutions. Since most crisis situations are not simple, we can safely say that there are no quick fixes.

Resiliency. The ability to persevere despite terrible things happening is a basic definition of resiliency. Crisis situations can create opportunities for resilience to occur. The thousands of studies, articles, and various works discussing resiliency all look at the numerous factors that contribute to some children, who have gone through horrific experiences, emerging stronger. One of the common factors for kids who are resilient is that there was at least one adult who cared about them unconditionally. Adults, as well as children, can be resilient, provided they have the right support. Not everyone demonstrates resiliency in the aftermath of a crisis, but many people can and do. We must remember that any crisis can lead to resiliency and growth—in ourselves and others.

Types of Crisis Situations

In addition to the distinctive characteristics of a crisis, there are several types of crisis situations. These include developmental, situational, existential, and ecosystemic crises. An individual or community may experience one or more at any given time.

Developmental Crises. The normal flow of human growth includes changes and shifts throughout one's life and can be experienced as points of crisis. Some examples include graduation from high school or college, birth of a child, death of a loved one, divorce, retirement, and aging milestones. Note that many of these crises are generally considered positive events, such as graduation or the birth of a child, but they can be perceived and emotionally experienced as a crisis.

Situational Crises. Nearly everyone will experience an uncommon and extraordinary event that occurs randomly and without warning at some point in their lives. Some events have a higher probability of occurrence, such as a relationship breakup, illness (medical and/or mental), injury, job termination, and car accidents. Other examples of devastating situational crises include a house fire, death of a child, severe weather (e.g., hurricane, tornado, flood, or blizzard), and terrorist attacks.

Existential Crises. When a person experiences an inner conflict that raises issues related to their purpose, responsibility, freedom, choices made, or place in the world, they are having an existential crisis. A spiritual crisis would also fall under this category. The person having a spiritual crisis may be pondering and/or questioning why there is pain in the world, what is one's relationship with God, or why people die and what happens to their soul afterward.

Ecosystemic Crises. This type of crisis involves a group or community of people simultaneously experiencing the same conditions, which may be ecological, political, or economic. Examples of ecological events include drought, disease epidemic, and toxic pollution (e.g., lead in the water supply, an oil spill). Political events include discontinuation of human services, lack of access to education or health care, war, genocide, and refugee. Examples of economic events include closure of factories, stock market fraud, devaluation of currency, and economic recession/depression.

A crisis need not fit into a single type of category. An individual could easily experience a situational crisis (e.g., car accident) during a development crisis (e.g., a divorce), which could also be causing an existential crisis (e.g., spiritual crisis). Experiencing one or multiple types of crises may result in a mental health emergency.

When a Crisis Becomes a Mental Health Emergency

A crisis becomes a mental health emergency when its severity or circumstances require professional intervention. Mental health emergencies can be chronic (long term) or acute (short term). High-risk clients are those who experience a mental health emergency. The focus of the clinical intervention may be to avoid harm, such as when a person is unable to care for themselves and/or is suicidal or homicidal. The focus of the intervention could also be to determine the cause of the emergency as well as any precipitating events. Is the mental health emergency due to a medical condition, substance abuse, or trauma? Whereas the presenting symptoms of a high-risk client can be related to an existing mental illness, the cause is often more than a diagnosed mental illness alone.

The Six Ways That Individuals Respond to Crisis

People respond to crises, and stressful situations, in specific ways. How people respond to a crisis could be due to their personality, culture, upbringing, or any number of other factors. Although there may be more than six ways that people respond to a crisis, for the purposes of this text, we will focus on the following six reactions.

Aggression. This is often demonstrated by a physical or verbal attack on others or oneself. Examples include the following:

- "I am going to kill you"
- Suicidal ideation or attempt
- Self-harming as a maladaptive coping mechanism
- Physical assault or attempted assault

- Verbal assault or threats
- Throwing objects, punching walls

Passive-Aggressive. A person acting passive-aggressively typically demonstrates their response to crisis by verbal statements or subtle behaviors. The individual is often afraid or unsure of their own aggressive feelings and displays these emotions in ways to try to get others to act out their aggression:

- "I'm sorry, I thought you were a doctor, not just a social worker"
- Consistently late to appointments; undermines their success

Passive (Dependent). Individuals who respond this way become completely dependent on other people to act for them and even speak for them. They are often frozen in their own inaction:

- "You are so smart, what do you think I should do?"
- Silence

Depression. This response can include a major depressive episode and other dysphoric symptoms, or may include sadness, crying, somatic complaints, and appetite or sleep disturbances:

- Malaise: "Whatever …"
- Anhedonia
- Sleep and appetite disturbances are common

Psychosis. Psychotic symptoms include disorganized thoughts, hallucinations, and delusions. This response indicates a mental health emergency in most cases. Some people develop psychosis independently of a crisis (e.g., those with a psychotic illness such as schizophrenia). Every person has the capacity to become psychotic when placed under enough stress, deprived of sleep, or experiencing certain medical or mental health emergencies. Aggressive behaviors can also occur.

Catatonia. This response indicates a mental health emergency in all cases. Catatonia is the disconnection with external reality. We will examine the symptoms and different types of catatonia in Chapter 4.

Who Are High-Risk Clients?

Clients experiencing a mental health emergency are obvious high-risk clients. Of special concern are situations in which the life or safety of the client and/or others is in danger. This could be due to a medical problem that presents as a mental health issue or to an overdose on a substance of misuse. High-risk clients also include people who are violent and/or suicidal.

Clinicians must also remember that *every client* could be a high-risk client. I get irritated when I talk with clinicians who say that they only want to work with the "worried well." My usual response is to ask, "What will you do if you are faced with someone who is more than 'worried well?'" "What happens when a 'stable' client experiences a crisis or major life change;

they become a high-risk client?" Sometimes they stop to think this over, and a few times I have had people say, "Refer out."

Although I agree that some clients, and some mental health problems (e.g., eating disorders), require specially trained and equipped clinicians, quality clinicians should be prepared to deal with the majority of problems that clients bring to treatment. This includes clients dealing with suicidal or homicidal ideation, clients with extensive trauma histories, and clients with substance use disorders. Quality clinicians are prepared to deal with the problems of real people. Clinicians also need to remember that before they begin working with people, two things **must** be present:

- The clinician must give a damn. Clinicians must like people in general, regardless of the client's circumstances or behaviors or the opinions of the therapist.

- Clinicians should find something to like in the person with whom they are working and connect with them on a human level.

I tell my graduate students that their clients care nothing about their degrees, certifications, grade point average, or interests outside of school. They care about two things:

1. "Do you care about me as a person?" and,

2. "Are you competent to do your job?"

While my job is to help students and professionals become more competent, I have yet to find a way to teach someone how to care about people. This is something that must come from the individual and their value system.

Like many of my peers, I have met and even had to work with other clinicians who were either burned out or just didn't seem to care for their clients (or people in general). I remember thinking of one peer, "This person shouldn't be working with mammals, let alone people." Finding something to like about the person in crisis and having concern for their well-being cannot be omitted or substituted. The therapeutic relationship, no matter how brief, is key for the client's progress (Norcross, 2010, p. 114): "We can operationally define the *client-therapist relationship* as the feelings and attitudes that therapist and client have toward one another and how these are expressed."

Now that we have identified several types of crises and differentiated mental health emergencies from the broader types of crises, how do we work with high-risk clients? In my experience with a variety of crisis situations in different environments, there are specific things that the clinician can do to diffuse the crisis, calm the person down, and help connect with them. The following steps are presented in no particular order.

How to Approach a Person in Crisis

For eight years, I worked in several medical emergency departments (EDs) conducting comprehensive psychiatric evaluations. I found that using these steps helped me to connect with people experiencing a mental health emergency, or in the very least, to de-escalate a tense situation. They also helped me to keep myself and others safe, especially when working with an agitated person.

1. **Is the environment safe?** How safe is it for you and the client? What can you or other people do to make it a safer environment? If the environment is not safe, should you try to engage the client or wait for help? I am a firm believer in getting help when needed.

This is especially true for clinicians who work in the community or in clients' homes. If a situation does not seem safe, it probably is not. Seek help if you are unsure.

2. **Assume an open posture,** with your hands clearly visible and down at your sides, not clasped in front of you or behind your back. A client who is psychotic or paranoid may already assume that you wish to harm them. Seeing your hands in an open, relaxed, and palms-out position shows them you are not carrying anything. Having your hands in your pockets suggests you might be hiding something. Also, having your hands out and to your sides allows you to protect yourself should the client become violent.

3. **Make sure you have access to an exit,** while also not "cornering" your client and preventing them from having a safe exit as well.

4. **If the client appears to be calm, offer to shake their hand (but understand if the client refuses to shake your hand), introduce yourself, and ask what they would like to be called.**

5. **Again, if it appears safe, sit down in a position that is nonthreatening and safe for the client and yourself.** I sit at least three to four feet away from the client, and at a slight angle so I am not facing them head on. This tends to reduce pressure on the client as they do not feel as if they are being interrogated.

6. **Offer them something to drink and ask if they are comfortable.**

7. **Use positive language by being polite and respectful.** This usually goes far in building rapport.

8. **Go low** (lower the volume of your voice).

9. **Go slow** (slow the pace and speed of your voice). "Going low and slow" is something I learned by watching more experienced clinicians when I started my career. I noticed how I quickly reacted to anxious and energetic clients and how this usually made the interaction unhelpful. By slowing down, especially our speech, our clients typically mirror this and calm themselves down.

10. **Be honest;** tell the truth.

11. **Listen.**

12. **Ask a combination of closed-ended questions**, which often helps the person to focus, and leads to open-ended questions. How can I help you today? How long has this problem been going on for you? What has worked for you before? Who else knows you feel this way? Notice that some of these questions can be answered with a simple answer, while other questions require greater explanation from the client. All of the questions, however, provide opportunities for further discussion between clinician and client.

CHAPTER 2

Assessment

All approaches to a mental health emergency start with a comprehensive assessment. This includes gaining a clear understanding of the presenting problem, the client's perception of the problem, and additional information provided by people who support or know the client. The assessment also includes a mental status exam (MSE), a trauma assessment, and a substance use assessment. Given that we are dealing with high-risk clients experiencing a mental health emergency, detailed family history and cognitive exams are typically abbreviated during the initial assessment and obtained later. We examine the assessment process through the following case study.

CASE STUDY–VERNON

ASSESSMENT

Vernon was a 31-year-old man who was brought to the ER by his girlfriend. He stated that he had stopped using prescription opioids eight days earlier. Vernon had been selling and using opioids for the past 11 years. He believed he was going through opioid withdrawal, and he described his symptoms as problems managing his behaviors, especially his anger. Curiously, he did not endorse any symptoms related to a typical opioid withdrawal profile, which would normally include nausea, vomiting, diarrhea, cold sweats, body aches, sleep disturbance, and a variety of additional symptoms that are examined in Chapter 9.

Vernon was polite when I entered the room, and he consented to allow his blood to be drawn. He appeared to be disheveled, but his clothing was clean and his hygiene appeared to be good. He was sitting in a chair across from the hospital bed in his room, and his girlfriend was standing to his right. I sat across from him so that we both had access to the open door, which was to his left and my right. A nurse stood behind me. Vernon then started rapidly talking about "my friend, the professor." He started to cry as

---

he spoke about the professor's intelligence and how he (Vernon) felt he "let the professor down." Vernon started to shout at someone who was not present, looking over his left shoulder and toward the ceiling. After several attempts, I redirected him to focus on me, but I struggled to keep him focused during the rest of the interview.

Vernon said that he believed someone else was in the room (besides the nurse, Vernon's girlfriend, Vernon, and me), and he was upset that no one else could hear this person. As I noted later in my written record, Vernon was clearly responding to internal stimuli as evidenced by thought blocking, and he appeared to be delusional. Vernon correctly stated that the day of the week was Friday, but he was unable to name the correct year and the current president. He added that he came to the hospital for help, so he consented to let me speak with his girlfriend. He then resumed engaging the professor in conversation.

Vernon's girlfriend said that she has known him for eight years and has never seen him like this. She said that this behavior had not occurred until eight days ago, and Vernon's actions had gotten worse over that timeframe. Vernon's girlfriend added that he had pending charges for distribution of opioids, and his first court appearance was scheduled for two weeks from the present day.

Vernon appeared to be psychotic and in need of services. While Vernon was receiving a computerized tomography (CT) scan of the head, he began to be more responsive to his delusions. Interestingly, when Vernon first came into the ER. he specifically said, "I am having delusions and hallucinations." However, during his interview with me, he did not report this, but rather was acting as if he were experiencing hallucinations and delusions.

As indicated in the case study, Vernon presented as someone who was acutely psychotic. He said that he was hearing a distinct voice, and he consistently looked to the same part of the room when he said he heard the voice. There was no evidence of any previous psychotic episodes, but this could have been his first "break."

Vernon could also have been under the influence of any number of substances. His urine drug screen revealed that he was negative for each of the drugs tested; however, there are many chemicals that urine drug screens do not or cannot detect (Cary, 2012). He claimed that he had stopped using opioids several days earlier, but his symptoms were not consistent with opioid detoxification (Rose, 2012). It was possible that Vernon was experiencing atypical withdrawal symptoms, but this would be unusual. It was also possible that Vernon was using or had used a different drug than he had intended, which was causing his symptoms.

Another concern was that Vernon could have been suffering from a medical condition that was manifesting as a mental health problem. Vernon's vital signs were normal for a person of his age. His blood work did not reveal any infections or other abnormalities. The attending physician ordered a CT scan of his head to rule out a stroke, brain bleed, or brain tumor. The results of these medical tests revealed no abnormalities that could suggest a medical cause for Vernon's symptoms.

I had to seriously consider that Vernon was malingering; or feigning a psychiatric illness for secondary gain. My reasons for thinking this were that Vernon did not have a history of psychosis and he stated in triage that he was "having hallucinations and delusions." A person experiencing psychosis typically believes that what they are sensing is real and would not think they were experiencing mental health symptoms. Vernon had an upcoming court date that he may have been trying to avoid; so, he could have been seeking admission to a psychiatric facility to delay his hearing or avoid going to jail altogether.

In the end, I admitted Vernon to the hospital's behavioral health unit, as it appeared his condition was worsening and he would soon be unable to care for himself. His girlfriend shared these concerns as well. I knew it would take time and more information, including observing Vernon on a closed psychiatric unit, to figure out what was happening to him. Here is my provisional admitting diagnosis that includes multiple possibilities:

- Brief psychotic episode
- Psychotic episode due to an unknown or unspecified substance intoxication or withdrawal syndrome
- Malingering

ASSESSMENT

Which of the previous diagnoses do you believe is most accurate? List the symptoms that support your decision.

What else could explain Vernon's symptoms that I might have left out?

Vernon's case is interesting due to its complexity and the variety of things that could have been causing his behaviors. These situations are not uncommon in acute behavioral health centers and EDs. But what about other crisis situations that, while not as grave as Vernon's, still require a comprehensive assessment to determine what is going on?

Let's use Vernon's situation to examine the components of a complete assessment. Keep in mind that assessment is a continuous process—clinicians should constantly reassess their clients, as changes occur throughout treatment. Remember that in crisis situations, the assessment is often completed quickly out of necessity, and some of the more detailed historical information may not be gathered until the client is more stable.

Interviewing the Client

The first meeting with the client is the most important. The initial interview has two main goals: To begin the relationship-building process and to begin gathering information. Both goals can be reached if the client is given the opportunity to tell their story, regardless of their setting. This is sometimes referred to as "meeting the client where they are." This starts with ensuring that the client is comfortable and feels safe. In loud, busy, or chaotic environments like an ER. this can be challenging. However, by planning and communicating with other providers, we can create an area of calm in the middle of a very busy space.

During my work within the hospital system, I typically only saw patients when they presented to the ER. About half of my patients on a given day were returning ones, and the rest were people I was meeting for the first, and possibly only, time. One might ask, **"What is the purpose of focusing on the clinician-patient relationship if I am only going to speak with them this one time?"** My response is that a clinician is not only building an individual professional relationship with the patient but is also building a team/hospital relationship with them. While I was the first mental health clinician the patient encountered, I would not be the only clinician they met and with whom they worked. Therefore, I was building an institutional relationship with them. My hope was that the rapport the patient and I created would be sustained as they worked with psychiatrists, nurses, mental health clinicians, and other social workers if they were admitted.

The interview starts before either the clinician or client says anything. I encourage all clinicians, whether they are new or experienced, to first observe the setting and the initial appearance of the client; this is part of the MSE. It is equally important to be aware of the context in which you will be speaking with the client. Are you on an inpatient psychiatric unit or in the ER? Are you meeting the client in their home, a community center, or your office? Are you able to obtain any information about the client from previous medical records or registration information? (If you have access to any previous information, review it before meeting the client.) Are they seeing you voluntarily? Are they being coerced by someone, or are they being court ordered to see you? On seeing the individual for the first time, what do you observe? Are they sitting, standing, or lying down? (This might be more expected in a hospital setting compared with an outpatient office) Are they awake or asleep? Do they appear to be aware of their surroundings; are they alert or drowsy? How do they respond when you walk into the room?

I start interviews by introducing myself and asking the client what they would like to be called. I also offer to shake their hand unless the client appears to be extremely agitated. If they refuse to shake my hand, I let it go; some people do not like to touch or be touched. When I was in private practice or working in a community mental health setting, I would usually make small talk with the client(s) as I led them back to my office. I often asked, "Did you have any problems finding the office?" since our building was surrounded by identical office buildings. Or, I might say something about the weather.

With most clients, once seated or in the space where we are going to meet, I usually get right to the point by asking, "What brings you here today?" or "How can we help you today?" I used the term *we* in the hospital setting because the staff works as a team. My purpose in being direct is to encourage the client to explain in their own words what they perceive to be the presenting problem.

Vernon initially told the triage nurse that he was experiencing delusions and hallucinations, and his behaviors appeared to support this. Identifying what the client perceives to be the problem provides context and an initial direction for the therapeutic encounter.

After the client states why they are presenting for treatment, I usually let them explain their presenting problem(s) in more detail. I often ask, "How long has this [situation] been a problem?" I then add, "Why are you coming here today to deal with this problem?" Finally, I ask, "Have you ever had to deal with this problem before? If so, how did you handle it then?" I have found that most clients want to explain what is going on in their own words with little interruption; they want to be heard.

Giving them this opportunity helps create a relationship and allows the clinician to begin observing some of the client's mannerisms, thought process, thought content, attention, speech volume, and other factors that are integral parts of the MSE.

Throughout an interview, I ask a mixture of open- and closed-ended questions. This provides the client with additional prompts and encouragement to tell their story in their own way. **Keep in mind that some clients, specifically younger children and people with an intellectual and/or developmental disability, may find it difficult to answer open-ended questions. Closed-ended questions may then be more useful.** However, it is important to understand that many people with moderate to severe intellectual disability may say "yes" to a variety of questions, regardless of the true answer, as they are not used to being asked a lot of questions and they often believe that answering "yes" will please their interviewer. One option that can help with these populations is to ask multiple-choice questions, such as, "Did you drive, ride the bus, or walk to get here today?" (Morrison, 2014).

Identifying Information

In both inpatient and outpatient clinical settings, most patients' identifying information is collected and recorded prior to the clinician's first meeting with them. This information includes the patient's name, address, age, and medical insurance information (if applicable). Additional information is also collected on sex, ethnic identity, and often the presenting problem/ chief complaint.

As clinicians become more aware of and educated about the diversity of gender identity and gender expression, documentation should also reflect how the patient identifies their own gender. I regularly interview clients who were born, or assigned, a sex (female or male) with which they no longer identify. This can cause some confusion with medical records. The patient may consider their birth name to be their "dead name." As a rule, I identify people by the gender pronoun(s) of their preference and address them using their desired names and titles, such as Mr., Ms., Dr., etc.

Additional identifying information includes the client's occupation, education level, and satisfaction with school, work, and home life. Awareness of the context of the referral for services is key in building rapport.

In the hospital setting, a patient must be assessed for, and ideally cleared of, any possible medical illness or physical injury prior to a mental health interview taking place. Some injuries may be obvious, but others are not as apparent.

Once the presenting problem is identified and identifying information is collected, I move on to a lethality assessment or MSE. The choice of where I go next with the assessment depends on the patient's presenting problem. Roughly half of the patients I saw each day in the ER had a chief complaint of suicide attempt or suicidal ideation. I preferred to get right to the lethality assessment in these cases. In many situations in which suicidality is not the presenting problem, I proceed with the MSE, but I still conduct a lethality assessment during any interview.

Identifying Information

Name:

Sex:

Age/Date of Birth:

Ethnicity:

Sexual Orientation:

Gender Identification and Expression:

Occupation:

Education Level:

Who Do You Live with:

Children, Ages:

Chief Complaint:

How Long Has This Been a Problem?

Referral Source:

Lethality Assessment

I cannot emphasize the importance of a clear and concise lethality assessment as part of all client assessments in any setting, regardless of the chief complaint. The following assessment is the one I used with the patients I assessed in the ER. In Vernon's presentation, he did not mention suicidal ideation or a suicide attempt as his chief complaint, but I still conducted a lethality assessment. The lethality assessment can be divided into three parts: Suicidal ideation, homicidal ideation, and risk factors.

Suicidal Ideation. As a professional and teacher, I have discovered that many clinicians, students, and family members are hesitant or feel uncomfortable asking people about suicidality. Part of this hesitancy comes from the belief that asking a person about suicidal ideation will cause them to act on it. There is no evidence of asking about suicidal ideation being a risk factor for suicide; if anything, *not asking* is a greater risk. Clinicians may avoid asking about suicidal ideation because they feel unequipped to respond to a client who is experiencing it.

Are you having thoughts of killing or hurting yourself? I sometimes ask this as two different questions, since some people want to hurt themselves (e.g., to feel physical pain or see blood) while not intending or even wanting to die. I usually do not use the word *suicide* at this point in the assessment but instead ask about thoughts of killing themselves. My main reason for this is that not everyone knows what the word *suicide* means. If the person answers "no" to this question, I ask the following question.

Have you had thoughts of killing or hurting yourself or wished you were dead in the past two weeks? Some clinicians ask patients if they have *ever* had thoughts of killing themselves. For most people, these are fleeting thoughts with no real plan or intent to harm themselves. I use a specific timeframe that should be easy for the patient to remember and still recent enough to be relevant. I use a two-week span because it is identical for the minimum symptom duration for major depressive disorder. If the patient answers "yes" to either of the first two questions, I follow up with the next four questions.

In what way(s) have you thought about killing or hurting yourself? Directly asking this question is important when determining the detail of the client's suicidal ideation or their intent to kill themselves. How lethal is their plan (e.g., are they thinking of jumping off a bridge [highly lethal] or drinking half a cup of bleach [not as lethal])? Do they or do they not have the means to carry out their plan (e.g., they are having thoughts of shooting themselves with a gun, but they do not own a gun and do not have immediate access to one)? The more detailed a suicide plan, the greater the risk.

What has happened that has led you to think of killing yourself? Many people who report suicidality identify one or more stressors or events that have led them to feel this way. I have often found that individuals want to talk about what has happened. Sometimes, clients respond to this question by saying, "I don't know." I usually follow up this response by saying, "It's not unusual for someone who feels what you are feeling to not be able to identify a specific reason for why they want to kill themselves." I elaborate on this by noting that some people become depressed or anxious because of an event or situation, while other people develop anxiety or depression seemingly independent of external stressors. This question can elicit memories of a traumatic event or series of events for the client. Be prepared for the client to become emotional (e.g., sad or angry), demonstrative (e.g., crying) or dissociative (e.g., mentally checking out), all of which can be responses to their memories.

How long have you been feeling this way? How long has the client felt like completing suicide? What have they done during this time to potentially endanger themselves or protect themselves? If the client feels like harming themselves right now, why do they feel this way at this moment? Is this different from how they have felt other times in the recent past, and if so, what is different now?

What has kept you from killing yourself even though you feel like killing yourself? This follow-up question for clients who have not attempted suicide despite feeling suicidal is an effective way to discover potential protective factors and possible risk factors. Many patients tell me that they have people who are depending on them, and this is the reason they have not killed themselves. Others will say, "It says in the Bible that if you kill yourself, you'll go to hell." When I am told this, I respond, "So, your spirituality is important to you? Can you tell me more about this?" I have also had people respond that they have not yet thought of a way to kill themselves that will not cause them pain.

Have you ever tried to kill yourself? What did you do? Previous suicide attempts are the strongest risk factor for another suicide attempt. Gathering detailed information is important, specifically looking at the number of attempts and the lethality of those attempts.

What happened because of this suicide attempt? Situations in which a client does not tell anyone about their attempt(s) are particularly concerning, because it demonstrates secretiveness and unwillingness to ask for help, both of which are suicide risk factors.

Have you ever been admitted to a psychiatric hospital? For what reason? I ask this question in the assessment regardless of whether the client reports suicidal or homicidal ideation. This is part of gathering the patient's history and can help the clinician get more information. I also ask if the person voluntarily admitted themselves to the hospital or if they were involuntarily committed.

Do you currently see a psychiatrist or counselor in the community? Have you seen either in the past? What resources does the patient have, and what services have they received in the past? How effective were these services? Does the patient feel that they were treated well by their providers? I also ask, "Have you ever been diagnosed with a mental illness?" Far too often, I've asked this question and the patient has responded, "I have bipolar schizophrenia." Sometimes the person is making this up, but often they have been told they have bipolar disorder by one psychiatrist and schizophrenia by another. In most of these cases, the patients were using alcohol and/or other substances, and/or they had suffered significant trauma. Many of those diagnosed with bipolar disorder had never had a manic episode, and those diagnosed with schizophrenia had never experienced psychotic symptoms without using substances.

Has anyone in your family ever died by suicide? This is admittedly a tough question to ask but an important one that is easily missed. It is imperative that a family history of suicide be considered as a strong risk factor for any patients who are experiencing suicidal ideation. There is some debate on genetic factors that can predispose a person toward suicidal behavior (Sadock, Sadock, & Ruiz, 2015).

What do you think happens to us when we die? While this sounds like an existential question, the reason I ask this is I want to see if a patient who reports suicidal ideation has thought through their own death. Does the person believe that they will go to heaven, hell, be reincarnated, or simply cease to exist? Is there a reunion fantasy: Does the client believe that dying will reunite them with a deceased loved one? The more a person has thought through their death, the greater the lethality risk.

How do you think the people who care about you will feel, or how will they react, if you kill yourself? This question also seeks to find out if the patient is seeing past their own death. Are they fantasizing about their own funeral? Are they hoping that their death will bring peace to someone else, or do they hope their death will devastate someone?

Do you have access to a gun, knives, or medications? Given that half of all suicides are completed using a firearm, access to a gun represents a major risk factor for people who are suicidal. Obviously, access to a firearm poses an increased risk in the hands of a person who is having homicidal thoughts. Knives can also be used as a means of harming oneself or others. Prescription and over-the-counter medications, along with herbal supplements, are all means that people can use to overdose.

Who else knows you feel this way? On several occasions, I have interviewed people whose chief complaint was suicidal ideation. A patient reporting suicidal ideation may not have told the friend or partner who had brought them to the hospital and instead used an excuse like chest pain as their reason to come to the ER. The desire to keep suicidal thoughts a secret or to avoid seeking help are major suicide risk factors. This question can also help us identify people who could serve as part of a safety plan for the patient, but only if the patient is willing to bring them into the creation of a safety plan.

Homicidal Ideation. In addition to assessing for suicidal ideation, a lethality assessment must include questions about whether the client is having thoughts of harming someone else. For Vernon, this was not the case, but for some clients, homicidal ideation is a presenting problem.

Are you having thoughts of killing or hurting anyone else? I sometimes ask this as two separate questions, because, just as with suicide and self-harming behaviors, some people have thoughts of hurting, but not necessarily killing, someone else. I find that clinicians are more likely to omit an assessment for violence or homicidal ideation as part of the lethality assessment, mainly because we have been taught to focus on suicidal ideation and behaviors.

Have you had any thoughts of killing or hurting someone else in the past two weeks? If they say "yes" to this question, I ask who the person is they want to hurt or kill. If their response includes specific individual(s), I then have a duty to protect those individuals (more on this in Chapter 6). If the client says "no" to this question as well as to the first one, I skip to the last question.

In what way(s) have you thought about killing or hurting someone else? The more specific the patient's plan to harm or kill another person, the greater the risk. Are the patient's thoughts primarily homicidal ideation, or is their actual intent to wound or kill someone?

Why do you want to hurt or kill this person? Many patients have real, or sometimes imagined, reasons for wanting to harm someone else.

How long have you been feeling this way? The longer the duration and greater detail, the bigger risk of violence.

What has kept you from hurting this other person even though you feel this way? I have had people tell me that the only reason they have not harmed the person they want to hurt is because they have been unable to locate them. Most patients, once they have been talking for a while, will admit that they will not hurt the person because they do not want to get into trouble. Other clients may have moral or religious beliefs that keep them from harming someone else (e.g., fear of going to hell).

Have you ever been charged with assault or malicious wounding? What happened because of this? The risk of violent behavior is highest among those patients who have a history of violence (Steinert, 2006) so it is important to assess past violence. Has the person already harmed an individual? Often, patients will tell me, "I feel homicidal, but not toward anyone in particular unless someone were to really piss me off!" I found that in a hospital setting, people are usually honest about this question. Sometimes, I ask broader questions, such as "Have you ever been in prison or jail? Why were you there?"

At the end of the lethality assessment, I review the patient's responses with them just to ensure that I have the correct information. I do this whether or not the person has reported suicidal or homicidal issues, just to be certain I have understood the client's responses.

Lethality Assessment

Are you having thoughts of killing or hurting yourself?

Have you had thoughts of killing or hurting yourself or wished you were dead in the past two weeks? In the past month? In your lifetime?

In what way(s) have you thought about killing or hurting yourself?

What has happened that you are thinking of killing yourself?

How long have you been feeling this way?

What has kept you from killing yourself even though you feel like killing yourself?

Have you ever tried to kill yourself? What did you do? What happened as a result of this attempt?

Are you having thoughts of killing or hurting anyone else?

Have you had any thoughts of killing or hurting someone else in the past two weeks?

In what way(s) have you thought about killing or hurting someone else?

Why do you want to kill this person?

How long have you been feeling this way?

What has kept you from hurting this other person even though you feel this way?

Have you ever been charged with assault or malicious wounding? What happened as a result of this?

Have you ever been admitted to a psychiatric hospital? For what reason?

Do you see a psychiatrist or counselor in the community? Have you seen either in the past?

Has anyone in your family ever died by suicide?

What do you think happens to us when we die?

How do you think the people who care about you will feel, or how will they react, if you kill yourself?

Do you have access to a gun, knives, or medications?

Who else knows you feel this way?

Mental Status Exam

General Appearance, Behavior, and Attitude. The client's attitude in conjunction with the clinician's initial approach to the client and the interview have the biggest impact on the quality of the information obtained. Attitude contributes greatly to the rapport that needs to be established between clinician and client. This is obviously a subjective aspect of the interview but one that needs to be recorded nonetheless. Was the client cooperative, friendly, pleasant, and involved in the interview? Or, were they hostile, guarded, nonchalant, or argumentative?

How alert does the patient seem? Are they asleep when you enter the room? (This is not unusual in a hospital setting.) I have been called to an ER to assess a patient and learned on arrival that the patient had to be medicated because they were a danger to themselves or others; thus, the interview had to wait. If the patient is not alert, are they drowsy? If the patient is sleepy, how easily are they roused? Does the patient appear to be stuporus or intoxicated? When the person is speaking with you, what do their facial expressions reveal? We assess some aspects of the client's facial expression when we examine affect, especially when their affect is different from their stated mood. Does the client smile spontaneously? Do their facial expressions reveal any inconsistencies with anything else they say or do?

The patient's behaviors are an important part of the MSE that can easily be underreported. How was the patient's gait when they walked in? If you did not see the patient walk, ask them to stand and walk a few paces around the room. How easily is the patient able to stand? Can they walk without assistance? Do they walk with a limp? By extension, is the patient sitting in a wheelchair when you interview them? How well do they ambulate? Can the patient complete their activities of daily living (ADLs) without assistance or some assistance, or are they completely dependent on another person to complete them? ADLs include feeding, cleaning, dressing, and toileting oneself.

Abnormalities of behavior should be noted and often point to areas that need to be addressed medically and/or psychiatrically. This includes gait, mobility, and assessing for fall risk. It also includes observing for behavioral tics and tremors. Tremulousness in the limbs could be a sign of substance withdrawal, Parkinsonism, or other medical issue.

Gross abnormalities of behavior include an increase in arousal or movement. This is sometimes referenced as *hyperactivity. Akathisia* is a sense of inner restlessness, causing the patient to feel they cannot sit still or they must constantly move. Some patients may jump up suddenly from a prone position, pace back and forth, or shift their legs continuously as they are lying in bed (Sadock, Sadock, & Ruiz, 2015). This is a possible side effect of antipsychotic medications, especially older ones.

Akathisia represents one of many extrapyramidal symptoms (EPSs) that are not uncommon among patients who use or once used older, first-generation antipsychotics. Indeed, one of the driving factors in developing second-generation, also called atypical antipsychotics, was the EPSs that often led to treatment nonadherence by people with psychotic disorders (Preston, O'Neal, & Talaga, 2013). In addition to akathisia and Parkinsonian symptoms, other EPSs worth noting during this portion of the MSE include *dystonia*, spasms and muscle contractions, and *tardive dyskinesia,* jerky movements of the hands, tongue, and lips (Sadock, Sadock, & Ruiz, 2015). We discuss some of these symptoms in further detail in Chapter 7.

Other gross abnormalities of movement include a decrease in or slowing of movement, also called *bradykinesia* or *psychomotor retardation*. The person could also be unresponsive, sometimes called stuporus, which could be due to delirium or another medical emergency or to substance intoxication. *Akinesia*, rigidity of muscles, can also be present as an EPS or as a symptom of another medication-induced condition.

Catatonia is a condition in which the person is completely unresponsive to the external environment and is something that clinicians must be aware of. **People experiencing catatonia can be excited to the point that they are pacing around the room, or they may lie prone in bed and not move. Some demonstrate waxy flexibility, whereby their limbs are held rigidly and can only be moved slowly and with some force, as the client resists any movement.**

Clients can also posture, where they hold a position for a prolonged time. Some posturing includes *catalepsy*, in which the client maintains an odd or unusual position in which they are placed. Other people experiencing catatonia can engage in *echopraxia*, in which they involuntarily mimic another person's words or actions. Catatonia is expanded on more in Chapter 4.

Eye contact is a behavior that is also assessed during the MSE. Part of developing rapport includes the clinician maintaining eye contact with the client. The quality of eye contact can help the clinician assess the patient's emotional state. Many clients experiencing a major depressive episode find it difficult to maintain eye contact. Repeatedly glancing to one side or appearing to be distracted by, or focusing on, something that is not there can be an indication that the client is responding to internal stimuli, a symptom of a psychotic episode.

When assessing eye contact, the clinician must be aware of cultural norms, especially if the client's cultural background differs from that of the clinician. In some cultures, maintaining eye contact is viewed as disrespectful. It would be unfortunate if a lack of cultural understanding resulted in erroneous conclusions in the assessment.

Additional behaviors that need to be assessed during an MSE include *stereotypies*, repetitive and purposeless movements. They can include rocking or head banging. Stereotypies can be a part of autism spectrum disorder or an intellectual disability, or they could be due to EPSs or another medical condition. People with schizophrenia, bipolar disorder, mania with psychotic features, or depressive disorder that is severe with psychotic features can demonstrate odd or distinct mannerisms.

Speech. With some exceptions, from this point forward in the MSE, many clinicians use the phrase *within normal limits* (WNL) to denote a range of behaviors or a presentation that falls within an accepted range for the patient's age, cultural background, level of intellectual functioning, and current situation. There is obvious subjectivity whenever we assign a value of "normal" to anything. In clinical practice, we must be careful to not pathologize the diversity in human behavior, but at the same time we need to address behaviors that are causing problems and meet criteria for a mental illness, drug problem, trauma, or medical issue.

When considering a client's speech, does the client stutter, mumble, speak with a lisp, or demonstrate any other speech impediment? Does the patient have an accent that may allude to their country or region of origin? Does the quality of their word choice suggest their education level or overall intelligence? Is the patient able to speak at all? If the person is deaf or hard of hearing, do they utilize sign language? If they sign, which system (e.g., American Sign Language [ASL]) do they use?

The rate and volume of the patient's speech can provide clues to potential mental health problems. Slower speech can indicate a depressive disorder and/or intoxication on depressants and/or opioids. Rapid, and often loud, speech could indicate a manic episode and/or intoxication on a stimulant medication.

What is the patient's speech volume, regardless of their speech rate? Are they shouting or whispering? Some people experiencing mania or a psychotic episode will speak in a loud voice regardless of their hearing ability. Conversely, patients who are experiencing stuporus catatonia may not speak at all, just like those demonstrating selective mutism. Also, many patients experiencing a major depressive episode may demonstrate slowing and softening of their speech.

A person experiencing a manic episode will often demonstrate pressured speech. The best way I can describe pressured speech is that the individual talks so rapidly that another person cannot get a word in unless they interrupt them. I have tried to interview people whose speech was so pressured that I was unsure if they were taking time to breathe.

People with pressured speech often demonstrate *loose associations*—jumping from one topic to the next, usually with little connection between the contents of the varying subjects. I once spoke with a young woman with pressured speech who told me that she felt that if she stopped talking she would die. Pressured speech should be contrasted with people who are *hyperverbal,* which essentially means talking a lot but following goal-directed flow in their conversation and allowing the person they are speaking with time to talk. Vernon displayed hyperverbal speech, with occasional episodes of pressured speech. Conversely, people who speak very little are said to be *hypoverbal.*

When assessing speech, the clinician must also consider the native and/or spoken language(s) of the client. It is difficult for most clinicians to fully assess a patient who speaks a language that they do not. Steps must be taken to ensure that people who speak a language other than the language spoken by the dominant culture have access to competent interpretation services. Family members should not be used as interpreters. In addition, interpreters should be trained to know that correcting any deficiencies in the client's speech is inappropriate and they should instead translate the client's speech word-for-word. If the translation is done in this manner, a clinician should be able to discern some aspect of the patient's thought content and quality of speech when assessing a client who speaks a different language.

Mood and Affect. The terms *mood* and *affect* have become interchangeable in much of clinical nomenclature. For our purposes, *mood* refers to what the patient says that they are feeling (e.g., depressed, anxious). *Affect* is an objective term applied to how the patient's emotional state appears to the clinician. We determine a patient's affect by assessing their speech, facial expressions, posture, gait, eye contact, and expressed emotions (e.g., tearfulness) and the tonal inflections inherent in vocal communications.

I usually ask patients to describe their mood by asking, "How are you feeling today?" This is not something I would say if the patient is crying or appears to be very angry, as such a question would be insensitive. Most people respond with brief answers: fine (in which case I would record WNL), happy, sad, okay, angry, irritable, depressed, anxious, afraid, ashamed, or any number of additional feelings. I generally write down exactly what the client says in response to my question. Be aware that some people have a condition known as *alexithymia*, which means they cannot describe how they feel. Some clients may also demonstrate *anhedonia*, meaning they cannot experience pleasure, including with things they used to enjoy (Sadock, Sadock, & Ruiz, 2015).

Many of the same words that are used to describe mood can be applied to describing a patient's affect. When the patient's stated mood and affect are identical or similar, we record that the patient's affect is *congruent* with their stated mood. Likewise, if the client is crying loudly and appears to be sad, yet says, "I am happy," we record that the affect is *incongruent* with the patient's stated mood.

In assessing affect, we also consider the range of emotions that are demonstrated. The following diagram illustrates one range of emotions:

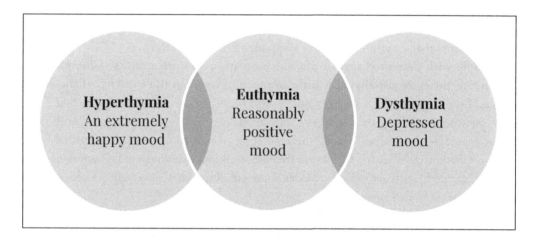

In this equation, *euthymic* equals *WNL*. I typically describe affect with an expanded range, whereby the more "energetic" affective response flows toward the least demonstrative affective response. This expanded range of affect is exampled in the following diagram:

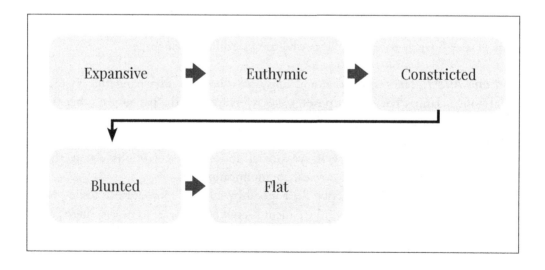

- **Expansive:** Exaggerated emotions, often seen in the presence of a manic episode
- **Euthymic:** Stable, affect WNL
- **Constricted:** The patient demonstrates a euthymic range of emotions, but the emotions are not strong; often seen in people with depression or posttraumatic stress disorder (PTSD)
- **Blunted:** A very limited range of emotions; seen with a variety of mood disorders, trauma disorders, and psychotic disorders
- **Flat:** Little to no expression of emotions; mainly seen in people with severe major depressive disorder with or without psychotic features and schizophrenia

In addition to describing the client's affect itself, we need to consider the lability and appropriateness of their affect. *Variability* is the mobility of a person's affect. Most people display variety in their affect even over a small period of time. When we refer to lability in the clinical sense, we are referring to extreme swings in emotion over a short time. This can be seen in people who are experiencing a manic episode, a depressive episode, a traumatic response, or drug intoxication. Variability of mood is a hallmark symptom of borderline personality disorder (BPD).

Appropriate affect means that the patient's affect is consistent with the situation. Note that this is different from congruence or incongruence of affect and stated mood. A client whose partner recently died from cancer and who reports being sad would be expected to have a sad, constricted, or blunted affect.

A person who has experienced a recent traumatic event and is laughing and exuberant despite saying that they are sad would be said to have an inappropriate affect. Does the patient's affect appear to be forced, like they are trying to appear to have a different mood than what they have stated they feel? Is the person nonchalant as they describe a horrific situation? Inappropriate affective response can indicate a possible organic or neurological cause, delirium, dementia, or substance intoxication, any of which suggests the need for a more comprehensive medical or mental health assessment. Inappropriate affect could also be due to the patient trying to appear sick to gain admission to the hospital or services and/or to avoid consequences.

Thought Process. We can infer a client's thought process only by their speech. Thought disorganization, also known as a formal thought disorder, is a primary symptom of psychotic disorders. We can view some thought disorders on a continuum from a normal goal-directed thought process through increasing levels of abnormal though process, including several types of loose associations.

Note that there are a variety of terms used to describe each type of thought disorder, and some of these terms are defined differently by varying clinicians. Rather than simply stating that the client's thought process is (for example) tangential, I recommend following this with a brief description or even a direct quote of what the client is saying. This graph illustrates the progressive breakdown of thought process from goal-directed thinking.

Goal-Directed → Circumstantial → Tangential → Looseness of Associations → Word Salad

Goal-Directed Thinking. Most people communicate with goal-directed thinking daily without realizing they are even doing it. Think of this as going from point A to point B in a conversation.

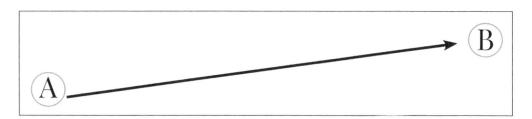

> **INTERVIEWER:** Have you had any problems with your appetite in the past two weeks?
>
> ***CLIENT:*** Yeah. I don't want to eat. I don't feel ill, and I like food, but I just haven't had an appetite.

Notice that the client answers the interviewer's question directly and without any apparent difficulty.

Circumstantial Thinking. The first sign of a thought disorder in which there is a loss of goal-directed speech is circumstantial thinking. In conversation, the client brings in a lot of unnecessary details but usually gets to the main point after some circuitous diversions.

> **INTERVIEWER:** Have you had any problems with your appetite in the past two weeks?
>
> ***CLIENT:*** Hmm … Well, I haven't wanted to eat out much, or cook dinner for that matter. I wonder what I have in the pantry at home? Or, what will the kids want to eat? No, pizza sounds too boring. I guess I'd have to say that I haven't felt as hungry as I usually do.

Note how the client takes a circuitous route to answer the question. It takes time for him to get there, but he does after a lot of unnecessary details and information.

Tangential Thinking. This is a further degradation from circumstantial thinking. Instead of eventually getting back to the main point, the person never returns to it. This can be seen in a person experiencing a manic or psychotic episode. Patients presenting with tangential thinking often find things in the environment to distract them and help drive them further away from the topic at hand. Clinical questions usually go unanswered because the client keeps moving away from the topic.

> **INTERVIEWER:** Have you had any problems with your appetite in the past two weeks?
>
> **CLIENT:** We rarely eat in the formal dining room, we mainly use the eat-in kitchen or breakfast nook. Breakfast is my favorite meal of the day. I really like waffles. But I don't like to order waffles in a restaurant. The syrup gets really messy, especially when the kids use too much of it.

Notice how the answer has little to do with the question other than that they both pertain to food. Also, the client goes off on a tangent and does not appear to be anywhere close to answering the question. Vernon demonstrated tangential thinking throughout much of his interview, although he experienced moments of lucidity. I spent a lot of time with Vernon trying to keep him on topic. To do this, I had to keep repeating his last lucid comments to remind him where we had left off in our conversation before he went on a tangent.

Loose Associations. This is sometimes referred to as *derailment* and the term *loose associations* is sometimes used interchangeably with *flight of ideas*. This represents a further breakdown in thought processes, in that there is little logical connection between ideas. The client's words might make a recognizable sentence, but the sentence itself makes no sense on its own or in the context of the conversation. Rather than moving from point A to point B, many other points are brought up, and point B is never reached. This is often seen in people experiencing a manic episode and/or psychosis.

A	F	O	P	X	C
T	Y	W	Q	L	

> **INTERVIEWER:** Have you had any problems with your appetite in the past two weeks?
>
> **CLIENT:** Today is Sunday, a fun day. Make way! Say hey! Hay! Horses eat hay. Ride the horses, ride the horses. We used to ride the horses down the street and watch the kids dance to the beat. You got movin' feet?

Notice how this is not really a conversation at all. The client is also engaging in a type of thought disorder called *clanging*, sometimes called *rhyming* or *alliteration*, in which they keep rhyming words together. Other loose associations include *punning* (using words associated by their double meanings) and *echolalia* (repeating the words or some of the words used by the interviewer).

Word Salad. With this, also called *incoherence*, the client's speech is so disorganized that sentences do not make sense in and of themselves. Sometimes the words themselves do not make sense. When confronted with someone demonstrating incoherence, always be aware that the person could be having a stroke. Emergency services should be summoned immediately if a person suddenly demonstrates incoherence, a facial droop, one-sided weakness or blindness, and problems with gait. Word salad is almost exclusively seen in patients with schizophrenia.

> **INTERVIEWER:** Have you had any problems with your appetite in the past two weeks?
>
> **CLIENT:** God, I am God, loathsome spider, brackingly, shoo, downingly the way, not, not, not. Slash, thrash, blee, shot, pot, shree, fee, me …

Note how the client seems to be oblivious to the interviewer's question. Some forms of word salad are called *neologisms*, which are made-up words or words comprising parts of other words. Another form of incoherence is *verbigeration*, when the patient repeats a word or several words for no obvious purpose. Additional thought process problems exist that are not on the continuum I outlined previously. These can occur by themselves but often accompany other thought process problems. Two parallel thought process problems may include perseveration and thought blocking.

Perseveration. This describes a speech pattern where the individual repeats the same thought or phrase, often in response to stimuli. Several years ago, I had a patient who used the F-word in the most creative ways imaginable (verb, noun, adverb, and adjective). She would interrupt her tirade with a brief pause and then exclaim, "Now let the church say, 'Amen'!" and repeat these words many times before pausing and returning to her creative use of what, at the time, was her favorite word. When I saw her on the psychiatric unit toward the end of her stay when she had stabilized, she was able to engage in goal-directed conversations with no use of profanity or perseveration on spiritual words.

Thought Blocking. This describes a thought process where the client suddenly stops talking, usually in the middle of a sentence or statement. Clients may stare into space, look to the side, or keep moving their mouth while still looking at the interviewer. This condition lasts for a few seconds, then the client returns to what they were talking about or starts talking about something else as if they cannot remember the original topic. I have seen thought blocking most often in people experiencing loose associations or tangential thinking. Some clients can appear to use the stop in communication to focus on what they are talking about, as if they are trying to "block" auditory hallucinations or other distracting things.

Thought Content. Closely related to the client's thought process is their thought content, which we infer from what the client is saying and from their behavior. *Thought content* usually refers to the theme of the client's presentation. This includes the client's ideas/beliefs, delusions, hallucinations, illusions, obsessions, preoccupations (which may include suicidal and homicidal ideations), phobias, and any evidence of depersonalization or derealization. We can divide thought content into two major categories, *thoughts* and *perceptions*. Thoughts, in increasing order of severity, include preoccupations, obsessions, and delusions.

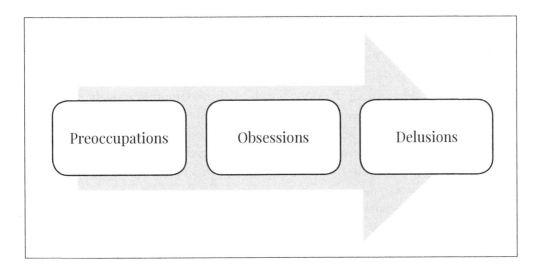

Preoccupations are thoughts that are not fixed, false, or intrusive but have an undue prominence in the person's mind. Clinically significant preoccupations would include thoughts of suicide, homicidal thoughts, suspicious or fearful beliefs associated with certain personality disorders, depressive beliefs (e.g., that one is unloved or a failure), or the cognitive distortions of anxiety and depression. If a lethality assessment has not been completed by this point in the assessment, this is where a clinician could include questions related to suicide or homicide.

Obsessions are thoughts that can be conceptualized somewhere between preoccupation and delusion. An obsession is an overvalued idea; specifically, a false belief that is held with conviction but not with delusional intensity. Prominent examples of obsessions include *hypochondriasis* (an overvalued idea that one is suffering from an illness), *dysmorphophobia* (an overvalued idea that a part of one's body is abnormal), and the *body dysmorphia* seen in anorexia nervosa (an overvalued idea of being overweight).

An obsession is undesired, unpleasant, or intrusive and cannot be suppressed through the patient's volition. Obsessions often involve intrusive thoughts of violence, injury, sex, obsessional doubt, or obsessive ruminations on intellectual themes (e.g., religion). These same themes occur in people who experience delusions; however, the intensity is much higher in people who are delusional. People with obsessive-compulsive disorder generally know that their obsessive thoughts are irrational, but they feel compelled to perform specific actions to ameliorate the anxiety about their obsessions.

A **delusion** is an unshakable false idea or belief that is not congruent with the patient's educational, cultural, and social background and is typically held with extraordinary conviction and subjective certainty. Delusional thinking is maintained by the patient even in the presence of unmistakable evidence to the contrary. Clinicians need to be aware of the client's cultural and educational background when determining if the person is delusional. Delusional themes may be described as persecutory or paranoid, delusions of reference, guilt, grandiosity, erotomania, controlling, bizarre, jealous, and/or misidentification of others.

Paranoid or persecutory delusions are more likely to occur with a psychotic disorder such as schizophrenia or stimulant-induced psychosis. Clients with this type of delusion believe that individuals or agencies are surveilling them and/or seeking to do them harm.

With *delusions of control,* the individual has the experience of the mind or body being under the influence or control of an external force or agency. Delusions of control are also typical of schizophrenia or delusional disorders. Other examples of this type of delusion are thought withdrawal (someone or some force is taking the patient's thoughts), thought insertion (some force has placed thoughts into the patient's mind), or thought broadcasting (a force is broadcasting the patient's thoughts to the world).

With *thoughts or delusions of reference,* simple, everyday things have become incorporated into the patient's delusions. For example, the patient believes that people being interviewed on television are speaking about them, or a patient sees two people having a discussion and assumes it is about them.

With *erotomanic delusions or delusions of grandeur,* the patient believes that someone, often someone famous, is in love with them. People experiencing delusions of grandeur may believe they are incredibly famous, brilliant, or some other gift to humanity.

Some people with *delusions of death* may believe that they are already dead. Alternatively, they may believe that everyone around them is dead.

Delusions may be described as mood congruent (the delusional content is in keeping with the mood), which is typical of manic or depressive psychoses, or mood incongruent (the delusional content is not in keeping with the mood), which is more typical of schizophrenia. Regardless of the type, intensity, or congruence of the delusion, the patient typically sticks to their delusional beliefs despite what the clinician or the patient's loved ones say. In many situations, patients with delusions are unable to care for themselves and, at times, may even be a danger to themselves and/or others.

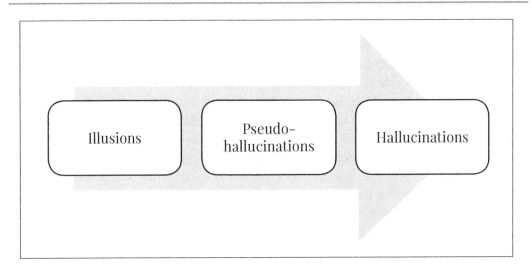

| Illusions | Pseudo-hallucinations | Hallucinations |

Perceptions are any sensory experience. *Perceptual distortions* can be understood along a continuum, with illusions at one end and hallucinations at the other. Although hallucinations are the most well-known of the perceptual distortions, they only represent one extreme of the perceptual spectrum. Illusions and pseudo-hallucinations, while not as severe as hallucinations, can also be debilitating.

An *illusion* is defined as a sensory misidentification or misperception in the presence of an external stimulus. Several years ago, a man was brought to the ER by police under a temporary detention order (TDO) because he was unable to care for himself. Once in his room, he became agitated and irritable because he was certain that the sprinkler head in the ceiling of his room was really a death ray operated by the government that would vaporize him if he said the wrong thing. In this situation, there was an actual object that I could see, but the patient was misinterpreting the identity and purpose of the object.

A *pseudo-hallucination,* also called a *nonpsychotic hallucination,* does not mean a false hallucination, which is more akin to factitious disorder or malingering. Instead it is the distortion of a sensory experience in an individual's internal or subjective space in cases where the person is aware that the experience is coming from within their own mind, not from external sources. Auditory pseudo-hallucinations are suggestive of dissociative disorders, posttraumatic stress disorder, and occasionally borderline personality disorder.

Many of the visual effects of hallucinogenic drugs are more correctly described as visual illusions or visual pseudo-hallucinations because they are distortions of sensory experiences and are not experienced as existing in objective reality. Pseudo-hallucinations are difficult to differentiate from true hallucinations in some cases. Other sensory abnormalities include a distortion of the patient's sense of time (e.g., déjà vu), *depersonalization* (a distortion of the sense of self), and *derealization* (a distortion of the sense of reality).

A *hallucination* is defined as a false sensory perception in the absence of any true external stimulus. Hallucinations can occur in any of the five senses, although auditory and visual hallucinations are encountered more frequently than tactile (touch), olfactory (smell), or gustatory (taste) hallucinations. Any type of hallucination may indicate organic conditions such as neurologic disorders, delirium, drug intoxication, and drug withdrawal syndromes (so a medical/neurological workup may be recommended) or may indicate malingering.

With auditory hallucinations I always ask the client to point to where the voices are coming from in the room. If they point to their own head, I become suspicious that the person's claims of hallucinating are due to pseudo-hallucinations or malingering.

Features of psychotic depression or schizophrenia may include *third-person hallucinations* (voices talking about the patient) and hearing one's thoughts spoken aloud, or *second-person hallucinations* (voices talking to the patient) that are threatening, insulting, or telling the client to commit suicide. To the patient, these voices are real. I therefore become suspicious when a person comes to the ER and says they are hallucinating. This was the main reason I suspected that Vernon was malingering: He said, "I am experiencing hallucinations." Most people who are psychotic are not able to differentiate between their hallucinations and reality. Notable exceptions to this are people who have lived with schizophrenia for many years and who have developed insight into their illness. Several patients who have this insight have explained to me, "I know the voices aren't real, but they seem real to me."

Assessing for hallucinations can be difficult. I typically observe how the patient acts when they are by themselves. This is easier to do in a hospital, even in an ER. where other professionals, particularly nurses, can observe how the patient acts.

Do you ever hear voices that no one else can hear? Do you ever see things that no one else can see? If the person answers "yes" to either of these questions, I follow up by asking, *Is it possible that these experiences are your own thoughts?* A response of "yes" strongly indicates that the client's experience is not a hallucination.

What do the voices sound like? How many voices are you hearing? Do the voices sound as clear as my voice? Typically, the greater the detail in the client's answers to these questions and the more distracted they appear to be due to the voices, the greater the likelihood that they are experiencing true hallucinations.

Are the voices telling you to do anything? How compelled do you feel to follow what the voices are telling you to do? Command hallucinations occur primarily with schizophrenia and can be especially worrisome when they tell the patient to harm themselves or others.

Cognition. Cognition involves several factors that must be assessed during a mental health assessment: how the client processes, retains, and communicates. Many aspects of the patient's cognition (e.g., memory, language, and judgment) can be determined during the rest of the interview. A detailed cognitive assessment may not be possible, or even desirable, during a crisis assessment. Here, we focus on a basic cognitive exam that I have found to be useful in most assessments I have done in crisis situations.

Orientation. A patient is fully oriented when they know who they are, where they are, the time/date, and the context of their situation or presentation to treatment.

Can you tell me your full name again, please? If the client can answer this, they are oriented to person.

What day of the week is it? I've found that it is better to ask this of clients than asking them to say the date, as most people take some time to remember that. I also sometimes ask the month, the year, or the season if I ask for the date and they are off by a day or two. If they can answer these questions, they are oriented to time.

Where are we? Some people can name the specific hospital in which we are located, but others reply that they know we are in a hospital, and that still counts in my opinion, and they are oriented to place.

Why are you here? If the patient can generally explain why they are meeting a clinician, they are oriented to situation. A patient cannot be fully oriented if they are oriented to time, place, and person but not to situation. The person must know the context and reasons for their current situation and location to be considered fully oriented.

Alertness is a global observation of level of consciousness. Is the person aware of and responsive to their environment? Alertness can be described as alert, clouded (possibly due to thought blocking or substance intoxication), drowsy, or stuporus (catatonic, in a coma, or unconscious).

Attention and Concentration. One's attention and concentration can often be ascertained during the overall interview. How closely has the client followed and responded to questions? Whereas *attention* is defined by the patient's ability to focus on the interview or task at hand, *concentration* measures attention over time. Some clinicians assess concentration using the *serial sevens test:* Asking the patient to subtract 7 from 100, then subtract 7 from that, and so on. Most adults can reach 65 with only one mistake (Morrison, 2015).

Another test of attention and concentration is to ask the person to spell a five-letter word backward. Many clinicians use the word **world** for this task. The danger of using world or the serial sevens test is that treatment-savvy clients may have memorized the answers to these questions because they have been asked them so many times; thus, this would not be a true test of attention (Morrison, 2015). We also need to consider the person's education level and any intellectual or developmental disability. Reduced attention can indicate a psychotic disorder or severe depression. I do not use tests of attention unless I suspect a problem with attention during the previous parts of the interview.

Memory. Our memory is divided into three parts: Immediate, short-term (recent), and long-term. Immediate memory is closely linked to attention; namely, it refers to what the patient can retain after five to ten seconds. An interviewer could request, "Please repeat these three things back to me: George (a proper name), blue (a color), 15 Meadow Street (an address)." After five minutes, the clinician asks the patient to repeat these things. This is a test of short-term memory. Failure to repeat all three words suggests a major cognitive problem or interference with memory due to a psychotic, mood, or dissociative disorder.

Some assessments add a fourth type of memory, intermediate. Since this is a vague concept and defined in several ways, I have not included it. Long-term memory is typically considered longer than several weeks. To test for long-term memory, I typically ask the patient to recall some well-known facts. *Please tell me the name of the current president of the United States.* If the person gets this correct, I follow up with, *"Who were the two presidents before the current one?"*

Language. Language is assessed by the patient's ability to name objects and repeat phrases and by observing the individual's spontaneous speech and response to instructions. It is important to assess language in older patients, people with an intellectual or developmental disability, and patients with a potential medical illness. It is also important to be aware of whether your patient understands English or whatever language you are using. Language comprehension is determined by the client's ability to follow an instruction. The ability to name objects can be ascertained by pulling out a pen and asking the client to name the object and any other common things found in the room.

Patients may be embarrassed about any problems they have with reading. I encounter many clients who dropped out of school, were kicked out of school, or never learned how to read. In discussing this with them, I explain to them that their treatment will not be impacted by their reading level. I add that I want to measure their reading ability so that if they have problems with reading, I can communicate with other staff to verbally go over their medication(s), treatment plan, or discharge instructions with them so they can best care for themselves. Reading and writing can be measured by asking the client to read a short paragraph or to write a sentence that you dictate to them.

Reliability. A patient's reliability is established by their ability to give a consistent history. If the person provides vague or no details in describing their chief complaint, reliability is suspect. Also, if the client gives conflicting information, for example changing the dates of when they last attempted suicide, reliability can be questioned. A psychotic disorder, severe mood disorder, cognitive disorder, or some personality disorders can cause problems with reliability. We must also consider that the patient is confabulating (lying) to obtain something as secondary gain.

Insight. This describes the person's understanding of his or her mental illness. This is evaluated by exploring the client's explanatory account of the problem and understanding of the treatment options. In this context, insight can be said to have three components: the recognition that one has a mental illness, one's compliance with and motivation for treatment, and the ability to re-label unusual mental events (such as delusions and hallucinations) as pathological. Impaired insight is characteristic of psychosis and dementia and is an important consideration in treatment planning and in assessing the capacity to consent to treatment. To assess insight, an interviewer may ask, "Do you think something is wrong with you? If so, what?"

Judgment. Judgment refers to the client's capacity to make sound, reasoned, and responsible decisions, particularly regarding their treatment. Some clinicians inquire about how the patient has responded or would respond to real-life challenges and contingencies (e.g., "What would you do if you found a stamped letter on the ground?"). Instead of this, I ask, "What do you hope will be better when you are discharged from the hospital?" Is the patient future oriented? Do they have realistic expectations of their treatment? Do they have an awareness of what is expected from them during treatment?

Assessing judgment also considers the individual's executive decision-making capacity regarding impulsiveness, social cognition, self-awareness, and planning ability, all of which we have been measuring throughout the assessment. If a person's judgment is impaired due to mental illness, there might be implications for their safety or the safety of others. This is where I examine the client's ability to keep themselves and others safe.

Appetite and Sleep. When was the last time you had something to eat? What did you have? Have there been any changes to your appetite recently? A decrease in appetite is a common symptom of depression, although people with atypical depression can experience a significant increase in appetite. Another thing to consider is that the person may not be eating because they lack access to food or money to purchase food.

Have there been any changes to your sleep recently? Have these changes happened on their own, or because of any changes in your health or your living environment? Sleep problems often precipitate many psychiatric problems; insomnia or hypersomnia are also common symptoms of a variety of mental health problems. Sleeping problems are reported in most people in crisis I assess. For some people, the sleeping problems could be due to environmental cues or situations that can trigger a mental health crisis. For other people, their mental illness creates problems with their sleep, which in turn exacerbates their symptoms. The goal is to help our patients understand the need to set and keep a regular sleep schedule. This is easier said than done, given the paucity of appropriate safe and structured living environments for our patients with serious mental illnesses.

Mental Status Exam

Client's Appearance (Check All That Are Applicable):

☐ Within Normal Limits/No Evidence of Impairment

☐ Rigid

☐ Shows Poor Hygiene

☐ Tense

☐ Unkempt

☐ Appears Stated Age

Attitude (Check All That Are Applicable):

☐ Cooperative

☐ Hostile

☐ Suspicious

☐ Uncooperative

☐ Guarded

☐ Regressed

Behavior (Check All That Are Applicable):

☐ Within Normal Limits/No Evidence of Impairment

☐ Akathisia

☐ Restless

☐ Combative

☐ Shows Poor Impulse Control

☐ Evidence of Catatonia/Stupor

☐ Stereotypies

☐ Psychomotor Agitation

☐ Good Eye Contact

☐ Rigid

☐ Displays Tremors

☐ Shows Problems with Gait

☐ Psychomotor Retardation

Mood (Use the Client's Own Words to Describe How They Are Feeling and/or Check All That Are Applicable):

☐ Euthymic

☐ Anxious

☐ Euphoric

☐ Sad

☐ Irritable

☐ Displays Anhedonia

☐ Depressed

☐ Angry

☐ Withdrawn

☐ Frightened

☐ Expansive

☐ _____

Affect (Check All That Are Applicable):

☐ Full Range of Affect

☐ Blunted

☐ Labile

☐ Constricted

☐ Flat

☐ Incongruent with Stated Mood

Speech (Check All That Are Applicable):

- ☐ Spontaneous/Typical Speech
- ☐ Slow
- ☐ Hyperverbal
- ☐ Slurred
- ☐ Soft
- ☐ Loud
- ☐ Pressured
- ☐ Echolalia

Thought Process (Check All That Are Applicable):

- ☐ Goal directed
- ☐ Tangential
- ☐ Loose Associations
- ☐ Thought Blocking
- ☐ Circumstantial
- ☐ Word Salad
- ☐ Shows Preservation

Thought Content (Check All That Are Applicable and Note Specific Symptoms):

- ☐ Preoccupations
- ☐ Suicidal Ideation
- ☐ Homicidal Ideation
- ☐ Phobias
- ☐ Delusions
  - ☐ Grandiosity
  - ☐ Paranoia
  - ☐ Somatic Delusions
  - ☐ Delusions of Control
  - ☐ Ideas of Reference
- ☐ Obsessions
- ☐ Perceptional Distrubance
- ☐ Illusions
- ☐ Pseudo-hallucinations
- ☐ Hallucinations
  - ☐ Auditory
  - ☐ Visual
  - ☐ Tactile
  - ☐ Olfactory
  - ☐ Gustatory

Level of Alertness (Check All That Are Applicable):

- ☐ Alert
- ☐ Drowsy
- ☐ Clouded
- ☐ Stuporus

Orientation (Check All That Are Applicable):

- ☐ Time
- ☐ Person
- ☐ Place
- ☐ Situation

Memory (Check All That Are Applicable):

- ☐ No Evidence of Impairment
- ☐ Short-Term Memory Impaired
- ☐ Immediate Memory Impaired
- ☐ Long-Term Memory Impaired

Insight (Check All That Are Applicable):

- ☐ Recognition That One Has an Illness
- ☐ Motivation for Treatment
- ☐ Compliance with Treatment

Judgment:

Mental Health History

Not every individual being assessed during a mental health emergency has a mental health history, but it's a safe assumption that many high-risk clients have had some previous contact with mental health providers. Gathering a complete mental health history is an important part of the extended assessments required for ongoing therapy and inpatient hospital stays. However, when assessing a person in crisis, the interviewer may have time to only gather basic (but still important) information.

Symptoms. Have you ever had these symptoms before? Have you ever experienced intense feelings of sadness or emptiness? What about feelings of intense worry or fear?

Duration and Intensity. How long have you experienced these symptoms? How did your symptoms impact your everyday life: relationships, school/work, or any other part of your life?

Treatment. What did you do to address these symptoms? If the client entered treatment, what kind of treatment was it, how long were they enrolled in treatment, and how effective was the treatment? Based on your assessment and the patient's report of their previous symptoms, was this the right type of treatment for the problem?

Medications. Have you ever taken medications for depression, anxiety, bipolar disorder, attention deficit disorder, or schizophrenia? If so, which medications? This is often where I see poor drug selection for the diagnosed problem. Examples include a patient being prescribed benzodiazepines for extended periods to address a dubious diagnosis of bipolar disorder or an antidepressant without a mood stabilizer for the same diagnosis.

Did you take the medication regularly? If not, why not? Did you have any side effects with any of the medications you took? If so, what were they? Side effects and high drug prices are two of the main reasons patients tell me that they stop taking their medications.

Family History. Is there any family history of mental illness? If so, who in your family, and what type of illness did they have? Has anyone in your family attempted or completed suicide? If so, who? Has anyone in your family ever been admitted to a psychiatric hospital? If so, how are they related to you? Why, and for how long were they admitted?

The reason for asking these questions is that mental illness appears to have a genetic component, thus understanding the client's family history could help to identify what is happening with the client.

Medical History. Just as we must assess for past mental health symptoms and any corresponding treatment, we should not neglect gathering information about past medical illnesses and treatments, as this could have a bearing on the client's treatment. One of the benefits of electronic medical records is that much of this information is available in the patient record, and the clinician can review it without having to ask extensive questions of the patient. At the same time, quality clinicians do not take medical records as 100 percent accurate; I recommend discussing medical records with the client to determine the validity of the records.

Have you ever had a serious medical illness that required you to come to the hospital? If so, what happened and what treatment was provided to address the illness? Have you ever been seriously injured? If so, what happened? Are you now, or have you ever been, pregnant? What current medications are you taking, and why are you taking them? Do you have any medication allergies or food allergies?

Mental Health History

Symptoms

- Duration:

- Intensity:

Treatment

- Type:

- Duration:

- Effectiveness:

Medications

- Side Effects:

Family History of Mental Illness, Including Suicides, Suicide Attempts, and Psychiatric Hospitalizations:

Appetite (Check All That Are Applicable):

☐ Within Normal Limits/No Evidence of Impairment

☐ Decreased

☐ Weight Loss

☐ Increased

☐ Weight Gain

Sleep:

☐ Within Normal Limits/No Evidence of Impairment

☐ Hypersomnia

☐ Insomnia

Major Medical Conditions

Illnesses (and Treatments):

Injuries (and Treatments):

Current and Past Medications:

Medication Allergies:

Family History:

Medical:

Mental Health:

Developmental History:

Trauma and Abuse History

One of the primary things we must investigate during the assessment process is the individual's safety in their home. Some people are unable to care for themselves due to a disability or an unsafe environment. We also need to consider whether there is any ongoing abuse or neglect, the immediate safety of the client, and past abuse and trauma, as well as the impact of these experiences on the client's current functioning.

If the clinician is meeting with their client in the client's home, it can be easier to discover problems with abuse or neglect. However, since most clinicians are not visiting the client's home, they must rely on findings from the MSE and direct questioning of the patient and any collateral informants.

Do you feel safe at home? This direct question is a good way to start a conversation about abuse in the home. Clients often ask me what I mean by this, and I elaborate on the question by asking if they have what they need to feed and care for themselves and any dependents at home, and if anyone in the home is hurting them. Asking, "Have the police ever responded to a call at your home? If so, why, and when was the last time this happened?" is another way to further explore any history of violence within the home setting.

Who is the one person in your life whom you feel you can count on the most? It's okay to say you don't know or "no one" if that is the case. This question helps the clinician determine what the patient's support system is like. This can also help us test the reliability of the client's responses. Especially if, earlier in the assessment, the client talked about people who are supportive of them. Likewise, when a suicidal client tells me they have no one to help them, I become very concerned about the client's safety outside the clinic or hospital.

I don't need to know any details, but could you just tell me "yes" or "no" if you have ever been physically, sexually, or emotionally abused? This is a tough question to ask and an even tougher question to be asked. It may be difficult to ask this question of a patient with a different sex or gender than the interviewer. After asking the question, I usually add that I am asking this difficult question because I want to make sure we are sensitive to the client's needs on the inpatient unit if they have a history of abuse. Many people with a mental health problem do have a trauma history. ALL patients should be treated with the assumption that they have a trauma history, but sadly, this is not always the case. Sometimes, this information was already shared in the earlier parts of the interview. Some patients answer the question by talking about their past abuse, and others answer the question with a brief "yes" or "no." Some respond in the negative and then add that they do not want to talk about it. I then respond with, "That is absolutely okay, and I appreciate you telling me."

The primary care PTSD screen is a good way to examine the possibility of PTSD during an initial or follow-up assessment (Prins et al., 2003).

Have you ever had an experience in your life that was so frightening, horrible, or upsetting that you:

- Had nightmares about it or thought about it when you didn't want to?
- Tried hard not to think about it or went out of your way to avoid situations that remind you of it?
- Were constantly on guard, watchful, or easily startled?
- Felt numb or detached from others, activities, or your surroundings?

Positive responses to three of these questions indicates the possible presence of acute stress disorder (ASD) or PTSD if the precipitating event meets criteria for a traumatic event. Traumatic events may include exposure to death, sexual violence, physical violence, or threats and/or witnessing of any of these types of violence in person.

Abuse and PTSD Screening

"Who do you live with?"

"What are your relationships with each person living in your home?"

"Do you feel safe at home?"

"Have the police ever responded to a call at your home? If so, when was the last time this happened?"

"Who is the one person in your life whom you feel you can count on the most? It's okay to say you don't know or 'no one' if that is the case."

"I don't need to know any details, but could you just tell me 'yes' or 'no' if you have ever been physically, sexually, or emotionally abused?"

"Have you ever had an experience in your life that was so frightening, horrible, or upsetting that you" (Prins et al., 2003):

- "Had nightmares about it or thought about it when you didn't want to?"
- "Tried hard not to think about it or went out of your way to avoid situations that remind you of it?"
- "Were constantly on guard, watchful, or easily startled?"
- "Felt numb or detached from others, activities, or your surroundings?"

"What do you like to do to relax?"

"How do you spend your free time?"

"What would you say are some of your strengths?"

"What are some of the things you and your friends do together?"

"Tell me a little about your spouse/partner."

"Do you have a faith system, church, religion, or any spiritual practice that is important to you?"

Additional Comments:

Substance Abuse History

Clinicians often fail to complete a comprehensive substance abuse history as part of an assessment, just as many fail to assess for trauma. This often leads to erroneous diagnoses and missed opportunities to address real problems. When I was trying to figure out what was going on with Vernon, one thing I considered was the role that drugs may have played in his presentation in the ER. Although in Vernon's case, his apparent psychotic state prevented us from completing a detailed assessment, most patients will not be as impaired and will be able to complete an assessment.

In Chapter 9, we examine the wide variety of plants, chemicals, and other inebriants that can intoxicate a person. Researchers note that half of all people with a mental illness also have a substance use disorder (Inaba & Cohen, 2014). I believe the actual number to be much higher than 50 percent. A general understanding of the variety of drugs that people use is essential in working with any person experiencing a mental health emergency. I recommend the following questions.

What substances do they use? Be specific about the more common drugs used. Clients tend to minimize their responses when asked, "Do you use drugs?" This vague question also can leave out the three most-consumed drugs: tobacco, alcohol, and cannabis (as many people do not consider these to be drugs). Instead, ask, "Do you smoke cigarettes or use tobacco in any form? Do you drink alcohol? Do you smoke or use marijuana?" I would continue by asking about the use of cocaine, heroin, prescription drugs (specifically opioids and benzodiazepines), hallucinogens, inhalants, and other inebriants. I tend to expand my questions about specific drugs when the client admits to using some of the initial drugs I ask about.

> **INTERVIEWER:** You've told me that you smoke cigarettes and marijuana and you drink alcohol. Do you use, or have you ever used, cocaine?
>
> *CLIENT:* Yeah, sometimes. I used a lot in the past, but only about once a month now.
>
> **INTERVIEWER:** What about heroin?
>
> *CLIENT:* I used to use that, it's been a while; a year or so.
>
> **INTERVIEWER:** I appreciate you telling me this. What about pills like oxycodone (Percocet or OxyContin) or Xanax?
>
> *CLIENT:* I use Xanes (street name for Xanax) and Perks (street name for Percocet) when I can get them and they're cheap. I like things that boost me up more.
>
> **INTERVIEWER:** Like cocaine?
>
> *CLIENT:* Yep.
>
> **INTERVIEWER:** What about methamphetamine?
>
> *CLIENT:* I tried it. It lasts longer but doesn't get me as high as crack. Reminds me of when I used to get Adderall on the street.
>
> **INTERVIEWER:** What about LSD [lysergic acid diethylamide] or PCP (phencyclidine), anything like that?

> **CLIENT:** Nah, I don't like that trippy shit. I did try Special K (street name for ketamine) once, and that was weird.
>
> **INTERVIEWER:** You ever huff or inhale any gases or things to get you high?
>
> **CLIENT:** Nah, huffing is stupid kids' stuff.

When was the client's last use of the drug, duration of use, amount used, and routes used? Once the clinician understands what the client is using or has used, we need to know the last time the client used. Was the use so recent that the client is currently intoxicated? **An impaired client, even one who does not appear to be intoxicated, is more likely to be a poor historian, and the results of the MSE will likely be inaccurate**. Sometimes the client will admit that they are intoxicated, and other times a clinician can infer the client is intoxicated by their behaviors or quality of speech. There have been many times when I have interviewed a client who appeared anything but intoxicated, only to find out through the results of a subsequent drug screen that the client was likely impaired.

Once we have an idea of the last time the patient used each drug, we need to know how long they have been using each drug. Start by asking their age when they first started using the drug and then how old they were when they started using regularly. Ask if they have had any periods of sobriety and what they did to accomplish this. Were they in an inpatient or outpatient drug treatment program? Were they, or are they, involved in Alcoholics Anonymous, Narcotics Anonymous, or another type of support group? Were they in jail or prison, and if so, how did they remain sober while incarcerated? Once we know about any "clean time," is this something that we can build on for future sobriety?

How much of each drug is the person using? For legal drugs, including prescription medications, this is easy to determine: How many packs of cigarettes does the person use each day? How much alcohol do they consume? How many milligrams of each prescription medication? **For illicit drugs, this can be more difficult to determine**. If a person says they smoke "five or six blunts" per day, this does not tell us how much of the chemical this actually entails. Since blunts are cigars in which the tobacco has been replaced by marijuana, the size of the initial cigars only tells part of the story.

We also need to consider the strength of the cannabis and other factors. Since this is information that is difficult to get a complete picture of, I typically just document what the person said they use. I work with a lot of people who use heroin, and I try to stay up on how much heroin costs in our area. Sometimes I ask patients, "How much do you spend on heroin each day?" This question usually leads to other questions that help me learn more about their living situation and any potentially risky behaviors in which they are involved. Many of the people I work with have jobs to support their habit; others sell their plasma, prostitute, steal, or panhandle to support it.

Finally, we need to ask how the client uses each drug. Do not assume that because the client uses heroin that they are injecting it. Many heroin users start out with insufflation (snorting through the nose). If your client says they use cocaine, ask how they are using it. Do they smoke it, snort it, or shoot (inject) it? Drugs, including alcohol, are now being used in novel ways (using alcohol through an enema or by vaporizing and inhaling it).

Once we have this information, we need to examine how each drug has had an impact on the client. Tolerance means that the person needs to use more of a drug to feel its effects.

Withdrawal symptoms, as mentioned previously, occur when the client stops using the drug. Although the exact definitions of addiction and substance dependence have changed over the years, tolerance and withdrawal symptoms are generally agreed on as being primary symptoms of addiction. We discuss withdrawal symptoms in greater detail in Chapter 9.

There are several ways to measure tolerance. One is to ask how much (amount) of a substance a person needs to feel its effects and then work backward to see how this has increased over time. Another way is to use the CAGE questionnaire. This widely used, empirically valid, and reliable scale is easy to administer as it consists of four questions (Inaba & Cohen, 2014):

- Have you ever tried to **C**ut down your use of substances but have been unable to do so?

- Have you ever become **A**nnoyed when someone complained about your substance use?

- Have you ever felt **G**uilty about your substance use?

- Have you ever needed an **E**ye-opener (use of a drug) in the morning to get your day started?

A positive answer to two or more questions strongly suggests tolerance.

Substance withdrawal symptoms vary based on the substances used and the length of time the person has been using them. There is also a wide range of symptoms with which different individuals present. Vernon said that he was going through opioid withdrawal, but his symptoms were not typical of an opioid withdrawal profile. Regular users of opioids, for example, will begin to experience withdrawal symptoms six to eight hours after their last use (except with methadone, see Chapter 9). Opioid withdrawal symptoms include nausea, vomiting, diarrhea, chills, body aches, yawning, runny nose, sleep disturbance, and extreme cravings. Psychotic symptoms are almost never present, but again, Vernon could have been the rare individual with the presenting symptoms he was reporting, or he could have been intoxicated or withdrawing from a substance we could not detect with our drug screens. For the purposes of assessment, record the client's answers when asking them about their withdrawal symptoms.

What kind of impact has the individual's drug use had on their life? How has their drug use impacted their relationships, education, vocation, health, or any other aspect of their life? Has their drug use brought them to the attention of law enforcement or the justice system? Are they entering treatment because they are being compelled by someone with whom they are in a relationship ("Get sober or you're outta here!"), or have they been court ordered to treatment? **Even in the absence of court-ordered treatment, try to assess how the patient perceives their drug use has impacted them and their loved ones**. It can be helpful to interview collateral sources, as many people who struggle with addiction have difficulty seeing how their use has impacted themselves and others.

Finally, what is the client's family's history of drug use? Are drugs used by others in the family, either currently or in the past? How has this impacted the individual?

When we look at any of these areas of questioning about drugs, we should also consider that the information we get often is not complete and may be untrue. People who use drugs are frequently in denial to themselves and others about the extent of their drug use. My recommendation is to take the client at their word, barring any credible evidence to the contrary, such as a viable drug screen. As you develop rapport with them and they progress in treatment, you may need to revisit the initial substance use assessment and update it as new or amended information becomes available.

Substance Abuse

Substance	Route	Amount Used (per day)	Age of First Use	Last Used	Tolerance	Withdrawal Symptoms
Nicotine						
Caffeine						
Alcohol						
Cannabis						
Other:						
Other:						
Other:						
Other:						

Past Treatment; Periods of Sobriety or Recovery: _____

Family History of Substance Use: _____

Final Assessment Questions

I usually use these questions to close out the interview unless I asked them earlier. What do you like to do to relax? How do you spend your free time? What would you say are some of your strengths? What are some of the things you and your friends do together? Tell me a little about your spouse/partner. Do you have a faith system, church, religion, or any spiritual practice that is important to you? If the patient is in obvious distress, is hypoverbal, or is potentially psychotic, I typically skip these questions except for the last one. My experience has shown me that many clinicians do not incorporate spirituality into the assessment process. Given the importance of spiritual and religious beliefs to many people, we need to know about their belief system, as we may be able to incorporate their beliefs into their care or provide for their spiritual needs.

Cultural Considerations

The clinician should be aware of potential problems when the MSE is applied in a cross-cultural context: when the clinician and patient are from different cultural backgrounds. The patient's culture might have different norms from the clinician's regarding appearance, behavior, and display of emotions. Culturally normative spiritual and religious beliefs also need to be distinguished from delusions and hallucinations. This is an important part of the client's culture and demands respect. Patients often speak of the spiritual world as being connected to relatives who recently died, and these beliefs are generally positive and supportive. In talking with them about their experiences, it is typically easy to differentiate these experiences from psychotic symptoms.

Cognitive assessment must take the patient's language and educational background into account. The clinician's racial bias is another potential issue to address. One of the best ways for a clinician to address and resolve bias is to learn about the communities and cultures in which they are likely to serve. The hospital where I most frequently worked predominately served an African-American community, and many of my coworkers were African-American. I found that by taking the risk of being uncomfortable, asking genuine questions, listening, and being sincere myself were the best ways to be culturally competent. Of course, as our communities grow more diverse, this is an ongoing process.

Ending the Interview and Disposition of Care

Once I have asked all the assessment questions, I encourage the client to ask any questions they may have. Often, clients are presented with options regarding the next steps in providing for their care; therefore, it is important that the client and their family have the chance to ask questions and explore their options. Patients who are clearly unable to care for themselves or are a danger to themselves and/or others usually require inpatient psychiatric admission; this can be a frightening process for the patient and their family. Explaining the admission process, visitation policies, and the rights of the patient can decrease patient and caregiver/family anxieties.

CASE STUDY—VERNON

ASSESSMENT, PART II

Let's revisit Vernon. He was involuntarily admitted to the behavioral health unit of the hospital because he was deemed unable to provide informed consent to voluntarily admit himself. While I was considering three provisional diagnoses, I believed that he was malingering to avoid going to court. My main reasons were his apparent lack of mental health symptoms prior to this episode and that he stated, "I am having hallucinations and delusions," when he presented to the ER.

Vernon was transferred to the psychiatric unit without any problems. His attending psychiatrist was as perplexed as I was regarding the cause of Vernon's behaviors. There was still a possibility that Vernon was under the influence of a chemical that was not detected in our drug screens. Vernon was not started on any medications during the first two days on the unit but was observed. Had he been using a chemical(s) that caused his behaviors, the thinking was that once they had worn off, he would return to a stable state that was within normal limits.

The opposite happened: Vernon got worse. He became more responsive toward internal stimuli and very paranoid. He was started on an antipsychotic medication, which he tolerated well. His fiancée and family visited him regularly. After five days on the medication, Vernon's behaviors were close to what his family described as "normal." Vernon stayed on the unit nearly 14 days, and he reached stability to where he was free of any psychotic symptoms. He went to his court hearing and was able to defend himself; he accepted a plea bargain for a reduced jail sentence.

I spoke with Vernon's psychiatrist toward the end of Vernon's stay. While I did not provide direct-care services for Vernon while he was on the behavioral health unit, I was curious as to the cause of his behaviors. The doctor speculated that Vernon had likely had a previous psychotic break, but since he was heavily using prescription opioids at that time, no one noticed that he was acting differently. Most likely, being off opioids allowed his symptoms to be visible when his current episode began. The fact that Vernon responded well to antipsychotic medication was another indicator that Vernon likely had an organic psychotic illness.

I asked about Vernon's initial statement, "I am having hallucinations and delusions," to the triage nurse and how this did not match with the limited insight often observed in people who are experiencing psychosis. It turned out that Vernon's fiancée was enrolled in a local university, where she had taken a psychology course the previous semester. Recognizing Vernon's symptoms for what they were, she directed him to say, "I am having hallucinations and delusions," when he entered the ER. As a good fiancé, he did exactly what his future wife told him to do.

Practice Activities

The case studies of Jay and Dee are presented as an opportunity for you to test your assessment and decision-making skills. Questions follow both stories. Following the questions, I explain what I did after I assessed Jay and Dee. I think there may be more than one possible outcome for these stories, so please see my actions as one possible response and not the only correct one.

CASE STUDY—JAY

ASSESSING PSYCHOSIS

Jay was a 20-year-old man who was brought to the ER by his family. Jay had not slept in four days but said there was nothing wrong with him. His family stated that he had been spending most evenings pacing around the house. Jay had also not been caring for his personal hygiene, and this was not typical for him. Jay's family added that for the past six months, Jay had become increasingly paranoid. One year ago, his best friend was shot and killed as he stood next to Jay on a street corner. Jay had been smoking cannabis three to four times a day for the past two years.

Jay and his family denied that these symptoms had occurred before. Jay was a high school graduate who had been employed sporadically in entry-level jobs but typically failed to keep them for more than 3 months. He was currently unemployed. Jay was single, did not have any children, and had lived with his parents his entire life.

ASSESSING PSYCHOSIS

What are Jay's symptoms, and what do you think could be causing them?

How would you assess for psychosis, and what questions would you ask?

If you conclude that Jay is psychotic, what could be causing his psychotic symptoms?

What is the most immediate concern now?

My Response

I concluded that the cause of Jay's symptoms was less of a concern to me than their severity. This young man was not sleeping or caring for his personal hygiene, and he was becoming more paranoid. I believed that he would not have sought help without the insistence and persistence of his family, especially his mother. Despite his mother's pleas, Jay would not voluntarily admit himself to the hospital and had to be admitted involuntarily. He calmly, though guardedly, accepted this decision.

Once on the behavioral health unit, Jay was observed for a couple of days to see if his symptoms were caused entirely by his use of cannabis. His symptoms worsened, and he was placed on an antipsychotic medication. Within a few days, Jay demonstrated decreased paranoia, irritability, and guardedness, and he began to interact with other patients on the unit. Jay's mother noted that he was close to "acting like his old self again." Jay's mother also provided a valuable piece of information when speaking with Jay's hospital social worker, remarking how seeing Jay in the hospital reminded her of her mother. When pressed further, Jay's mother stated that her mother had battled with schizophrenia for much of her adult life and had spent a lot of time in state hospitals. This information confirmed what Jay's attending doctor suspected; this young man had suffered his first psychotic break. This illustrates the genetic predisposition toward psychotic disorders that exists within some families. Because Jay's family was active and supportive, his prognosis was better than for most people his age who have schizophrenia.

CASE STUDY—DEE

ASSESSING BIPOLAR DISORDER

Dee was a 28-year-old woman who stated that she had bipolar disorder and was feeling out of control. She called an ambulance to bring her to the ER because of this feeling, leaving her two young children in the care of her sister. Dee consented to let her blood be drawn, and she also provided urine for a urinalysis and urine drug screen (UDS). Before entering the room, I noted that her UDS was positive for tetrahydrocannabinol (marijuana) and cocaine.

Dee was calm, fully oriented, and cooperative as we started to talk.

"Okay, when were you diagnosed with bipolar disorder?" I asked.

"When I was about 17, I guess. I'm just real angry one minute and then happy the next."

"When was the last time you had a manic episode?" I asked.

"What's that?" Dee responded.

"Has your doctor ever explained to you what a manic episode is?"

"No," Dee replied, "He doesn't say much, just gives me prescriptions for Prozac and Xanax."

"Does he give you any other medications?" I asked, slightly concerned, as Xanax is not used to treat bipolar disorder and should not be given regularly over extended periods of time in most cases. Prozac, in the absence of a mood stabilizer, can precipitate a manic episode in many people with bipolar disorder.

I went on to explain the symptoms of a manic episode, but I left out the criteria of the symptoms having to last at least one week.

"Yeah, that sounds right," replies Dee.

"What is the longest time these symptoms last?"

"Maybe an afternoon," Dee replied. "No more than that. You know, though, I really only get like that when I use cocaine."

"I really appreciate your honesty," I replied. "I noticed that your drug screen was positive for cocaine and marijuana before I came in here. So, you mainly have these manic symptoms when you've been using cocaine?"

"Mostly," said Dee. "I smoked cocaine last night, and that was the last time that I felt that way."

Dee denied any suicidal or homicidal ideations. Dee also did not appear to be manic at that time. She seemed to enjoy having someone listen to her. She reported that she lived in a stable environment, and she wanted to be a good mother.

"I wanna be different from my mom," Dee volunteered.

"How so?" I asked.

She explained, "I never really knew my dad; he was locked up most of my life—he's dead now. Mom had this guy—I guess you could call him my stepfather. Anyhow, when I became a woman … you know what I mean? I started to develop."

"I got ya," I replied, nodding. I was still surprised at Dee's willingness to talk.

"Well, he started messing with me, and he eventually fucked me, even though I kept telling him no."

There was a pause in the conversation. "I am so sorry," I replied, "That should not have happened."

"I think so, too, and you want to know the worst part of it? When I told my mom what happened, she beat me, sayin' I was lying. Then when she found out it was true, she hit me again and blamed me for coming on to him."

Dee had tears in her eyes at this point. I passed her a small box of tissues and again reassured her and said I was sorry for what she had gone through.

"I didn't stay at home much after that," Dee continued. "I mainly spent a lot of time outside the home, on the streets. I was fighting all the time, angry one minute and happy the next. I was, like, relieved when I was told I was bipolar because it explained me."

I responded, "That part makes total sense to me. But what if there is more to it? You said that you feel manic when you use cocaine. Did you ever tell your psychiatrist that you used cocaine?"

"Nope. He never asked," said Dee.

"And you told me that you feel this way when you use cocaine. Do you want to stop using it?"

"I think so, but I'm not totally sure," said Dee.

ASSESSING BIPOLAR DISORDER

What is the next thing you would do?

What else do you want to find out from Dee in this interview, which is your first session with her?

Why do you think Dee is so eager to talk?

My Response

I responded by praising Dee for her honesty in admitting to her recent use of cocaine. I was equally honest with her: I told her that I did not believe that she needed to be on a psychiatric unit but would benefit more from substance abuse treatment. Dee accepted this from me and, more importantly, accepted referral information to drug treatment providers in her area that she could access and afford.

CHAPTER 3

Diagnosis

In the United States, mental illness diagnoses are determined by the criteria listed in the *Diagnostic and Statistical Manual of Mental Disorders, 5th edition (DSM-5®)* and the tenth edition of the International Statistical Classification of Diseases and Related Health Problems (ICD-10). The diagnostic process is extremely important in determining the best course of care. A basic understanding of the *DSM-5®* and diagnostic criteria is important to providing the right intervention for the client.

The American Psychiatric Association (APA), the *DSM*, and much of modern psychiatry are focused on the biological aspects of mental illness, specifically the neurochemical and neuroanatomical aspects. The *DSM* is built on consensus—what most psychiatrists (the predominate discipline) agree are the basic signs and symptoms of various mental illnesses (Paris, 2015). The *DSM* is not true science but it is the best tool we currently have, and it is what we use to identify and understand mental illness, determine treatment and interventions, and bill insurance companies.

The purpose of diagnosis is to guide treatment along industry-accepted practices. A diagnosis is not fixed or static but is dynamic and should only be provided to direct treatment—not to simply label a person. I see diagnosis as something more than just representing the *DSM* criteria, which is why I, as a social worker, include a biopsychosocial-spiritual-environmental perspective as well.

CASE STUDY—DAVE

DIAGNOSIS

Dave was brought into the ER by his wife, Cathy. Dave was 55 years old. He and Cathy had been married for 30 years, and they had two grown sons. A week earlier, Dave had been discharged from a hospital near his home after being admitted for kidney stones. Since he had a history of depression and anxiety and was not seeing a counselor, a hospital social worker referred Dave to a former colleague of mine in private practice. My former coworker, on meeting with Dave, realized he was experiencing suicidal ideation and extreme anxiety. Therefore, she sent him to the hospital for medical treatment and further assessment.

By the time Dave and Cathy arrived at the hospital, Dave's speech was difficult to understand. Medical assessment revealed that Dave was septic, the result of a hospital-acquired infection he contracted while in the other hospital. He was also going through benzodiazepine withdrawal, as he had stopped taking the medication for unknown reasons. Dave's family doctor had prescribed him Xanax for more than 20 years, and Dave had been taking doses exceeding 5 mg per day.

It took a while for the medical hospitalist to see Dave in the ER and then for the doctor to consult with the attending psychiatrist. During this time, I talked on and off with Cathy for several hours. She was relieved that Dave was getting help but concerned about his use of Xanax. She noted that his doctor had tried for years to wean him off the medication, but Dave had insisted that he could not stop using it.

Cathy was clearly afraid for her husband. His depression had recently increased after he had been forced to retire because of heart disease and an implantation of a pacemaker the prior year. She stated that Dave was often more irritable and morose. I was impressed by Cathy's kindness toward everyone in the ER and her love for her husband, especially during this challenging time.

While waiting with Dave in the ER, Cathy told me more about her husband. She shared that he could be a difficult person to live with, even when he was not sick. Dave was self-centered and arrogant. He brokered no opinion but his own. As a workaholic, he was not involved in his sons' childhood, leaving much of their upbringing to Cathy. When the boys became older, Dave's domineering ways alienated both sons. Cathy was understandably upset by this.

Dave was an engineer at a prestigious firm in town. Two years earlier, after a series of doctor visits, he was diagnosed with congestive heart failure and had to have a pacemaker installed. Because of his declining health, he was forced to take early retirement from his firm. Cathy suggested that the firm may have taken advantage of her husband's illness to push him out the door, as his abrasive personality made him difficult to work with, despite his brilliance. The loss of his job, which had been his focus in life, contributed greatly to Dave's depression and anxiety. He did not find another job or develop any interests to fill his time, and he sank into an even deeper depression.

Dave was admitted medically, and once his sepsis was cleared, he was transferred to the behavioral health unit for treatment of his depression and Xanax dependence. His antidepressant medication was increased, and his

Xanax was changed to Klonopin, with a plan to gradually wean him off the benzodiazepines over a period of several months.

Dave's social group appeared to be largely limited to Cathy. His sons did not visit or call him while he was in the hospital. Cathy visited him on the medical floor, and when he was transferred to the behavioral health unit, she visited him there, too.

Dave attended group therapy on the behavioral health unit but did not say much. He primarily communicated with the psychiatrist, as Dave appeared to be disdainful of the nurses, social workers, and medical techs. Dave did not like that his Xanax was changed to Klonopin but said very little about this to the doctor and instead complained to Cathy. He was resistant to the doctor's and Cathy's attempts to help him reconnect with groups and activities to reestablish structure in his life now that he was no longer working.

After a week on the behavioral health unit, Dave asked to be discharged. He denied having any suicidal ideation. Cathy was in support of this decision and participated in a safety plan with Dave and a hospital social worker. Cathy secured the medications and knives in the home and reported that they had no guns. Dave agreed to return to the outpatient counselor he had tried to see when he was discharged from the medical hospital the first time: That initial visit was disrupted because the counselor sent him to ER, noting that he was ill.

Dave's discharge diagnosis was as follows:

- Major depressive disorder, recurrent, severe, without psychotic features
- Generalized anxiety disorder
- Benzodiazepine dependency (iatrogenic)
- Narcissistic personality disorder
- MRSA sepsis history
- Congestive heart failure
- History of renal stones
- Status post pacemaker placement

In the days that followed his discharge from the hospital, Dave became increasingly agitated and was no longer in favor of stopping his use of Xanax.

A week after he left the hospital, Dave went to his mother's empty home (his mother was deceased). He left a note on the door with specific instructions for the first responders as to what they would find inside. He then dowsed himself with a flammable liquid and lit a match. As he burned, he stabbed himself in the stomach with a knife. A passing motorist noticed smoke coming from the house and called the police. Dave had also left a note for Cathy explaining that he had been "living in hell" for a long time, and now it was time for him to put himself in the real hell.

The diagnosis was a start in determining the appropriate treatment provided for Dave, even though it could not encapsulate all of who Dave was as an individual. Let's unpack what these words and phrases mean and examine Dave from a biopsychosocial-spiritual-environmental perspective.

Biopsychosocial-Spiritual-Environmental Perspective

The five components of this perspective are equal, with none of the five components superseding any of the other parts. One of my problems with a medical model of treatment is that it places far too much emphasis on the biological component, at the expense of the other elements. Dave was diagnosed with major depressive disorder, among other things. How much of this was due to a chemical imbalance? How much was due to psychosocial stressors? What about his environment? Let's look at the separate parts of the model.

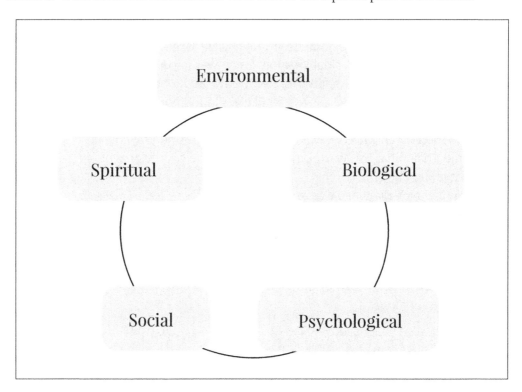

Biological. The biological component of the biopsychosocial-spiritual-environmental perspective concerns the physical body and its separate, yet interrelated, systems. These include the cardiovascular, reproductive, neurological, endocrine, and gastrointestinal systems. The biological component includes specific medical illnesses, prescribed treatment, and the medications used to treat them. This component involves the examination of how physical injury or disability impacts the individual. The biological component also considers the individual's genetic profile, which includes his or her physical characteristics and inherited traits. Many medical and mental health problems likely have a genetic component.

Both major depressive disorder and generalized anxiety disorder have genetic components, including possible heritability (Sadock, Sadock, & Ruiz, 2015). In addition, Dave had become dependent on benzodiazepines due to the long-term usage of a large dose of a high-potency medication, Xanax. For reasons unknown, Dave stopped taking his Xanax after leaving the hospital. He appeared to be displaying withdrawal symptoms, including suicidal ideation and anxiety.

Note that the attending psychiatrist documented that Dave's substance dependence was *iatrogenic,* which meant that the addiction was caused by a physician. In Dave's case, he was prescribed Xanax by a family doctor and continually provided this medication for years. The medication's addictive potential was never explained to Dave, and according to Cathy, Dave was never offered counseling to address the root causes of his anxiety.

When Dave and Cathy presented at the hospital's ER, he was medically admitted for sepsis: He was suffering from a hospital-acquired infection and had become delirious as a result. Dave acquired sepsis while being treated for kidney stones several days earlier. In addition, Dave had a history of congestive heart failure, diagnosed a year earlier, which had required the placement of a pacemaker.

Psychological. The psychological component of the perspective includes mental health issues and a broader understanding regarding how we see the world and make sense of it. Psychology also examines how we see ourselves and make sense of "I," which is sometimes referred to as the *ego.* The psychological component is also the foundation of an individual's personality, which may be impacted by life stressors, substance use, trauma, and grief/loss.

Dave's depression and anxiety likely had biological components, but there were also psychological components. His estrangement from his sons and difficult relationship with his wife were likely due to both the depression and anxiety; in parallel, his symptoms likely worsened due to his relationship problems. The psychiatrist also diagnosed Dave with narcissistic personality disorder, another component of the psychological aspect of the biopsychosocial-spiritual-environmental perspective.

Dave's physical health appeared to have had a major impact on him psychologically, resulting in his isolation and lack of structure once he stopped working. People with narcissistic personality disorder often do not accept help or support unless it is from someone they deem worthy of helping them. Although Dave could have benefitted from psychotherapy, he never pursued it and may have viewed counseling as a pseudoscience and only for the weak minded, comments I have heard from other people with narcissistic personality disorder.

Social. The social component of the biopsychosocial-spiritual-environmental perspective includes the groups, in addition to family, of which the individual is a part. This includes the realms of work/employment, school/alumni, church/mosque/temple or any other spiritual gathering, neighborhood, friends, hobby/sporting groups, and any other community groups or gatherings. The social component also includes how the individual views society as a whole, humanity, and their place within the social environment.

What we mean by *family*, as part of the social component of the biopsychosocial-spiritual-environmental perspective, differs among groups and has changed over time within cultures. For some people, *family* is defined as their immediate nuclear family (parents and children), while for others, it is defined as an extended network of aunts, uncles, grandparents, grandchildren, and cousins. As the definition of *family* continues to evolve, it includes same-sex partners and blended families. A broader definition of *family* includes people who are not biologically or legally attached—one's "family of choice."

Dave's participation in several of his social groups had decreased. He had to leave his job, which was a huge loss for him, and he had not been able to replace this social outlet. Much of his identity and self-esteem appeared to have come from his work. He had estranged himself from his adult sons, and there was no report of any siblings. Cathy was active in a Christian church, but other than at Christmas, Dave refused to participate. His isolation likely played a big part in his increased depressive symptoms.

Spiritual. Clinicians may overlook or minimize spirituality because it is not a priority in their lives or they are afraid of pushing their own beliefs onto their clients. A big reason for this is a general confusion regarding the difference between religion and spirituality. Religion is an expression of a person's spirituality; a person can have spirituality that is independent from any religion. Spirituality seeks to address the existential aspects of our lives. It concerns our connection with something greater than ourselves and our attempts to make meaning of the world. Spirituality also tries to address the meaning of life and attempts to answer the questions: Why am I here? What is right and what is wrong? Why must I die?

Spirituality did not appear to be a concern or source of support for Dave, even though Cathy's beliefs were extremely important to her. Dave stated that he did not want to harm himself or others, and he was able to participate in his safety plan; therefore, no other reason kept him in the hospital.

Environmental. The environmental component examines the forces outside, or surrounding, the individual and how they influence them. This component of the biopsychosocial-spiritual-environmental perspective is often subsumed into the social component, as it examines cultural factors, institutions, organizations, and even sociopolitical dynamics that impact the individual. I use it to examine the physical environment in which the individual lives. For example, at the hospital where I primarily worked, many of the people receiving services lived in one of the six public housing projects within Richmond City.

By default, these inner-city environments are affected by poverty, which impacts the rates of crime, gang-related activities, drug distribution/use, and sex trafficking. This environment adds a tremendous amount of stress to patients and their families. Compounding these challenges, there is a profound lack of resources in these communities, including access to fresh fruits and vegetables. These factors create an environment that is not very supportive to the needs of the people and is often adversarial to an individual's recovery and well-being.

Dave's *DSM* diagnosis did not explain who he was, how he lived, or ultimately predict that he would die by his own hand. A diagnosis explains signs and symptoms and, if utilized correctly, can guide treatment. As I hope I have demonstrated with Dave's case, a diagnosis alone does not tell us everything about the patient and does not provide all the information we need to intervene in a mental health emergency. The initial intervention was recognizing Dave's symptoms as delirium related to sepsis: something requiring immediate medical attention. Once Dave was stabilized, the second area of concern—suicidal ideation, depression, anxiety, and dependence on Xanax—could begin to be addressed.

Diagnosis and the *DSM-5*

Once the initial assessment is completed, the next step is to develop a provisional diagnosis. This provides a "road map" for selecting initial treatment interventions and developing a more comprehensive/long-term treatment plan. We must remember that a diagnosis is a dynamic, not static, process that usually proceeds through a process of elimination. It often includes further observation, trial-and-error pharmaceutical drug treatment, and/or psychotherapeutic interventions.

Sometimes, we lack useful information from a client, and there may not be any additional sources of information. I agree with Allen Frances (2013a) that in these situations, it is wise to defer to the more conservative diagnosis. Let us say I am assessing a new patient for whom I have no medical or mental health history. He is clearly responding to internal stimuli, appears to be delusional, and is presenting with gross abnormalities of thought. It would be easy to slap a diagnosis of schizophrenia on him, but is this accurate? Has the patient been experiencing these symptoms for the timeframe called for when diagnosing schizophrenia? Furthermore, could he be under the influence of a drug or other chemical that would not appear on a standard UDS?

When making a diagnosis, remember that individuals can differ dramatically in how they present with the same disorder. Consider schizophrenia and its broad diagnostic criteria: hallucinations, delusions, disorganized speech, grossly disorganized behavior (or catatonia), and/or negative symptoms. Two or more of these symptoms, one of which must be hallucinations, delusions, or disorganized speech, must have been present [for a significant portion of time during a month period] (American Psychiatric Association, 2013). Consider the various combinations of these symptom groups and how they can present. Despite this variety, all patients displaying these symptoms could be diagnosed with schizophrenia. Once a clinician has arrived at a diagnosis, care must be taken to avoid allowing a diagnosis to turn into "cookie-cutter" intervention planning and delivery.

When making any mental health diagnosis, the clinician must take several factors into account. First, one must determine that the disorder is not the result of a medical condition. Second, one must ensure that the disorder is not the result of a substance of abuse or a medication. Third, the symptoms must cause a significant disturbance in the individual's life over a stated minimal timeframe that is specific to the diagnosis, (e.g., two weeks, six months). Last, the disturbance must impact several of the patient's life domains (e.g., relationships, health, academics, vocation), unless otherwise specified. Quite often, patients are misdiagnosed because one or more of these criteria are ignored or not investigated.

Factors of Misdiagnoses

Once the patient is medically "cleared," we must still consider possible injuries and illnesses that could be causing behaviors that might be mistaken for a mental illness. In addition to medical illness, we must assess for trauma. Trauma-informed care has become the industry standard of any type of clinical intervention. When people ask me to explain *trauma-informed care*, I define it as 1) not doing more harm to the client while trying to help them and 2) acknowledging that a variety of life experiences can impact an individual in countless ways. Some of these experiences create symptoms consistent with a mental illness, while other experiences can create a variety of physical symptoms (van der Kolk, 2014). We examine trauma as a mental health emergency in Chapter 8.

Factitious Disorder and Malingering. A thorough assessment and close attention to diagnostic criteria can help a clinician determine the possibility of factitious disorder or malingering. *Factitious disorder* is defined as the falsification of physical and/or psychological signs and symptoms, or induction of injury or disease, associated with the chosen disorder for deception—the patient does not receive any obvious secondary gain. Factitious disorder is difficult to diagnose unless there is established medical information that all but proves that the patient is not truly ill. It is more difficult to diagnose than *malingering*, which is indicated by behavior that demonstrates explicit evidence that a patient is feigning psychiatric problems for secondary gain.

Clients who malinger are seeking psychiatric admission, services, or a label of a mental illness for clear secondary gain. On an average week in the emergency departments I have worked, up to 25 percent of the patients I saw who reported mental health symptoms were malingering. Many of these individuals were seeking a diagnosis of a mental illness so they could either obtain or maintain disability payments. Others were seeking a place to stay because they had been kicked out of their homes. Still others were seeking admission because they had warrants out for their arrest and were trying to avoid going to jail.

The context of the presentation and a marked discrepancy between the individual's claimed stress/disability and the clinician's objective findings and observations are key indicators of malingering. A patient's lack of cooperation during the diagnostic evaluation may also indicate malingering (Brady, Scher, & Newman, 2013). The presence of antisocial personality disorder can also co-occur with malingering.

I recommend treading lightly when it comes to diagnosing malingering or factitious disorder. Even in cases where I was all but certain that the person was malingering, I would usually admit them when I lacked any additional information, such as past assessments or psychiatric admissions where the discharge diagnosis was malingering. I would rather admit someone who was seeking admission for secondary gain than not admit them and have them hurt themselves or someone else. When I did have a lot of evidence, which was not uncommon with access to medical records, I often decided against admission. In these situations, I still offered outpatient or walk-in services to the individual.

Co-occurring Disorders. A final factor we must consider is the use of alcohol and other drugs; specifically, is the person under the influence of chemicals or experiencing a withdrawal syndrome? More than half of people (a low estimate, in my opinion) with a serious mental illness also have a serious substance abuse problem (Inaba & Cohen, 2014). *Co-occurring disorders*, or *dual diagnosis*, are defined as the existence of at least one independent major mental disorder and one independent substance use disorder (Sadock, Sadock, & Ruiz, 2015).

Because many mental illness and substance use disorder symptoms are identical, it is often difficult to determine whether the symptoms present are due to a mental illness or the effects of a drug. In most cases of a co-occurring disorder, the primary cause is the substance use disorder (Inaba & Cohen, 2014). Therefore, it is important to address the substance use first to help the patient achieve sobriety or greatly reduce their use before trying to treat a mental illness with medication.

In many cases, achieving and maintaining sobriety will cause the mental health symptoms to decrease in intensity or disappear altogether. The *DSM* (American Psychiatric Association, 2013) includes several diagnoses that explain how the use of various chemicals can contribute to or cause mental illness symptoms. The following is a summary of the drug classes that relate to specific mental health symptoms.

Substances That Can Mimic or Cause Psychotic Symptoms

- Stimulants (e.g., cocaine, amphetamines, methamphetamine, caffeine, cathinones)
- Anabolic steroids
- Cannabis (in some cases); synthetic cannabinoids may be more likely to cause psychosis
- Hallucinogens (e.g., LSD, mescaline, N,N-dimethyltryptamine)
- Dissociates (e.g., phencyclidine [PCP], dextromethorphan [DXM/DM], ketamine)
- Entactogens (e.g., methylenedioxymethamphetamine [MDMA/Ecstasy/Molly])
- Alcohol (long-term alcohol use, which leads to a thiamine [vitamin B1] deficiency, can cause Wernicke-Korsakoff syndrome)
- Depressants (e.g., major tranquilizers, benzodiazepines, barbiturates, alcohol, opioids), which can cause a withdrawal syndrome

Substances That Can Mimic or Cause Depressive Disorders

- Alcohol (withdrawal syndrome after chronic or excessive use, including alcohol intoxication)
- Stimulants (withdrawal syndrome after chronic or excessive use)
- Cannabis (withdrawal syndrome after chronic or excessive use)
- Entactogens and hallucinogens (symptoms occur during the resolution phase, which occurs after the active phase)

Substances That Can Mimic a Manic Episode or Cause Manic Behaviors

- Stimulants
- Cannabis (in some individuals)
- Hallucinogens

- Dissociates
- Sedatives, hypnotics, or anxiolytics (can cause depressant paradoxical stimulant reactions in some people, who become excited or agitated with use)

Substances That Can Mimic Anxiety Disorders or Cause Anxiety

- Stimulants (from overdose or withdrawal or just general use)
- Opioids (during withdrawal)
- Alcohol (during withdrawal)
- Benzodiazepines (during withdrawal)
- Hallucinogens, entactogens, or dissociates (panic during use)
- Cannabinoids (may cause adverse reactions)

Substance-Induced Mental Health Disorders

There are several mental health diagnoses that denote that a drug or drug class is responsible for the mental health symptoms. To meet the diagnostic criteria for any of the following diagnoses, the patient must be using the drug (indicated by the client admitting use or determined by a drug screen) or have been using the drug and experiencing withdrawal (American Psychiatric Association, 2013). In most cases, stopping the use of the drug in question causes the mental health symptoms to remit.

- Alcohol-induced depressive disorder
- Alcohol-induced anxiety disorder
- Alcohol-induced bipolar disorder
- Alcohol-induced psychotic disorder
- Alcohol-induced neurocognitive disorder (dementia)
- Alcohol-induced delirium
- Alcohol-induced sleep disorder
- Alcohol-induced sexual dysfunction
- Cannabis-induced … (e.g., depressive disorder, anxiety disorder, etc.)
- Opioid-induced … (e.g., depressive disorder, anxiety disorder, etc.)
- Stimulant-induced … (e.g., depressive disorder, anxiety disorder, etc.)
- Hallucinogenic-induced … (e.g., depressive disorder, anxiety disorder, etc.)
- Inhalant-induced … (e.g., depressive disorder, anxiety disorder, etc.)
- Sedative-, hypnotic-, or anxiolytic-induced disorders … (e.g., depressive disorder, anxiety disorder, etc.)

Biopsychosocial–Spiritual–Environmental Exercises

Many clinicians learn to use the *DSM* alone to diagnose clients. Consider also seeing the client's situation from the broader biopsychosocial-spiritual-environmental perspective. The following case studies include exercises to fill out for practice. The first one has been completed as an example.

CASE STUDY —CARLOS

DIAGNOSIS

Carlos is a 16-year-old male who was brought to your agency by his mother. He makes it clear that he does not want to be meeting with you, but he does answer most of your questions. He states that he was recently placed on probation for possession of marijuana. He admits to using marijuana on a regular basis and selling a little bit to his friends. Carlos lives with his mother and younger brother. His father was killed three years earlier in a car accident involving a drunk driver. Carlos' mother had to take a second job to support the family, leaving Carlos to take care of his younger brother most evenings.

Carlos gets good grades and states, "I don't even have to study and I get straight Bs." He says he thinks about becoming either a physical therapist or a lawyer. He says very little about his father. Despite being angry about having to take care of his little brother and missing out on being an adolescent, he tries to look out for his young brother. He notes that there are not a lot of Latinos in the community and that sometimes he is made fun of, even at the Roman Catholic Church that he attends at the behest of his mother.

Biological:
Physically healthy, smokes cannabis, lives with biological mother and brother.
Psychological:
Intelligent, angry, father was killed three years earlier, feels isolated, teased, future oriented. Talks in counseling even though he does not want to be there.
Social:
Must watch his brother, so he misses out on things; not many Latinos in his community. Involved in the criminal justice system, which is mandating counseling.
Spiritual:
Attends church, but he is teased there; he goes at the behest of his mother—does he want to attend? How has Carlos dealt with the death of his father?
Environmental:
Limited opportunities for him to do things he wants to do. Mother must work two jobs to make ends meet.
Additional Information Needed:
Quality of the relationship between Carlos and his mother, suicide assessment, does the younger brother have needs, does Carlos smoke cigarettes or use any other chemicals?

CASE STUDY—LATISHA

DEPRESSION DIAGNOSIS

Latisha is a 26-year-old woman who comes to you with a primary complaint of depression. She is a single parent of a 5-year-old daughter. The daughter's father is marginally involved. Latisha has type 1 diabetes. Her 5-year-old daughter is entering kindergarten. Latisha and her daughter live in a housing project near your agency. Latisha makes it clear that she does not like living there. She strongly desires something better for her daughter, and she is frustrated that she cannot get out of her neighborhood. Latisha graduated high school and attended a year of community college. She has tried to work before but has found that if she works (even for little money) she loses the health benefits for her and her daughter. She notes that she needs the benefits because she needs her medications to remain healthy.

Latisha has cut off contact with her mother and siblings, as they are all regular drug users. She is an active Jehovah's Witness and feels supported by her spiritual community. She denies having suicidal ideation but complains of decreased appetite and sleep problems.

| **Biological:** |
| **Psychological:** |
| **Social:** |
| **Spiritual:** |
| **Environmental:** |
| **Additional Information Needed:** |

Biopsychosocial-Spiritual-Environmental Perspective

Biological:

Psychological:

Social:

Spiritual:

Environmental:

Additional Information Needed:

Conclusion

The diagnostic process requires attention to the assessment details as well as the selection of potential diagnoses. Through a process of ruling out possible diagnoses, the clinician narrows down the diagnoses that may best explain their client's behaviors, thought process, and pathology. Just as assessment and information gathering continues throughout treatment, so does the diagnostic process. Both continually evolve as we work with the client. By their nature, mental health emergencies occur quickly, and the clinician must make quick decisions, sometimes with limited information. When we encounter new information, we need to decide our next steps. This includes determining what type of mental health emergency the individual is experiencing.

There may be more than six types of mental health emergencies, but most high-risk clients fit into one or more of the categories discussed in the following chapters. Sometimes our clients fit into a single category; for example, a person diagnosed with major depressive disorder, recurrent, severe, without psychotic features, who develops suicidal ideation with a plan. Other times, we may have a patient with complex issues reporting suicidal and homicidal ideation, multiple medical issues, trauma due to childhood abuse, and addiction to cocaine and heroin. One of the things we focus on is determining what is the most dangerous presenting issue: What could kill the patient or someone else first?

CHAPTER 4

Inability to Care for Self

People who are unable to care for themselves, and as a result present a danger to themselves or others, include clients who are suicidal and/or homicidal. In this chapter, however, we focus on those individuals who are not suicidal, homicidal, medically ill, or intoxicated but still cannot care for themselves for various reasons. Persons in this category are often said to be unable to manage their behaviors or avoid dangerous situations.

The definition of being able to care for oneself varies from state to state. Child Protective Services (CPS) and Adult Protective Services (APS) may need to be involved in situations where people are unable to care for themselves and/or persons in their custody. The definition of imminent harm due to one's inability to care for oneself also differs from locality to locality. It is up to the reader to determine the laws and responsibilities of their localities and their responsibilities concerning children and adults who cannot care for themselves.

CASE STUDY—RONNIE

INDEPENDENCE

It was the middle of January, and the time was approximately 11:00 pm. The outside temperature was 8 degrees Fahrenheit. I was in the ER seeing another patient when Ronnie was brought in by the police. Ronnie, a 23-year-old man, was dressed only in his boxer shorts, and he had a blanket around his shoulders. He was also barefoot.

"The blanket is mine," said the officer accompanying Ronnie. "He was running down the middle of the street heading for the highway in just his boxers. Figured this is where I should bring him."

Ronnie threw the blanket off his shoulders and flexed his arm muscles.

"Things are great!" Ronnie exclaimed with a huge smile. "I am preaching the word of God, Jesus, Yahweh, Jehovah, Allah … I am his messenger! Y'all gotta smoke marijuana every day, bitches! I wanna be FREE! I gotta hook up with a Taurus, ya know? I love you guys!"

Right after saying this, Ronnie jumped up on the counter and started to dance. The police officer and I talked him down and led him into an exam room.

This was my first encounter with Ronnie. Ronnie lived with his mother about a block from the hospital, and Ronnie and his mother both have psychotic disorders. Ronnie's mother has schizophrenia, and Ronnie has a rarer psychotic disorder: schizoaffective disorder. Schizophrenia and schizoaffective disorder are chronic conditions that can impact a person's ability to care for themselves and/or create conditions where they put themselves in danger. Both Ronnie and his mother receive disability payments and intensive mental health services through the city's behavioral health authority.

Hierarchy of Needs

Abraham Maslow (d. 1970), a leader in humanistic psychology, developed a hierarchy of needs that is applicable to everyone (Sadock, Sadock, & Ruiz, 2015). Maslow noted that basic and fundamental needs like food, water, shelter, and safety had to be met before other needs, such as love, belonging, and esteem, could be met. Thus, someone who just lost their home to a fire is probably not interested in discussing how they *feel*. Could you imagine trying to do cognitive-behavioral therapy, without addressing basic safety concerns, with a person in a refugee camp in war-torn Syria? Of course not.

We must consider the setting and context in which we meet with our clients to determine what type of intervention we are to provide. When I was in private practice, I worked predominately with adolescents and adults who were dealing with adjustment disorders or relationship problems. Their issues would occupy Maslow's levels of love and belonging, esteem, and/or self-actualization. In the ER, most of my patients were high-risk clients dealing with physiological and safety issues that were most often due to severe mental illness, substance use, or another type of mental health emergency.

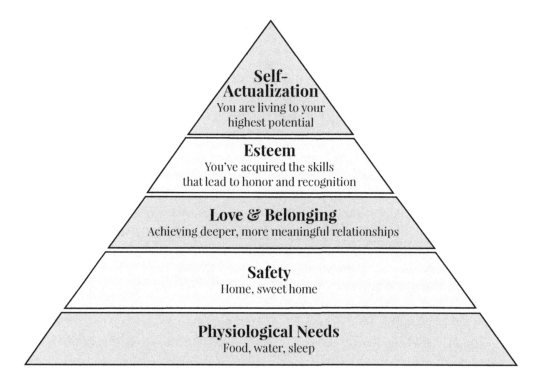

Reasons a Person May Be Unable to Care for Self

There are several things that could cause a person to not be able to care for themselves:

- A variety of medical conditions
- Trauma
- Drug intoxication or withdrawal syndromes
- Medication reactions
- Severe mental illness
- Age (the elderly and young children are more likely to be victims of abuse)

Abuse. Physiological and safety needs are more than abuse alone, but every mental health worker needs to know what to do when confronted with possible abuse or neglect. The rule I practice when dealing with physiological and safety concerns is that if I don't believe that the person can provide for their physiological and safety needs, then I act. Regarding child and elder abuse, state and local laws vary. In most localities, clinicians are mandated reporters for child and adult abuse; therefore, it is important to know the laws of the communities you serve and to follow them to the letter.

In Virginia, all cases of suspected child and elder abuse must be reported to the local Department of Social Services or to the State Department of Social Services. Local and state police are often involved as well. Like many social workers, I have had to make Child Protective Services (CPS) reports in situations where there was suspected physical abuse, sexual abuse, or neglect of a minor. I have also had to make reports for adults who were incapacitated, usually due to age or illness, and were being abused and/or neglected by a caretaker.

Mental Illness. Ronnie's situation mirrors this. The risk for Ronnie was that he was outside on a very cold night and was in danger of developing hypothermia or frostbite (remember he was underdressed, to say the least). Also, the police officer noted that Ronnie was running toward a highway overpass. Given the severity of Ronnie's delusions that he is a deity, it would not be implausible that he might try to "fly" off the overpass or go to the highway and try to stop traffic, which was going at least 70 miles per hour.

The presence of a mental illness in and of itself does not mean that the person is unable to care for themselves. Most people who have a mental illness do not have a problem caring for themselves and pose no risk of danger to themselves or others. Some mental illnesses, those I refer to as "severe," can create situations in which the individual cannot care for themselves; but again, many people with severe mental illnesses, like schizophrenia and bipolar disorder, are able to care for themselves when they have the proper support.

Let's look at the mental illnesses that are more likely to create a situation in which a client is unable to care for themselves. Again, we examine violence and suicidal behaviors in later chapters and look at trauma, particularly PTSD.

People who cannot or refuse to care for themselves, and in doing so place themselves in danger, almost always require involuntary admission to a psychiatric unit for stabilization. It is extremely important that all possible medical causes be ruled out before a psychiatric admission is considered.

The mental illnesses described in this text are from the diagnostic criteria listed in the *DSM-5® (APA, 2013)*.

- Autism spectrum disorder, severe
- Intellectual disability, severe
- Conduct disorder
- Bipolar disorder
- Major depressive disorder
- Schizophrenia and other psychotic disorders
- Panic attack
- Borderline personality disorder
- Anorexia nervosa
- Catatonia
- Dementia

Childhood and Adolescent Mental Health Disorders

In my experience, many children who have been diagnosed with a mental illness in fact do not have a mental illness. Several things can cause behaviors that are often misdiagnosed as the symptoms of a mental illness. These factors must always be taken into consideration when considering a mental illness in a child or adolescent. Failure to take these factors into account is one reason for misdiagnosis.

- Poor parenting, as exemplified by few limits, parental anxiety, poor boundaries, making the child's needs the center of the family, and treating young children like they are adults
- Childhood trauma, specifically sexual and physical abuse, usually resulting in poor attachment
- Parental drug use, which can lead to child neglect
- Poor nutrition (e.g., a diet containing an overabundance of processed foods and sugars)
- The trauma and anxiety that occur when living in a high-crime area
- Mental health providers, teachers, and other professionals being quick to label different or oppositional behaviors as due to a mental illness while not considering outside factors
- Limited resources, such as good schools, health care, and transportation, available to the child and their family

Of all the childhood and adolescent mental health problems, only four are likely to create a high-risk client/mental health emergency because of the client's inability to care for themselves or the risk of their being a danger to others: severe autism, severe to profound intellectual disability, major depressive disorder, and conduct disorder. It's true that children and adolescents may be diagnosed with disorders like bipolar disorder and schizophrenia, which can also cause an inability to care for self or danger to others, but often these are erroneous diagnoses that are better explained by factors such as abuse, neglect, or other forms of trauma

(Frances, 2013b). The few cases of childhood schizophrenia or bipolar disorder that appear to be legitimate are outliers. Childhood depression is a risk factor that must be addressed due to risk of suicide, and we do this in the next chapter.

Autism and Intellectual Disability. Autism spectrum disorder and intellectual disability are chronic disorders typically diagnosed in childhood. Most children diagnosed with an intellectual disability can live lives with minimal to moderate assistance. Ninety-five percent of people with an intellectual disability have either a mild or moderate level of impairment (Sadock, Sadock, & Ruiz, 2015). This means that they can care for themselves, attend school, and work with some assistance or support. People with a severe or profound intellectual disability, those comprising the remaining 5 percent of people with an intellectual disability, require much higher levels of care and usually need assistance with feeding, dressing, and toileting. Some require around-the-clock professional care. Autism spectrum disorder follows a similar severity distribution, with most people having milder forms of the disorder that do not require extensive care.

Conduct Disorder. Children with conduct disorder display a persistent pattern of violating the rights of others. They fight, bully, and intimidate others. They are cruel to people and animals and may force someone into sexual behaviors against their will. They are often truant from school and run away frequently. Children may also have a history of staying out late at night before age 13, despite parental prohibition. Stealing and fire-setting are also possible. Some children with conduct disorder can appear charming and disarming toward adults, which can make this a difficult disorder to diagnose (American Psychiatric Association, 2013).

Most individuals with conduct disorder are male, and their symptoms persist into adulthood. Many get into physical altercations and have symptoms that meet criteria for attention deficit hyperactivity disorder (ADHD). This disorder occurs at a higher rate among the children of parents with alcohol dependence or antisocial personality disorder. The prevalence of conduct disorder is 2 to 10 percent of all children, with a median of 4 percent (American Psychiatric Association, 2013).

Due to their lack of empathy and disregard for laws and rules, children with conduct disorder can present in a crisis center or ER because their behaviors have created an unsafe situation for others or themselves. I have worked with children as young as six years who have displayed these behaviors, and in some cases, I have had no choice but to hospitalize them because they could not keep themselves or others safe. On other occasions, I have assessed children initially diagnosed with conduct disorder who had experiences that better explained their behaviors.

Practice and experience has informed me to believe that many children diagnosed with conduct disorder and its less severe iteration, oppositional defiant disorder (ODD), are reacting to trauma they experienced in early childhood, usually in the form of abuse or neglect. This does not excuse their behaviors, but it can help us to better understand what is going on and possibly assist us in intervening to limit the trauma's damage.

Bipolar Disorder

Many clinical professionals agree that bipolar disorder is being overdiagnosed in children (Frances, 2013b; Paris, 2015). In my workshops, I point out that ADHD was the "disease du jour" of the 1990s, autism spectrum disorders were the diagnoses in vogue in the 2000s, and bipolar is the disorder of the decade for the 2010s. I want to make it clear that these disorders are real and can have a major impact on the individuals who have them: I do not wish to minimize this.

Features of Bipolar Disorder. The features of bipolar I disorder are specific and well researched. They include a manic episode that, by definition, must last at least one week. The following are features of a manic episode (American Psychiatric Association, 2013; Sadock, Sadock, & Ruiz, 2015):

- The person has an abnormally and persistently elevated, expansive, or irritable mood
- The patient's mood is often self-described as "feeling on top of the world" or "feeling high without drugs"
- Rapid shifts in mood may occur (happy, sad, angry, happy, sad, angry, repeat …), otherwise known as lability
- Persistently increased activity and energy is present for most of the day, nearly every day, for a period of at least one week
- Inflated self-confidence to supreme grandiosity can occur
- The patient may engage in multiple, overlapping projects while generally using goal-directed behaviors
- Engaging in risky or dangerous behaviors is not uncommon
- Decreased need for sleep is a major indicator: The patient feels rested after as little as two to three hours of sleep
- Speech is often loud and pressured; another person cannot get a word in edgewise
- The speech itself may make no sense and may include singing and/or a dramatic flair
- If the person is irritable, their speech is often hostile, threatening, and abusive, leading people close to them to say, "This is not at all like them; they never say things like that!"
- Racing thoughts are often present
- Increased sex drive or sexual activity may also be present; the client may engage in dangerous sexual activities that are out of character for them
- Agitation and restlessness are typical
- People in a manic state can be very sociable and engaging
- Excessive optimism can also be present
- Excessive spending and/or giving away of items can occur
- Individuals do not often think they are ill or need treatment; limited insight into their condition and judgment regarding their decisions is not uncommon

- They may perceive that everyone else is "moving too slow for me"

A manic episode, which includes the features listed previously, is required for the diagnosis of bipolar I disorder (American Psychiatric Association, 2013). Following the end of a manic episode, the patient may transition into a hypomanic episode or a depressive episode or may return to a sense of normalcy (euthymia), but many people go from mania to severe depression (Sadock, Sadock, & Ruiz, 2015).

Bipolar II disorder includes a major depressive episode and an episode of *hypomania* (a mood episode that is of shorter duration and less severity than a manic episode). Substance use can occur with bipolar disorders, and the clinician needs to be careful to avoid labeling the effects of a stimulant or another inebriant as a manic or hypomanic episode. Individuals experiencing a full-blown manic episode often require hospitalization for stabilization, especially when the mania is so severe that the patient develops psychotic symptoms.

Bipolar Disorder as a Mental Health Emergency. If the person is manic, they may present with pressured speech and a tangential thinking; thus, it may be difficult to get a word in edgewise. In these situations, remember that patients will often mirror others without realizing they are doing so. I respond by slowing my movements and speech ("Go low, go slow"). Many times, I find myself being directive but not forceful in my conversation. If the person keeps straying off topic, try simplifying the questions and use basic, closed-ended questions.

Ronnie was clearly manic, psychotic, or a combination thereof. Regardless of the mental illness that caused his behaviors, Ronnie, who was not using substances and who did not have any medical issues, was clearly unable to care for himself and keep himself safe.

Major Depressive Disorder

Five or more symptoms of a major depressive episode must be present to make this diagnosis. A depressed mood, loss of interest, or loss of pleasure must be one of those symptoms (American Psychiatric Association, 2013, Pgs 160-161). In addition, the following symptoms can be part of major depressive disorder: significant weight loss, increase or decrease in appetite, insomnia or hypersomnia, psychomotor agitation or retardation, fatigue or loss of energy, feelings of worthlessness or excessive guilt, diminished ability to concentrate, and recurrent thoughts of death or suicidal ideation. If a patient has ever had a manic episode, they cannot be diagnosed with major depressive disorder but must be diagnosed with bipolar disorder (American Psychiatric Association, 2013).

Features of Major Depressive Disorder. The following features are typically seen with major depressive disorder:

- Weight change and suicidal ideation do not need to be present every day to be considered "present"
- Fatigue or insomnia is usually a presenting symptom

- Some people with mild depression may appear to be functioning normally, but doing so causes them to expend a lot of energy

- Increased agitation and anger outbursts are not uncommon

- A sense of worthlessness or guilt is also present

- Individuals may misinterpret normal daily incidents as evidence to support their negative self-concept

- Difficulty concentrating and/or making even simple decisions is a common symptom

- Thoughts of death and suicidal ideation are common

- Affective symptoms include tearfulness, irritability, and/or brooding

- Excessive worry or anxiety can be common

- Phobias, somatic complaints, and chronic pain symptoms can also occur

- Suicide is one of the common mortality outcomes of depression

- Untreated depression, even if it does not result in suicide, leads to higher mortality due to associated medical illnesses

Like bipolar disorder, a major depressive episode can be severe enough to generate psychotic symptoms. Some of the symptoms of severe depression, mania, or psychosis can be difficult to identify and diagnose when they are all present at the same time. Any combination of these symptoms can create situations in which a client may not be able to care for themselves. Next, we look at ways to try and differentiate these symptoms after we examine psychotic illnesses.

Major Depressive Disorder as a Mental Health Emergency. Second to suicidality, the next more serious concern is the severely depressed patient's inability or unwillingness to care for themselves. This could include not eating, sleeping too little or too much, or not caring for their personal hygiene. If the patient's depression is severe enough to include psychotic symptoms, those must be addressed as well. The biggest concern for the person experiencing a mental health emergency related to major depressive disorder is suicidal ideation or a suicide attempt, and we discuss this in the next chapter.

Schizophrenia and Other Psychotic Disorders

Schizophrenia is one of the most variable disorders we discuss in this chapter. Its symptoms overlap with many other disorders, and none of the symptoms that define schizophrenia are specific to schizophrenia alone: They occur with many other disorders as well. What's more, two people can have schizophrenia with completely different symptom sets (Frances, 2013a).

Despite older views that schizophrenia only starts in late adolescence or early adulthood, we now know that schizophrenia can occur at any point in life. Arriving at a diagnosis of schizophrenia can only be accomplished by an extensive assessment process, collecting information from collateral informants, and systematically ruling out other mental health problems, substance use, and medical problems. Because of the severity of most symptoms of schizophrenia, many people who are actively experiencing symptoms may not be able to care for themselves.

Primary Symptoms of Schizophrenia. There are five primary signs of schizophrenia: delusions, hallucinations, disorganized thinking, disorganized speech, and negative symptoms (American Psychiatric Association, 2013):

Delusions. Delusions can have various aspects:

- They consist of fixed, false beliefs that involve a misinterpretation of perceptions or experiences
- They may involve a variety of themes, with persecutory being the most common
- *Ideas of reference* are also common, in which the person believes that certain gestures, television shows, song lyrics, or environmental cues are saying something specifically to them
- Delusions referred to as *bizarre* are clearly implausible (e.g., a person believes they can fly)

Hallucinations. Hallucinations can occur with any sense, but the most common with schizophrenia and related psychotic disorders are auditory hallucinations, as opposed to those with psychosis due to a medical illness or drug intoxication or withdrawal. Characteristics of hallucinations are as follows:

- The hallucinations are not under voluntary control
- They are usually experienced as voices that are distinctly outside of the person's thoughts
- Certain types of auditory hallucinations, especially command hallucinations or voices making a running commentary on the person's thoughts or actions, are indicative of schizophrenia

Remember that not all strange perceptual experiences are psychotic. Déjà vu or pseudo-hallucinations can happen within the context of other mental health disorders or in the complete absence of any mental health problem.

Disorganized Thinking or Speech. The following occur with disorganized thinking or speech:

- The person may move from one topic to another (loose associations)
- The patient's answers to questions may be partially or completely unrelated to the question
- Problems with speech may be so severe that the person does not make any sense at all

Grossly Disorganized Behaviors. Grossly disorganized behaviors may involve the following:

- A variety of behaviors, from childlike actions to unpredictable agitation

- Problems may be noted in any goal-directed behavior, leading to problems with performing activities of daily living, such as hygiene and eating
- The person may appear to be disheveled, dressed inappropriately for the weather, or acting bizarre

Negative Symptoms. Negative symptoms are aspects of a person's affect or behavior that would be expected to be present but are not and therefore represent a presentation that is not within the normal limits of functioning. Three negative symptoms are as follows:

- *Affective flattening:* The person's face appears flat and unmoving, with poor eye contact and limited body language
- *Alogia:* The client has decreased productivity of speech, with brief, empty replies
- *Avolition:* The person may sit for extended periods of time, showing little interest in work or social activities

Other Psychotic Disorders. Other psychotic disorders include schizoaffective disorder, schizophreniform disorder, brief psychotic disorder, and delusional disorder.

Schizoaffective Disorder. One can conceptualize schizoaffective disorder as schizophrenia intersecting with the major mood disorders: major depressive disorder and bipolar disorder (Frances, 2013a). To separate schizoaffective disorders from bipolar disorder with psychotic features or major depressive disorder with psychotic features, hallucinations and/or delusions must present for at least two weeks in the absence of any mood disorder. In other words, the diagnostic criteria for schizophrenia have been met.

For major depressive disorder with psychotic features or bipolar disorder with psychotic features, the psychosis is present only in the context of the manic or depressive symptoms. Because many people with schizophrenia understandably have accompanying mood symptoms, it is often easy for the practitioner to assume the patient has schizoaffective disorder. I suggest using either bipolar disorder with psychotic features or major depressive disorder with psychotic features as a provisional diagnosis until long-term observation of the patient reveals that they have symptoms of schizophrenia in the absence of a mood disorder. Ronnie was eventually diagnosed with schizoaffective disorder after multiple hospitalizations and intensive community intervention.

Schizophreniform Disorder. People with schizophreniform disorder have displayed the criteria for schizophrenia for between one and six months, no longer. Some people diagnosed with schizophreniform disorder do not go on to develop schizophrenia, while other patients have symptoms that last long enough to meet the criteria for schizophrenia (Sadock, Sadock, & Ruiz, 2015). Whether schizophreniform disorder is its own disorder or a precursor to schizophrenia is a matter of conjecture.

Brief Psychotic Disorder. The symptoms of brief psychotic disorder are identical to those of schizophrenia, except that the symptoms last one month or less. Like those with schizophreniform disorder, people with brief psychotic disorder can go on to develop schizophrenia, (or schizophreniform disorder for that matter), or their symptoms can remit (American Psychiatric Association, 2013).

Delusional Disorder. Delusional disorder is a psychotic illness in which the person experiences delusions but none of the other symptoms of schizophrenia. In some cases, hallucinations may be present, but they are related to the delusion and do not cause a disturbance in and of themselves (American Psychiatric Association, 2013).

Psychotic Disorder Differential Diagnoses. When making a diagnosis of any type, we must consider a variety of factors that could be causing the presenting signs and symptoms. There are many mental health disorders other than psychotic disorders that can include psychotic symptoms. As previously mentioned, major depressive and bipolar disorder with psychotic or catatonic features have psychotic symptoms only during the active phase of a mood disorder. PTSD is strongly considered when an actual event(s) seems to have caused the symptoms. Medical issues such as urinary tract infections in older adults can produce psychotic symptoms.

Substance-induced psychosis, specifically with the use of hallucinogens, stimulants, cannabinoids, dissociates, and entactogens, can induce psychosis; these symptoms typically remit once the substance is no longer active in the body. However, in some cases, severe hallucinations or delusions that developed during intoxication by or withdrawal from a substance or within one month of intoxication or withdrawal and persist after the person has stopped using the substance and withdrawal has ended may lead to a diagnosis of substance-induced psychotic disorder.

Schizophrenia or Other Psychotic Disorders as a Mental Health Emergency. Once problems of suicidal or homicidal thinking and behaviors have been addressed, we must examine if the person is able to take care of themselves. As we saw with Ronnie, his psychosis created a situation in which he was not able to care for himself and was putting him in danger. Many people with psychotic disorders have periods of stability despite their chronic illness. It is the acute exacerbations of the psychotic illnesses that create mental health emergency situations. In most of these situations, the patient must be admitted for stabilization and a return to baseline.

Panic Attacks

Panic attacks are a set of symptoms, and can occur with a variety of mental health disorders, including anxiety disorders, major depressive disorder, substance-induced disorders, and PTSD. Recurrent panic attacks can qualify for a diagnosis of panic disorder (American Psychiatric Association, 2013). Panic attacks are abrupt and intense, with the symptoms often described as "like a heart attack." Panic attack symptoms may include a pounding heart, chest pain, excessive sweating, feelings of choking or not being able to breathe, dizziness, nausea, an intense fear of dying, numbness to extremities, and intense discomfort (American Psychiatric Association, 2013).

I assessed many people who came to the ER with heart attack symptoms, only to discover that they had experienced a panic attack. When hearing this, they would often say, "I feel so stupid coming here for just a panic attack." I typically responded by asking what the symptoms of a heart attack are. When they listed them, I commented that they are nearly identical to those of a panic attack and asked, "So what are you supposed to do when you have these symptoms?"

"Get to the hospital," the patient usually responded.

"Exactly! If it is a heart attack, this is the place to be. If it's not, this is where we find that out. It's always better to be safe than sorry."

Features of Panic Attacks. Panic attacks are often unexpected and with no obvious triggers. The frequency and severity of panic attacks can vary. They usually last under 10 minutes, and rarely can last more than 10 to 15 minutes, often with residual symptoms. Many of the accompanying or secondary symptoms are due to decreased carbon dioxide levels in the blood because the person has hyperventilated (Frances, 2013a).

Expected panic attacks can occur because the person is triggered by cues from a previous panic attack. People are often consumed with anxiety that they will have a panic attack in a social situation. A person can also have nocturnal panic attacks in which they awaken in a state of panic. Many people with panic attacks worry that their symptoms are signs of undiagnosed medical problems. They may also engage in catastrophic thinking about any physical symptoms, medication side effects, etc. Others worry that their symptoms are a sign that they are "going crazy." Many such people reorganize their lives to avoid situations in which they might have a panic attack.

Panic Attacks as Mental Health Emergencies. Because the symptoms of a panic attack closely mirror the signs of a heart attack, a medical assessment, specifically an electrocardiogram (EKG or ECG), is the most immediate response. Once a medical condition is ruled out, reassuring the patient that what they experienced is not uncommon and providing psychoeducation about panic attacks and anxiety disorders in general can be helpful. Whenever working with someone who is anxious or who has had a panic attack, it is important for the clinician to "go low and go slow," so as not to react to the client's anxiety. This is not something that is easy to do: It takes self-awareness and practice.

Borderline Personality Disorder (BPD)

Clinicians working in acute care centers or ERs are likely to encounter a larger number of patients with BPD than clinicians who work in other settings (Paris, 2015). Clients with BPD are by nature in near-constant crisis. When I was in graduate school, one of my teachers told our class that the best thing we could do with "borderlines" if they ever presented for services was to refer them to another provider. I disagree with that statement, even though people with BPD can be needy, difficult, and emotionally taxing for even the most skilled clinician.

People with BPD often report extreme mood swings, and there is a high comorbidity with bipolar disorder and substance use disorders. Many people with BPD are misdiagnosed with bipolar disorder, even though they have never had a true manic or hypomanic episode (Paris, 2015). One reason for this misdiagnosis is that bipolar disorder is such a fad diagnosis right now; another reason is that many clinicians simply do not know enough about personality disorders in general (Frances, 2013a; Paris, 2015). People with BPD who present to an ER or acute care clinic typically endorse suicidal ideation, self-injurious behaviors, or hallucinations.

Diagnostic Features of Borderline Personality Disorder. For people with BPD, the fear of abandonment is intense, and they find being alone intolerable. I often ask a person I suspect of having BPD to imagine what it feels like to be alone. They typically respond with a look of extreme fear on their face, with eyes widening. Unfortunately, people with BPD consistently send mixed messages to the people with whom they are in a relationship: "I hate you, don't leave me" or "I love you, get away from me!" They can be very rude, sarcastic, and demanding. It can be difficult for many clinicians to develop empathy for people with BPD.

Stability is elusive for people with BPD. They often demonstrate extreme impulsivity, including self-injurious behaviors that are typically not truly suicidal in nature. However suicidal behaviors are common with BPD, and death by suicide (often accidental) occurs in between 8 and 10 percent of patients. They may have dramatic, sudden, and intense changes in how they define or express themselves. Ideas about other people and themselves are often black and white, but they can change "sides" quickly. People with BPD are easily bored and they typically undermine their own successes. Luckily, symptoms tend to decrease in middle adulthood (American Psychiatric Association, 2013).

Given the extraordinarily high number of people with BPD who experienced sexual abuse and/or a traumatic childhood, it is reasonable to see BPD as a way that some people who have had these horrendous experiences have learned to cope with their trauma (Dimett & Koerner, 2007). Medication and hospitalization have been shown to be ineffective for and even harmful to people with BPD. Correctly diagnosing BPD is the key to appropriate treatment, with dialectical behavioral therapy (DBT) being a preferred intervention.

Borderline Personality Disorder and Differential Diagnoses. The key diagnostic criterion is consistent instability in personality over time, regardless of the person's mood and situation. Several other personality disorders have similarities to BPD, but have some notable differences that the clinician needs to be aware of.

Histrionic personality disorder (HPD) is diagnosed in people who have a volatile mood and the need to be the center of attention but lack the self-destructiveness typically seen with BPD. People with antisocial personality disorder (APD) are focused on material gain or power as opposed to gaining the concern of others. They also completely lack any regard for others' needs and feelings, whereas people with BPD can have concern for others. With dependent personality disorder people react to abandonment by increasing their appeasement of others as opposed to responding to real or imagined abandonment with rage, as can occur with BPD (Frances, 2013a).

Borderline Personality Disorder as a Mental Health Emergency. People with BPD are often in a state of crisis and will present to clinicians with threats of suicide, homicide, hallucinations, delusions, or an inability to care for themselves. Because of this constant state of crisis, some people with BPD may not be able to care for themselves. Psychotic symptoms reported by those with BPD are typically pseudohallucinations brought on by extreme stress. Likewise, the patient's suicidal, and occasional homicidal, ideations are reactions to their mood lability and all-or-nothing thinking. Despite this, all threats of suicide or homicide should be taken seriously, as should any concerns about the patient's ability to care for themselves or others. Dismissing such symptoms as "just due to a personality disorder" ignores the risk of lethality and is unethical.

Dialectical behavioral therapy (DBT) has been shown to be more effective in treating BPD than any other intervention, although it is more intensive and time-consuming than other interventions (Dimett & Koerner, 2007). Due to the length of time and commitment associated with DBT, this is not something done in an acute care setting. However, in any setting, clinicians can be compassionate and understanding with patients with BPD while also maintaining boundaries and setting appropriate limits.

Anorexia Nervosa

Eating disorders, particularly anorexia nervosa and bulimia nervosa, are some of the most serious mental health disorders. The mortality among individuals with these disorders is higher than for nearly all other mental health disorders (Sadock, Sadock, & Ruiz, 2015). Clinicians should not treat an individual with an eating disorder unless the clinician has received additional professional training (I recommend certification) *and* the clinician is working as part of an interdisciplinary team that includes at the least a medical doctor and a registered dietician. Because anorexia nervosa involves an extremely unhealthy body weight (typically measured by a person having a body mass index [BMI] of less than 15 percent of "normal" weight for the client's age and sex), it creates the potential for both a medical and mental health emergency (American Psychiatric Association, 2013).

Features of Anorexia Nervosa. Here are some common characteristics of anorexia nervosa (American Psychiatric Association, 2013):

- Anorexia nervosa may manifest in children as not growing in height due to restricted food intake
- A BMI of 18.5 kg/m^2 is viewed as the lower limit of a healthy body weight
- The person's fear of gaining weight is very real, even for people who are significantly underweight
- This disorder wreaks a huge physical toll on the individual, complicated by the many things that they do to try and lose weight (e.g., using laxatives, inducing vomiting)

- About half of people with anorexia nervosa lose weight by only reducing food intake, whereas the other half diets and binges and purges (Sadock, Sadock, & Ruiz, 2015)
- The diagnosis for anorexia in the *DSM-IV* included an amenorrhea criterion (cessation of menstruation) that was eliminated to account for prepubertal or postmenopausal patients

Development and Course of Anorexia Nervosa. Females outnumber males from 10 to 1 to 20 to 1 in developing anorexia nervosa. It usually begins in late childhood to early adulthood (Sadock, Sadock, & Ruiz, 2015). Some people fully recover after an initial episode, while others experience a roller coaster of weight loss and weight gain. Anorexia nervosa behaviors are like those seen with substance addiction, obsessive-compulsive disorders, anxiety, and depression. Hospitalization is sometimes necessary: "Mortality is high, with more than 5 percent dying per decade after diagnosis, either from physical complications or from suicide" (Paris, 2015, p. 156).

Diagnostic Markers for Anorexia Nervosa. The following medical tests are necessary diagnostic measurements when considering the possibility of anorexia nervosa (Sadock, Sadock, & Ruiz, 2015):

- Serum chemistry: Dehydration is common among patients with anorexia nervosa, and most enzyme levels will be off
- EKG/ECG: Sinus bradycardia (heart rate of < 60 beats per minute [BPM]) is common. Arrhythmias are also possible
- Bone density test: Loss of bone mass is often seen
- Assess for amenorrhea or delayed onset of menarche
- Assess for emaciation
- Assess for lanugo: Lanugo, the development of fine body hair on an individual who is underweight, is an adaptive function the body uses to retain heat when its fat stores are depleted, as with anorexia

Anorexia Nervosa as a Mental Health Emergency. Of all the mental health emergencies we have discussed in this chapter, anorexia nervosa is the one that is most likely to present as a medical emergency rather than a mental health emergency. Typically, clients with anorexia nervosa present when their condition has worsened to the point that it is causing medical problems or concerns from loved ones. If the patient's weight drops too low, and this varies, they may require hospitalization. The need for collaboration between mental health clinicians and medical providers cannot be overstated when it comes to this illness. Most clinicians, on recognizing the presence of anorexia nervosa, will refer the patient to specialized treatment centers.

Catatonia

In the *DSM-IV TR*, catatonia was listed as a subtype of schizophrenia. In the *DSM-5*, catatonia was removed from the definition of schizophrenia in recognition that catatonic symptoms can accompany any number of medical and mental problems (Wakefield, 2013). Patients with catatonia no longer respond to their external environment. There are two subtypes of catatonia: catatonic stupor and catatonic excitement.

Catatonic Stupor. The following are characteristics of catatonic stupor:

- Posturing (the patient holds a position, even something uncomfortable, for a long time)
- Waxy flexibility
- Negativism (absence of any emotional or physical response)
- Rigidity/immobility
- Mutism
- Repetitive actions

Catatonic Excitement. The following are characteristics of catatonic excitement:

- Hyperactivity
- Speech that is hyperverbal or pressured and/or demonstrates verbigeration (repetition of random words)
- Restlessness
- Agitation
- Being in a confused state
- Bizarre stereotypes, mannerisms, grimacing
- Echo phenomena, such as echopraxia and echolalia

Etiology and Severity. Catatonia can also be classified based on its cause (etiology) and severity (strength of symptoms).

Etiology:

- Primary catatonia (catatonia that occurs due to a psychiatric problem):
  - … due to a mood disorder
  - … due to a psychotic disorder
  - … due to other psychiatric disorder
- Secondary catatonia (catatonia that occurs due to a medical problem):
  - … due to a neurological condition
  - … due to a medical condition
  - … due to substance toxicity

Severity:

- Simple catatonia
- Malignant ("lethal") catatonia
  - Usually associated with catatonic excitement
  - Can result in autonomic instability
  - May result in hyperthermia
  - Can lead to death

Catatonia can occur without warning, and signs of it can be easily missed. Ted's story is a good example of this.

CASE STUDY —TED
CATATONIA

Ted, a 19-year-old man, was brought to the ER by his father, Al. Al stated that Ted had not been "acting right." Ted was recently suspended from a military college after he wrote a disparaging letter to the commandant of the academy, which got him into trouble. Ted was subsequently suspended for a semester. Ten days ago, Ted went to North Carolina to visit a friend, and Al noted that Ted took a long time to drive back home and that he has been withdrawn and acting bizarre since that time.

Ted made poor eye contact throughout the interview. He had poor hygiene. He was marginally oriented; he knew who he was, where he was, and the day of the week but not much else. Ted admitted to smoking marijuana and drinking alcohol while he was in North Carolina, but he denied any other drug use. His urine drug screen was negative.

Although he denied hallucinations, Ted appeared to be responding to internal stimuli, as his eyes tracked unseen objects around the hospital room. He was paranoid and confused. His father was understandably concerned and wished for his son to be admitted for further observation. Ted did not appear to understand this, so he was evaluated by a crisis team member and subsequently admitted to a psychiatric hospital involuntarily.

Because Ted appeared to be psychotic, he was started on a regimen of an antipsychotic medication. He initially improved but then became more withdrawn and isolated. He stopped speaking two days later. A day after this, he needed help moving from one room to another as well as with feeding and toileting. He was stuporus, and his antipsychotic medication dosage was increased again in response to this.

As Ted entered his second week on the behavioral health unit, his blood pressure began to rise at an alarming rate. Ted's psychiatrist was at a loss to explain what was happening and asked for a consult from a colleague. The second doctor deduced that Ted was suffering from malignant catatonia. He immediately stopped Ted's antipsychotic medications and started Ted on benzodiazepines. Ted's blood pressure dropped back to normal, and within two days, he was interacting with the staff on the unit without any evidence of impairment. He was discharged after spending a total of two weeks on the unit. A week later, he visited the staff and brought them cookies he had made himself.

Forensic analysis failed to determine the cause for Ted's catatonic state. His family history was unremarkable for schizophrenia or catatonia. Ted's father noted that the friend whom Ted had visited in North Carolina had recently realized he was gay and had told Ted the weekend they were together, which surprised Ted. Ted's father wonders if this shock, coupled with his difficulties at college, simply created a breaking point for his son.

Catatonia as a Mental Health Emergency. The causes for catatonia cannot always be specifically determined. It appears that Ted developed neuroleptic malignant syndrome (NMS) because he was started on antipsychotic medications, which were then quickly increased. The NMS led to catatonia. Treating catatonia typically involves recognizing and correcting the underlying cause of the catatonia (Sadock, Sadock, & Ruiz, 2015). In this situation, medical professionals recognized and removed the offending medications before Ted suffered long-term consequences.

Dementia

Dementia and delirium are both major neurocognitive disorders. Dementia is a progressive deterioration in a person's cognitive baseline over a period of months to years. Dementia is more likely to occur in older adults but can occur in younger adults, particularly in cases where the individual has used alcohol excessively for many years (Sadock, Sadock, & Ruiz, 2015). Diagnostic criteria for dementia include problems with memory, learning, attention, language, executive function, social cognition, and perceptual motor skills (American Psychiatric Association, 2013). Dementia's typically slow onset usually means that an inability to care for oneself does not occur until the later stages of the disorder. There are several types of dementia.

Alzheimer's Disease. Alzheimer's disease is a slow, progressive dementia that is the most common form; 50 to 60 percent of people who have dementia have this type. The typical initial presentation of Alzheimer's is amnesia (forgetting recent activities or information), which increases over time. Personality and behavioral changes are often reported as well; family members may note, "This person is not at all like my mother."

As the disease progresses, the patient's memories regress further, to the point they may not remember close family members. Attention and frustration tolerance can wax and wane throughout the day, typically becoming worse toward the afternoon, a sign commonly referred to as "sundowning." Patients with Alzheimer's disease can also wander or drive purposelessly. It is usually in the later stages of Alzheimer's disease when the patient comes to the attention of crisis staff (Sadock, Sadock, & Ruiz, 2015).

There appears to be a genetic component in Alzheimer's disease, so genetic testing can be helpful but is not predictive. We are still not clear what causes Alzheimer's, and the presence of the disease can only be confirmed through a neuropathological examination of the brain. The average duration of survival after diagnosis is 10 years (Sadock, Sadock, & Ruiz, 2015).

Vascular Dementia. Vascular dementia is the second most common type of dementia, occurring in 15 to 30 percent of all cases (Sadock, Sadock, & Ruiz, 2015). Vascular dementia is caused by multiple areas of cerebral vascular disease and is most commonly seen in men, especially those with hypertension or cardiac issues. Stroke may or may not be present, but blocked blood vessels lead to infarction (cell and tissue death). Alcohol-related dementia, from heavy, long-term use, also falls under the category of vascular dementia.

Lewy Body Dementia. Lewy body dementia is less common than Alzheimer's disease, but the two types of dementia share many features. One distinctive difference between the two is that memory symptoms may not be as prominent with Lewy body dementia as problems with attention and visuospatial abilities. Fluctuating levels of attention and alertness and recurrent visual hallucinations can also occur with Lewy body dementia. Parkinsonian features are also present (Sadock, Sadock, & Ruiz, 2015).

Other Forms of Dementia: A number of other syndromes can cause dementia:

- Head trauma–related dementia

- Human immunodeficiency virus (HIV)-related dementia

- Parkinson's disease dementia

- Huntington's disease dementia

- Substance/medication-induced dementia

Dementia as a Mental Health Emergency. The most pressing issue for the patient with advanced dementia is their immediate safety. A broader concern is allowing the individual to have as much autonomy and independence as possible while also continually assessing their abilities to keep themselves safe and care for themselves. Often, the families of people with dementia keep them at home for as long as they can, not wanting to place their loved ones in a long-term care facility. While this approach generally works at first, as the dementia progresses, the family's ability to care for their loved one diminishes.

I have found that working with people with advanced dementia involves working with the patient's family as much as it does working with the patient. Family members often feel a lot of guilt about bringing their loved ones to a hospital or clinic. There also may be anger among family members because some may feel they have taken on a bigger burden than others in caring for the patient. I have found myself needing to take a much longer time in working with—mainly in listening to—families of people with dementia. Educating the family on the patient's condition and supporting the patient's ability to be as independent as they can be while also ensuring the safety of all involved can be a long, tiring process but also invaluable for those involved.

CHAPTER 5

Suicide

I once heard a clinical teacher say, "Suicide is our cancer." What he meant by this is a client's suicide is the worst thing that can happen to a clinician. Having experienced the completed suicide of two former clients, I understand what the speaker was trying to say, but I don't know if I agree with the comparison to cancer. People survive cancer every day, but a death by suicide is final.

Our goal as clinicians working with people experiencing a mental health emergency is to try and intervene before the patient completes suicide. This is not always possible; many people die by suicide without giving any warning as to their thoughts of killing themselves. Further, we should remember that most people who experience suicidal ideation do not try to take their lives. Even more remarkable is that 90 percent of suicide attempts do not result in a completed suicide (American Foundation for Suicide Prevention, 2018). This number includes the multiple suicide attempts made by some clients.

The key for the astute clinician is to determine whether the client they are assessing is having suicidal ideation with intent. *If* they do, what is the client's risk of attempting suicide?

CASE STUDY—MICHELLE
IDEATION

"I woke up this morning and decided I didn't have anything to live for. I told my dad that he would find me dead when he came home." Michelle, a 13-year-old girl, was sitting in a hospital bed. She had reddish hair, and she had been crying. Her father reacted to his daughter's declaration that morning by bringing her to the hospital. He called Michelle's mother, and she came to the ER. Michelle's uncle also found out and was present. Michelle agreed to speak with me by herself.

"So today was the first day you'd had thoughts of killing yourself?" I asked.

"Yes," she replied, "I woke up tired of feeling this way—you know, depressed."

"Have you thought about how you might try to kill yourself?"

"Not really; I figured I'd look around the house," she stated, then was quiet.

"Your parents seem really upset," I said, "Does that surprise you?"

"It does," she replied, "and it's probably why I don't really feel like killing myself now. I'm just so tired of feeling this way."

"Tell me a little bit more about how you're feeling?" I asked.

"Empty. Sad. I hate school."

Michelle was in the sixth grade. She had repeated the first grade and continued to struggle with reading comprehension.

"My biggest problem is being around so many people," she continued. "It's just hard to stay focused. Plus, I've missed a lot of school."

Michelle had been having severe abdominal pain for the past year, and this had caused her to miss school. Her doctors had not been able to determine the source of this pain.

"Are you in pain now?" I asked.

"It hurts now but not as much as it has before."

"Did this pain have anything to do with your suicidal thoughts?" I asked.

"No, I just felt like I needed to die today. I want to be with my mom."

"I'm confused. Are you talking about someone different than the woman who just stepped out of the room?"

"Yes. I'm talking about my dad's fiancée. I never lived with my biological mom [the woman who'd just left the room]—always my dad. My parents never married. My dad was engaged for a long time to a woman who treated me like her daughter. I called her mom. We were very close, and I miss her."

There was silence for a while.

"What happened?" I asked.

"About two years ago, she was diagnosed with cancer. About a year ago, she took an overdose of pills and died. I really miss her." More silence.

"And that also had something to do with you wanting to die this morning?" I asked.

"I guess."

"How have you and your dad talked about your mother's death?" I asked.

"We talked some," said Michelle, sitting up. "I know he was real sad, and that's why I could never really say much, you know? I didn't want to make him feel worse."

"And sometimes it's also hard to put feelings into words?"

"Yeah, maybe," she replied.

"If you were to kill yourself, how do you think it would affect your dad?"

Michelle's eyes got big. "I've been thinking about that since I told him I wanted to die this morning. It would kill him." She started to cry again. "That's why I really don't want to kill myself. I just hate feeling this way."

More silence passed.

"You ever talk about it with anyone other than your dad?" I asked.

"My guidance counselor at school, but only recently. For a long time, I didn't talk about it." Pause. "I still don't know what talking about it could do. I just wish I could go back in time."

"You were 12 when your mom died, right?" I asked.

"Yeah."

"Maybe it's taken a while for you to figure out how to talk about it?"

"Maybe," Michelle replied. Another pause. "So, what happens now?"

"I'm going to talk with your folks and get some information from them. Then we'll all come in and talk together and figure out the next step. Sound good?"

"Okay."

Defining Suicide and Suicidal Behavior

What do we mean by *suicide*? A variety of terms and words have been used to describe self-injury and the ways a person tries to, and sometimes succeeds in, kill(ing) themselves. For our purposes, we use the "terms comprising suicidal ideation and behavior" as defined by Sadock, Sadock, and Ruiz (2015) to explore the meaning of suicide.

Aborted Suicide Attempt. This is potentially self-injurious behavior with explicit or implicit evidence that the person intended to die, but stopped their attempt before physical damage occurred.

Deliberate Self-Harm. This is the willful self-infliction of painful, destructive, or injurious acts without intent to die. Most clinicians are familiar with patients who cut themselves while professing they are not trying to kill themselves. Although self-injurious behaviors were once considered by most people to be suicide attempts, over the past two decades, we have begun to distinguish suicidal behavior from self-injurious behaviors.

Most of the time, we can say that self-injurious behavior is different from suicidal behavior. Joiner (2005) postulated that some people may utilize self-harm to build their confidence to attempt suicide. Therefore, we need to not automatically assume that a person who cuts is *not* experiencing suicidal ideation, especially when we consider that a history of self-harming behaviors is cited as one of the strongest predictors of future suicidal behaviors (Ribeiro et al., 2016).

Lethality of Suicidal Behavior. Lethality is distinct from, and may not always coincide with, an individual's expectation of what is *medically dangerous*. I have worked with clients who took as little as 800 milligrams of ibuprofen thinking that this would kill them, when the most it did was cure them of a headache. The key is not only the actual lethality of the behavior but also what the client *thought* about the lethality of their plan.

Suicidal Ideation. Suicidal ideation is the thought of serving as the agent of one's own death. The seriousness of the ideation varies depending on the specificity of suicide plans and the degree of suicidal intent. Whereas Michelle did not have a specific plan, she was expressing thoughts of wanting to die. Suicidal ideation, without a plan, is the primary complaint to which I responded in the ER. Suicidal ideation is not uncommon among people with major depressive disorder, bipolar disorder, psychotic disorders, BPD, and many other mental illnesses and in people suffering from addictive disorders (Sadock, Sadock, & Ruiz, 2015). Hallgren and colleagues (2017) noted that "in the general population, alcohol or drug use disorders increase the risk for suicide by a factor of 10 to 14" (p. 150). Suicidal ideation, even without a specific plan, should always be taken seriously.

Suicidal Intent. This is a person's subjective expectation and desire for a self-destructive act to end in death. I see suicidal intent as in between suicidal ideation and a suicide attempt. The client has moved beyond thinking about killing themselves to *how* they could kill themselves.

Suicide Attempt. This is a person's self-injurious behavior with a nonfatal outcome accompanied by explicit or implicit evidence that the person intended to die. Examples of this include any of the ways in which people complete suicide. I have spoken with patients who shot themselves in the head in an attempt to complete suicide yet survived. I have also spoken with people who lived after jumping from buildings, sometimes several stories.

Suicide. This is sometimes called "death by suicide." It is a self-inflicted death with explicit or implicit evidence that the person intended to die.

Suicide—Epidemiology

More than half of the patients I saw in the ER daily had a chief complaint of suicidal ideation or a suicide attempt. In 2016, more than 44,000 people died by suicide in the United States (American Foundation for Suicide Prevention, 2017). Behind this number are more than 44,000 unique individuals who killed themselves. Each person was someone's child, parent, relative, and/or friend.

Individual suicide is not predictable, despite many efforts to try and predict it (Ribeiro et al., 2016). Sometimes, the means a person uses to complete suicide causes others to view the death as an accident. This may be due to denial on their part ("He/she would NEVER do THAT!"). Other times, a medical examiner cannot or will not definitively state that the person completed suicide (Katz, Bolton, & Sareen, 2016). Several years ago, the adult son of one of my friends hanged himself. In what I assume was an effort to spare the family additional pain, the investigating detective initially stated that the death was accidental. Later, the medical examiner ruled it a suicide. Rather than provide comfort, the initial declaration created confusion and additional grief for the family.

The statistics on suicide are sobering and disturbing (Centers for Disease Control, 2017):

- Suicide is the 10th leading cause of death in the United States
- Suicide is the second-leading cause of death for people ages 10 to 34
- There were 44,965 suicides in 2016
- The suicide rate is 13.9 per 100,000 people
- In 2016, there were an average of 123 suicides per day in the United States. In 2015, there were an average 121 suicides per day, and in 2014 the average was 117 per day
- Males are 3.5 times more likely to complete suicides, and females are four times more likely to make suicide attempts
- Since 1950, suicide deaths increased by 50 percent in males and 33 percent in females in the United States
- Suicide rates increase with age and are highest in white middle-aged and older men
- In 2016, there were 25 times more suicide attempts than completed suicides
- Ten percent of people admitted to a psychiatric hospital for a suicide attempt eventually do complete a suicide

To put this in further perspective, let's look at how suicide compares with other causes of death in the United States for the year 2016.

10 Leading Causes of Death By Age Group, United States — 2016

Centers for Disease Control and Prevention
National Center for Injury Prevention and Control

Rank	<1	1-4	5-9	10-14	15-24	25-34	35-44	45-54	55-64	65+	Total
1	Congenital Anomalies 4,816	Unintentional Injury 1,261	Unintentional Injury 787	Unintentional Injury 847	Unintentional Injury 13,895	Unintentional Injury 23,984	Unintentional Injury 20,975	Malignant Neoplasms 41,291	Malignant Neoplasms 116,364	Heart Disease 507,118	Heart Disease 635,260
2	Short Gestation 3,927	Congenital Anomalies 433	Malignant Neoplasms 449	Suicide 436	Suicide 5,723	Suicide 7,366	Malignant Neoplasms 10,903	Heart Disease 34,027	Heart Disease 78,610	Malignant Neoplasms 422,927	Malignant Neoplasms 598,038
3	SIDS 1,500	Malignant Neoplasms 377	Congenital Anomalies 203	Malignant Neoplasms 431	Homicide 5,172	Homicide 5,376	Heart Disease 10,477	Unintentional Injury 23,377	Unintentional Injury 21,860	Chronic Low Respiratory Disease 131,002	Unintentional Injury 161,374
4	Maternal Pregnancy Comp. 1,402	Homicide 339	Homicide 139	Homicide 147	Malignant Neoplasms 1,431	Malignant Neoplasms 3,791	Suicide 7,030	Suicide 8,437	Chronic Low Respiratory Disease 17,810	Cerebrovascular 121,630	Chronic Low Respiratory Disease 154,596
5	Unintentional Injury 1,219	Heart Disease 118	Heart Disease 77	Congenital Anomalies 146	Heart Disease 949	Heart Disease 3,445	Homicide 3,369	Liver Disease 8,364	Diabetes Mellitus 14,251	Alzheimer's Disease 114,883	Cerebrovascular 142,142
6	Placenta Cord. Membranes 841	Influenza & Pneumonia 103	Chronic Low. Respiratory Disease 68	Heart Disease 111	Congenital Anomalies 388	Liver Disease 925	Liver Disease 2,851	Diabetes Mellitus 6,267	Liver Disease 13,448	Diabetes Mellitus 56,452	Alzheimer's Disease 116,103
7	Bacterial Sepsis 583	Septicemia 70	Influenza & Pneumonia 48	Chronic Low Respiratory Disease 75	Diabetes Mellitus 211	Diabetes Mellitus 792	Diabetes Mellitus 2,049	Cerebrovascular 5,353	Cerebrovascular 12,310	Unintentional Injury 53,141	Diabetes Mellitus 80,058
8	Respiratory Distress 488	Perinatal Period 60	Cerebrovascular 38	Cerebrovascular 50	Chronic Low Respiratory Disease 206	Cerebrovascular 575	Cerebrovascular 1,851	Chronic Low Respiratory Disease 4,307	Suicide 7,759	Influenza & Pneumonia 42,479	Influenza & Pneumonia 51,537
9	Circulatory System Disease 460	Cerebrovascular 55	Septicemia 40	Influenza & Pneumonia 39	Influenza & Pneumonia 189	HIV 546	HIV 971	Septicemia 2,472	Septicemia 5,941	Nephritis 41,095	Nephritis 50,046
10	Neonatal Hemorrhage 398	Chronic Low Respiratory Disease 51	Benign Neoplasms 31	Septicemia 31	Complicated Pregnancy 184	Complicated Pregnancy 472	Septicemia 897	Homicide 2,152	Nephritis 5,650	Septicemia 30,405	Suicide 44,965

Data Source: National Vital Statistics System, National Center for Health Statistics, CDC.
Produced by: National Center for Injury Prevention and Control, CDC using WISQARS™

The 2016 data has one flaw that hides one of the highest groups of completed suicides (Shah et al., 2016). The oldest age range comprises a very wide age range. Most demographics take this growing age range (senior adults) and break it down into three groups (which matches the other adult divisions):

- Younger elderly: 65–74 years of age
- Middle elderly: 75–84 years of age
- Older elderly: 85 years and older

Men 85 and older have the highest rate of completed suicide (51.6 per 100,000 of the population). This ratio is buried when we expand the age group to those 65 and older. There are several theories as to why the suicide rate increases markedly in this older adult group. A prominent theory posited by Joiner (2005) is that older males are more isolated then their female peers and are more likely to perceive they are a burden to others, thus greatly increasing their reasons for suicidal behavior.

Suicide Deaths by Method

We must also consider *how* people complete suicide. The higher rate of completed suicide by men is due to greater lethality of the means that men use to kill themselves. Males continue to use more lethal means (gunshot, jumping, and hanging) compared with females, who tend to employ methods where there is a chance of rescue (poisoning and overdose). Two of three completed suicides among men were by a firearm, compared with one of three among women (Joiner, 2005). The "Other" category includes suicide by cutting oneself, self-immolation, jumping, and any additional methods not covered in the other sections.

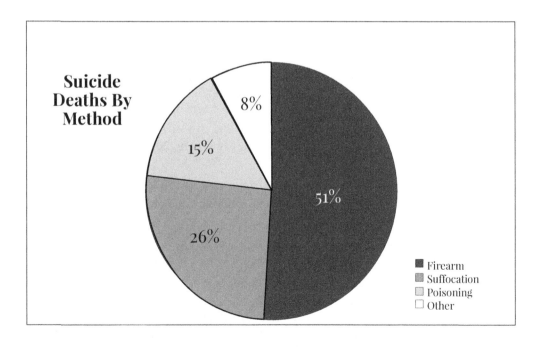

Suicide Risk Factors

There are many risk factors for suicide. Each of these, covered in the following sections, needs to be considered when assessing a patient's suicide risk.

Mental Illness. A mental illness is one of the biggest risk factors for suicide (Chesney, Goodwin, & Fazel, 2014). We must also be aware that:

- The severity of the mental illness increases suicide risk
- Multiple mental illnesses seem to increase suicide risk
- Substance use disorders, anorexia nervosa, BPD, and mood disorders appear to be the mental health disorders with a higher possibility of suicide (Chesney, Goodwin, & Fazel, 2014)
- A recent psychiatric hospitalization is a risk factor. Olfson, Marcus, and Bridge (2014) noted that 24 percent of completed suicides occur within the first three months following a discharge from an inpatient behavioral health unit. A major reason for this high rate is the general lack of post-hospital care or follow-up (Kessler, Warner, & Ivany, 2015)

Feelings of Hopelessness or Worthlessness. This is a major risk factor because clients who feel this way do not believe that things will get better, so suicide is a viable option. People with a physical illness (whether acute or chronic), particularly a recent diagnosis of a serious illness, often have these feelings.

Believing That One Is a Burden to Others. Joiner (2005) noted that feeling like a burden is likely a major reason why suicide rates are so much higher among elderly men; they believe that their continued existence imposes a burden on their loved ones.

Past Suicide Attempts. This is the strongest single suicide risk factor.

Minority Stress. Although suicide rates have been higher among whites than African-Americans, the differences in rates among races have been narrowing in recent years. In particular, the rate of suicide attempts among young African-American males has been increasing. High rates are reported in Native Americans (Joiner, 2005).

Marital and Parental Status. The highest risk occurs among those never married, followed in descending order of risk by those who are widowed, separated or divorced, married without children, and married with children.

Lack of Support. Having a limited support system, whatever the family structure, and living alone increase the risk of suicide.

Trauma History. Persons who have experienced abuse, especially physical or sexual abuse as a child or adult or having witnessed severe physical violence or killing are at greater risk of suicide (O'Hare, Shen, & Sherrer, 2014).

Family History of Suicide. Some researchers believe that there is a genetic predisposition for suicide (Sadock, Sadock, & Ruiz, 2015). Whereas this is certainly possible, we must consider that people who have experienced the completed suicide of a loved one may be influenced by this behavior, whether they are genetically related or not, and see suicide as a viable alternative for themselves. Given that major depressive disorder is a strong risk factor for suicide, we must also consider the genetic component of depressive disorders.

Reunion Fantasies. These are a common thread in many conversations I have had with people who are experiencing suicidal ideation and this appeared to be the case for Michelle: She wanted to see her mother again. Similar fantasies can include observing one's funeral or how other people would respond to the news of the client's death. Another fantasy involves suicide as revenge for a real or perceived slight or injury.

Recent Stressors. Financial and relationship changes are common stressors noted by people expressing suicidal ideation. Additional stressors can include a lack of services in the community and/or a lack of housing.

Access to Weapons. Having access to the means of killing themselves, particularly firearms, is a risk factor.

Suicide Notes. Letters written previous to suicidal actions were once seen as a common component of a completed suicide. Even today, people learning of a suicide sometimes ask, "Did they leave a note?" The fact is that many people who complete suicide do not leave a note. Still, some people leave notes, even in the form of marking on their bodies or posting messages on social media. Sometimes a social media posting is a way in which a person who is considering suicide can get help.

When I worked in the ER there were several occasions when a person had left a message on social media that alerted friends and family that the writer was either considering suicide or had made an attempt (overdose). People who read the post were then able to call the police and an ambulance to bring their loved one to the ER. Writing a suicide note is a risk factor because it shows attention to detail in their plans to kill themselves.

Treatment Resistance. An unwillingness to accept help is an often overlooked risk factor. I have worked with people who have attempted suicide and then refused to speak to anyone when they arrived at the ER. In nearly all of these cases, the individual had to be involuntarily hospitalized.

Hallgren and coworkers (2017) assessed 868 patients with substance use problems who had received primary care over a 7-month period. The authors found that nearly 26 percent of respondents had experienced suicidal ideation. The researchers noted elevated levels in participants who were female, lacked a high school diploma, were unemployed, reported a variety of mental health symptoms, and had used the ER or mental health services in the previous 90 days. One of the interesting things about this study is that participants had been seen by primary care providers. The results emphasize the need for more and better screening by primary care providers.

Suicide Protective Factors

Although we should be aware of the many risk factors regarding suicidal ideation or suicide attempts, we also must be aware of the factors that can protect against suicide (Sadock, Sadock, & Ruiz, 2015). We must remember, however, that whereas protective factors can reduce the risk of suicide, they cannot always prevent it.

Pregnancy. Pregnancy is often considered a protective factor. Obviously not everyone can get pregnant and getting pregnant can be a risk factor in some situations. However, for many women, being pregnant provides them with a sense of hope and a feeling that they are responsible for someone other than themselves. Despite pregnancy being a protective factor in many cases, the astute practitioner should continuously screen for pre- and postpartum depressive disorder, as there may be a higher level of suicidal ideation among women who are pregnant when compared with the general population (Gelaye, Kajeepeta, & Williams, 2016).

Parenthood. Being a parent, and especially having children in the home, is a major protective factor. Many adults experiencing suicidal ideation have told me that they do not want to harm themselves because they know it would negatively impact their children. Other patients have told me that they do not want to kill themselves in a place where their children might find their bodies.

Religiosity/Spiritual Connectedness. Having a relationship with one's higher power can also be a protective factor. Some people's beliefs include an admonition against suicide. Many patients have told me that they believe they will go to hell if they kill themselves and that this is the main reason they have not attempted suicide. My follow-up response is typically, "Your spirituality is important to you …," which can lead to further discussion about additional protective and risk factors.

Responsibility for Others. A sense of responsibility for family or other loved ones is another protective factor. In some cases, this is because there are children in the home, and other times, the patient may have the responsibility to care for another person.

Support Network. Social supports include family members, friends, a job, membership in a church or club, or any number of connections with other people. The greater the sense of social connectivity, the greater the protective factor. Michelle had invested family members and friends at school, and those relationships were helpful to her.

Future Goals. Being *future oriented* entails having thoughts and plans for the future. Michelle told me that she one day hoped to be a nurse or a counselor, which shows that she had at least some interest in her future.

Be Cautious with Contracts for Safety

As part of assessing or supporting a patient's ability to avoid acting on suicidal thoughts, the concept of "contracting for safety" or getting the client to agree to a "no-harm contract" has been used in clinical practice for many years. First described in the clinical literature in 1973, these contracts were originally designed for clients with whom the clinician had been working for a long time. No-harm contracts imply that patients can promise clinicians that they will not try to harm themselves when they are suicidal. A few problems with these contracts are that the terms are not consistently defined or used, and many clinicians do not receive formal training in performing suicide assessments. In addition, contracts for safety do not protect against legal liability (Garvey et al., 2009).

Furthermore, despite their continued wide use in clinical practice, there is little evidence that such contracts reduce suicide. As such, contracts may provide a false sense of security. The clinician may feel better, but is the client really safe? One of the things I often ask of other providers who use contracts for safety is, "Can a person with a serious mood or psychotic disorder truly understand, consent to, and participate in a contracting process?" I do not think they can in many instances. Instead of relying on a contract, clinicians should consider better tools, which include a detailed lethality assessment, open dialogue between patients and clinicians to establish a therapeutic alliance, and the performance of ongoing comprehensive assessments of suicide risk over time.

Safety Plans

Rather than rely on a contract, I prefer to utilize a comprehensive safety plan, which must have the following elements.

Consent. The patient must agree to and be able to participate in their own safety plan. If they have cognitive problems or are psychotic, this would usually preclude them from being safe if they are also suicidal.

Support. Another person, preferably a friend, family member, or professional caregiver, must be involved in developing a safety plan. This person will also be an immediate support for the client. Talk to the client about who else can be involved in addition to the person who is helping develop the safety plan.

Housing. Where will the patient be staying and for how long?

Removal of Access to Means. Weapons of any kind, including knives and cutlery, should be removed from the patient's access. Medication(s) should be stored in a secure place, and doses should be given to the patient individually and as prescribed.

Coping Skills. How will the next few days be structured? Come up with a plan of things to do to keep the client active. How will the client know when they are doing well? What are some of their warning signs if they begin to not feel well?

Referrals. What outpatient resources are available for the patient? How long will it take them to access these resources? What is the wait time? Resolve all financial (e.g., make sure that any providers take the patient's insurance) and transportation issues.

Contingency Plan. What is the plan if the patient's symptoms worsen? Provide a specific set of instructions for what the patient and their helper should do, including how to contact emergency services.

Safety Plan

Client's Name:

Persons Participating in This Safety Plan:

What Are the Client's Warning Signs or Triggers for Suicidal or Violent Thinking?

What Are Some Coping Skills for When These Thoughts Occur?

Where Will the Client Be Staying and for How Long?

Weapons/Dangerous Objects on the Property:

Where Will These Items Be Secured and By Whom?

Medications Present:

Where Will the Medications Be Secured and By Whom?

Who Will Be Responsible for Providing the Proper Medication to the Patient?

How Will the Next Three Days Be Structured? Who Will Be With the Client?

What Outpatient Resources Are Available to the Client?

What Is the Plan for the Client if Their Symptoms Return or Worsen?

Local Crisis Center or Hotline:

National Suicide Prevention Hotline:

Additional Issues to Consider When Assessing for Suicide

Condition of the Patient. When assessing a potentially suicidal individual, time is usually on your side, except in cases of overdose, poisoning, and/or when the client has ready access to a weapon. Sometimes, people need time to calm down and get their thoughts in order. I was often asked to assess patients who were intoxicated and saying that they were suicidal. I typically allowed them to sober up and receive fluids before completing my assessment and deciding whether to admit them. On many occasions, once the patient had sobered up, they denied having any suicidal ideation. Even in these situations, a safety plan must be completed.

Remember, your immediate safety is important, as is the safety of the patient and others in the community and during an emergency, call the police or EMS when there is a risk of harm to the client or another person (including you). Take all threats of suicide seriously, including nonverbal cues (e.g., poor eye contact, flat affect) and passive statements (e.g., "This will be over soon," "No one seems to care about me"). The more detailed the suicidal ideation, suicidal intent, plan, and means, the greater the suicide risk.

Risk Management. In situations where the client provides limited information and/or is unable to participate in constructing a reliable safety plan, I typically am very cautious about letting them go home (e.g., in these situations, I usually hospitalize them). I always ask myself: Is this a situation that will keep me awake at night if I let the patient go home and I'm just not sure about their safety? A lot also depends on the support the person has available to them.

Suicide: Thought-Processes and Intervention Strategies

In addition to safety plans, clinicians need to be aware of additional interventions for addressing ongoing suicidal ideations and/or suicidal behaviors of their clients. For example, many clients with chronic suicidal ideation or suicidal behaviors see their suicidality as a coping mechanism. Interventions for these clients would be to help them regulate their emotions in healthy ways. Since some clients have likely suffered trauma, utilizing the interventions listed in Chapter 8 (Trauma) could be helpful.

Other clients may view suicide as a viable option for problems (e.g., lost job, faltering relationship). An intervention for these clients could be to approach their thinking through cognitive-behavioral therapy to address negative schemas and work with clients to explore other options to solve their problems. Clients also may not be able to communicate their needs to others except by expressing suicidal ideation or behaviors. Interventions for these clients include listening (sometimes this is what is needed), along with developing healthier communication styles.

After the Crisis

What happens after hospitalization, or your client is released from the ER?

- Develop and stick to a safety plan—even if this means you need to refer the client back to the hospital

- Monitor for treatment (including medication) compliance

- Increase frequency of face-to-face and telephone contacts, and document each of these contacts

- Focus on emotional regulation and problem solving by anticipating potential problems and barriers and developing options for navigating them

- Try to broaden the client's support system as much as possible—bring in community resources (Alcoholics Anonymous/Narcotics Anonymous, National Alliance on Mental Illness, faith communities)

IDEATION

What are some of the risk factors for Michelle?

What are some of the protective factors for Michelle?

Now, develop a safety plan for Michelle. Persons participating in this safety plan:

Where will the client be staying and for how long?

Weapons/dangerous objects on the property:

Where will these items be secured and by whom?

Medications present:

Where will the medications be secured and by whom?

Who will be responsible for providing the proper medication to the patient?

How will the next three days be structured? Who will be with the client?

What outpatient resources are available to the client?

What is the plan for the client if their symptoms return or worsen?

Let's see if we came up with the same risk factors for Michelle:

- Family history of completed suicide (her father's fiancée—mother figure to Michelle)
- Impulsivity (which is not uncommon among adolescents)
- Depression (questionable if this was a reaction to her mother's suicide or if she was depressed before this)
- Initial sense of hopelessness (Michelle reported feeling empty)
- Reunion fantasy (Michelle hoped that when she killed herself she could be reunited with her mother)

Let's see if we came up with the same protective factors for Michelle:

- Active and engaged family members (father and uncle)
- No identifiable plan and no previous suicide attempts or suicidal ideations with a plan
- A willingness to accept help
- Future oriented (during the conversation, Michelle talked about being a nurse or a counselor when she reached adulthood)

The safety plan created by Michelle, her family, and myself included the following steps and components. I spoke with Michelle's father. He said he was comfortable taking his daughter home. I watched as he told her that he loved her and that she was the most important person in his life and he did not want to lose her. Michelle's father stated that there were no guns in the home, and as a precaution, he planned to secure all knives and medications in the home. Michelle's father also worked with his brother, who lived nearby with his family, to make sure that Michelle would never be alone over the next week. He and Michelle accepted referrals for counseling with appropriate providers for Michelle and him. Michelle and her father also agreed to return to the ER or call emergency services should her symptoms return or worsen.

CHAPTER 6

Violence

People who work with individuals who are experiencing a mental health emergency are at risk of becoming victims of violence. Half of all health care workers will be assaulted at some point in their careers, with some studies indicating that almost 100 percent of behavioral health nurses will be assaulted by a patient (McKenna & Paterson, 2006; Richter & Whittington, 2006).

In this chapter, we examine violence as a mental health emergency. We specifically address ways we can prepare for potentially violent situations and how we can respond if a situation were to unfold. We also look at how we should respond when working with a client who expresses a desire to hurt or kill someone else. Remember, people with a serious mental illness are not necessarily more likely to be violent than someone without a serious illness. It is often difficult to determine, at least initially, if a person experiencing a mental health emergency has an underlying mental illness: many other factors can be causing the situation.

Over the years that I have taught about mental health emergencies, I have identified two themes related to violence. The first is that many clinicians are afraid of being hurt, which is understandable. The second theme is that most mental health or medical agencies are not prepared to handle violent situations.

Fear of Harm. As mentioned, the first theme I've identified in my years as a clinician is that many clinicians are afraid of being hurt. This is not unusual, as most people do everything they can to avoid being hurt. When I teach clinicians about mental health emergencies, I ask participants to identify which group they prefer to work with and which group they would like to avoid. When people respond that they prefer to avoid working with people who are aggressive, the primary reason is the desire to avoid getting hurt.

I have been assaulted at least 10 times in my career, with all but one incident being perpetrated by an adolescent. I can now admit that, in all but two situations (one involving an adult and one involving a kid), I played a leading role in triggering the assaults. If I knew then what I know now, I probably would not have been assaulted. At that time, I tended to corner people who were agitated, thereby, limiting their ability to escape. This was sometimes done inadvertently, while other times, cornering was done on purpose because I was young and cocky and thought I was doing "treatment" by pushing my clients toward what I perceived to be a cathartic moment. Instead of helping, all I really did was trigger my clients' trauma responses and engage their fight-or-flight response. With me blocking the exit, they had only one way to get away—through me—and this sometimes meant becoming violent. I am not proud of this part of my career, and I would like to think that it knocked some sense into me and made me a better clinician, as I learned from my mistakes.

The two incidents in which I do not believe I triggered the aggression involved individuals who appeared to want to harm someone, and I was their intended target. One occurred on a camping trip with a young man who threw a rock at my head when one of my teammates set a limit with him. The other violent incident involved an adult who made it clear that he wanted to harm someone who worked for the hospital, and I was simply in the wrong place at the wrong time. Luckily, I was not seriously injured in either case.

I should mention that although clinicians certainly may examine people who become violent due to a mental illness or the effects of a substance abuse, I do not consider that the people who assaulted me did so because they were mentally ill or intoxicated. In my experience, most people who are psychotic and violent are acting out from a place of fear; usually something related to their thought disorder.

I have been in many situations in which I had to restrain patients with a thought disorder. Even when they were acting out violently toward me, it felt different compared with situations in which someone simply wanted to hurt someone else and tried to harm me. Although people who want to harm others may have a thought or mood disorder, my experience is that clients who aim to hurt others are predominately antisocial and derive a sense of power or even pleasure when harming someone else. Frankly, because of the intent (perceived or real) behind these actions, these types of assaults tend to be more damaging. As I mentioned, thankfully this group is small in most clinical settings (apart from prison or jail populations).

Lack of Preparation. The second theme I have identified in looking at violence is that most mental health or medical agencies are not prepared to handle violent situations. This includes hospitals with acute care behavioral health EDs or inpatient behavioral health units. These agencies appear to have a prevailing belief that if violence hasn't happened there before, it won't ever happen. This is called institutional denial. This lack of preparation is a primary concern among the people who attend my trainings. Imagining possible dangerous situations and preparing for them accordingly is necessary for all clinicians, regardless of the size and scope of their practice.

McKenna and Paterson (2006) noted that in addition to denying the potential for violence, institutions can also ignore violence itself or even the existence of a risk of violence. Some institutions may blame individual staff when violence occurs, some of whom are the victims of violence. In these situations, organizations make a scapegoat of the person, blaming the violence on perceived or real deficits of the staff person.

Epidemiology of Violence

There is no failsafe way to predict which clients will become violent and which ones will not. We must also remember that violence can assume many forms, including verbal aggression, physical violence, bullying, threats, sexual violence, and intimidation. We must also consider sources of violence other than just the client:

The literature investigating violence has consistently highlighted the patient/client as the perpetrator of violence. However, there is a growing recognition that work-related violence in health care is also attributed to relatives, friends, and members of the public. The challenge of maintaining safe, secure, and therapeutic clinical environments for staff and patients in mental health is complicated by the increased frequency in the number of relatives and visitors as a source of work-related violence. (Cowman, 2006, p. 253)

For the purposes of this chapter, we focus on physical violence from our clients; however, what we examine is applicable to other "actors" in a clinical setting. We include a discussion of security procedures and ways to determine who has access to the clinical environment.

Environment. Environment is the time, place, and circumstances in which an individual is/was raised or currently resides. Was the individual raised in a violent household or community? This experience can play an influential role on their views of violence. People who are exposed to violence every day may become desensitized to it; many of them or their loved ones may have been victims of violence.

Medical History. Does the client have an illness (medical or mental) that could lead to a higher potential for violence? It is important to assess for potentially dangerous organic causes of agitation as soon as this can be done safely (send them to an ER to be certain). Two common causes for aggression are delirium and dementia, which may be caused by a variety of conditions. An organic workup is necessary to rule out medical causes for violence. Along with vital signs, obtaining a urine drug screen (UDS) and a Blood Alcohol Level (BAL) is extremely important. In the ER drug and alcohol intoxication or withdrawal are the most common diagnoses in combative patients. Other tests include a rapid serum glucose (blood sugar level) measurement and pulse oximetry (blood oxygen content).

Interpersonal Relations. How does the individual relate to others? When I was an intern for a women's residential substance abuse treatment facility, most of the clients had experienced repeated acts of violence in their lives. For these women, there was no distinction between assertiveness and aggression: To be assertive, one had to be aggressive to survive. When a person's world and relationships are viewed through this lens, the only solution to being threatened, slighted, or not having one's needs met is to become violent.

Genetics and Epigenetics. Is there a genetic predisposition toward violence? This is an area that continues to be explored, particularly in populations that have experienced historical and systemic violence.

Neurochemistry and Endocrine Function. As we discuss further in Chapter 9, the more we learn about the brain, the less we seem to really know:

> While brain damage, nutritional deficits, and prenatal or birth complications are
> regarded as external organic causes of aggression, several functional deficits can be

described on the microlevel of the human brain. Well-known and presumed causal mechanisms are related to neurotransmitters such as serotonin, levels of which are found to be lower in aggressive humans. (Whittington & Richter, 2006, p. 53)

Substance Abuse. The presence of an inebriant, especially alcohol, is a common factor in violent situations. We go into detail about how substance use can present as a mood disorder and/or psychosis and may influence a person's behavior in the immediate and long term in Chapter 9.

Other Individuals. People accompanying the client to the clinical setting can instigate a client who is already upset. What's more, staff may unintentionally provoke the patient to become more aggressive (Whittington & Richter, 2006).

Risk Factors for Violence

Although we cannot predict which person may become violent, there are risk factors of which we need to remain aware. Steinert (2006) discusses some common characteristics of more aggressive patients. A history of violence is the most reliable risk factor. Male patients (who have a higher overall rate of violence than female patients) tend to demonstrate violence due to substance intoxication, whereas psychotic symptoms appear to be a higher cause for females. Drug or alcohol abuse increases the potential for violence, especially alcohol, as it is one of the most widely used and accessible drugs of abuse. It is worth noting that ethnicity, age, marital status, and education do not reliably identify as risks for violent behaviors.

Higher-Risk Diagnoses. Psychopathology is also considered a primary risk factor. According to Steinert (2006, p.115), "Probably the risk of violence generally increases with the severity of psychopathological symptoms, though contradictory findings with regards to this subject have also been mentioned." Regardless of the different findings of various researchers, a known psychiatric illness is a risk factor for violent behavior (Steinert, 2006). Attention should be paid in situations in which patients display signs and symptoms of the following disorders:

- Mania, particularly in situations where mania co-occurs with psychotic symptoms
- Depression with psychotic features
- Command auditory hallucinations
- Delusions involving violence
- Personality disorders
  - Antisocial personality disorder
  - Borderline personality disorder
  - A history of fire setting or cruelty to animals as a child, even in the absence of a formal personality disorder diagnosis
- Cognitive disorders

- o Intellectual or developmental disability
- o Neurologic impairment
- o Traumatic brain injury (TBI)
- o Autism spectrum disorder
- PTSD: Some people with PTSD experience flashbacks or other dissociative symptoms during which they can become violent, as their fight-or-flight responses become activated
- Behavioral disorders
  - o Conduct disorder
  - o Intermittent explosive disorder
  - o Oppositional defiant disorder

People with these disorders can exhibit violence, however, people without mental illness can be similarly, if not more, violent. "There is evidence that only a minor part of aggressive patient behavior is a direct consequence of psychopathological symptoms, whereas a major part can be attributed to similar psychological motives in those not mentally disturbed" (Steinert, 2006, p. 115).

Whenever there is a prominent act of violence in our country, the media suggest that the perpetrator has a mental illness and that is the cause of the violence. In some cases, this is true, but just as often, the person is acting on political or religious motivations or they seem to just want to hurt people. Regardless, our society's tendency to point the finger at mental illness as the primary cause of violence further stigmatizes an already marginalized group.

Preparation in Response to Violence

When working with people in any capacity, everyone's safety should be paramount. In any setting in which people might experience a mental health emergency, it is imperative that the environment be as safe as possible. Security procedures are essential in limiting the potential for violence; specifically, having a team of trained and responsive security personnel and the means to signal for their help.

Most clinicians working in private practice themselves may be the "security force." In larger agencies, there should be designated staff with additional training in verbal and nonverbal de-escalation techniques and/or physical restraint. Every agency must plan for the possibility of a violent patient, whether it has one employee or 500. I recommend examining the following issues as they pertain to the general clinic/hospital/office environment.

Limiting Access. Controlling access into the clinic helps to reduce the opportunities for violence. This can be done by limiting the number of entrances, controlling entryways (e.g., using remote-activated doors), and monitoring who enters. High-risk clinics should limit access to one or two entrances, especially during the evening hours. Clinics should also have a means to lock the doors to people coming into the clinic.

The hospital at which I worked the most would automatically lock all doors to the hospital whenever a patient came in who had been stabbed or shot. The hospital remained on lockdown until the situation was resolved by the police. The reason for this reaction was that people outside the hospital might want to do further harm to the person who had been stabbed or shot.

Caretaker Education. Regular, brief education sessions with clinicians, nurses, and ancillary staff on the prevention and management of agitated/violent patients may reduce the incidence of violence and improve worker satisfaction. Training should include role plays and drills for staff to practice how to respond to a violent patient or visitor. All staff who encounter patients should be aware of how their actions and reactions to a patient's behaviors can exacerbate a situation. According to Steinert (2006, p. 115), "It is common sense knowledge that staff behavior, staff attitudes, and staff personality traits play a major role in provoking or preventing violent conflict escalations, even if from a scientific viewpoint there is not yet much evidence."

Alarm Systems. Internal systems to notify hospital or clinic security are important in larger settings. In the hospital where my wife works, the staff carry "panic buttons" that can alert hospital security. In the hospitals where I worked, we had several emergency buttons spaced around the ER that notify the local police when pushed. It is imperative that these systems be tested regularly and that staff know when to utilize them. It is even more important that the systems be connected to outside services.

One of my coworkers, a medical provider, was in an isolated office in our hospital when she was confronted by a patient who was upset because she refused to prescribe the benzodiazepines he demanded. She pressed the panic button in her office expecting to get some response, but nothing happened. Luckily, my friend talked her way out of the situation without being physically harmed. After the incident ended, she learned that the hospital had paid to put the panic button in but not to have it connected to the local police station. My friend quit shortly thereafter due to her observation that the hospital administration was not prioritizing her safety.

Reducing Risk in the Clinical Environment

How we establish the setting for interviewing a client correlates to how the agency or hospital creates an overall safe environment. The setting of the patient interview should be private but not isolated. In most situations and with most patients, this is sufficient to ensure safety. When patients present as violent or threatening violence, additional steps should be taken. Some clinics have observation rooms specifically intended for interviewing potentially dangerous patients. In other cases, whenever a potentially aggressive or volatile patient is interviewed, security personnel or law enforcement officers should be nearby with the door left open to allow both intervention and escape by the clinician.

In all situations, the patient and interviewer should be seated roughly equidistant from the door, or the interviewer may sit between the patient and the door but not in a manner that traps or blocks the client. The patient should not sit between the clinician and the exit, nor should the exit be blocked. Blocking the door poses a risk of harm to the clinician if the patient feels the need to escape. The clinician should have unrestricted access to the door and therefore should never sit behind a desk unless they still have access to the exit.

Clinicians should take care when setting up their office if this is where they interact with clients. The interview room should not contain heavy objects that may be thrown. Be aware of lamps or other potential weapons, like electrical cords, needles, or hot liquids that could be used as weapons (or means of self-harm). One of my peers tells a story of his first day at a new private practice. He took time to walk around the office and meet the other clinicians. He noted that one of his new coworkers had a ceremonial dagger hanging on his wall. The dagger's owner was not concerned that it could be used as a weapon.

In addition to the office or physical surroundings, the clinician should be aware of any objects on themselves or the patient's body that could be used for harm. Pens, watches, and belts may be used as weapons, as can glasses, earrings, neckties, and necklaces. When I started working in the ER. an administrator once asked me why I was "out of uniform" (e.g., not wearing a tie). I replied that I would not wear a tie, as it posed a safety risk I was unwilling to take, given the potentially violent patients I saw. The administrator then asked the chief psychiatrist his opinion of my statement, and I think he was surprised when the doctor supported my decision and pointed out that he did not wear a tie either.

Aggression Cycle and Interventions

In most situations when a person becomes violent, there is a lead-up to the violent event. An act of aggression and violence can be viewed as the culmination of a sequence of events. I call this the Aggression Cycle.

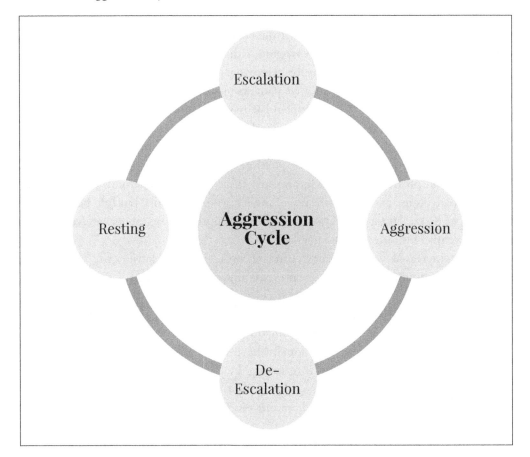

Aggression and violence are things we hope to avoid, which is why we have spent time examining the physical environment and how we prepare to prevent and/or manage violent situations. Once we have done this, we also must be aware of clients who are escalating so we can intervene before aggression occurs and more intensive methods, such as restraint and seclusion, would be considered.

Escalation. In the clinic, an obviously angry patient or someone who appears to be escalating should always be considered potentially violent. There are many signs of escalation to look out for. Steinert (2006, p. 115) noted, "Behaviors observed prior to violent incidents are confusion, irritability, boisterousness, verbal threats, physical threats, and attacks on objects." An angry demeanor may be exhibited as prolonged staring at providers and/or loud, aggressive, rude, sarcastic, or caustic speech. Provocative behavior may include tense posturing (e.g., gripping chair arm rails tightly or clenching fists) and frequently changing body position or pacing. Overtly aggressive acts would include pounding on walls, throwing objects, and/or hitting oneself.

If I suspect the client is psychotic or violent (or has a history of violence), I typically remain standing when talking with them. I always do this if the client remains standing. I also take a neutral stance with my hands visible, so the patient is less likely to assume that I have a weapon: This reduces a triggering of the fight-or-flight response. Eye contact is very important, as is mirroring the client. As I've noted previously, I try to practice a "go low, go slow" approach with my voice tone and always leave myself and the client an escape route.

When I have any concerns about potential violence, I also try to involve other staff who may have an existing relationship with the client or have developed some rapport with them. Just as involving staff who have rapport with a patient who is upset can be helpful to prevent escalation, so is preventing or removing contact between the patient and any belligerent accomplices or other provocative patients or staff.

Patients who are agitated but cooperative may be amenable to verbal de-escalation techniques. Nearly all patients who present with agitation or violent behavior deserve the chance to calm down in response to verbal techniques before physical restraints or sedative medications are implemented. The use of physical, mechanical, or chemical restraint varies state by state, and providing instruction on using these measures is beyond the scope of this text. I do not advocate or condemn the use of these types of restraints, but I do believe that all other forms of de-escalation techniques should be attempted before more coercive means are utilized. Preventive measures are also helpful.

Because increased waiting times correlate with violent behavior, the evaluation of these patients should be expedited to prevent any escalation of aggression. Often, the impression of preferential treatment will defuse patient anger. Ancillary staff sometimes resist this concept and dogmatically insist that the patient wait with everyone else. They must be educated on the importance of "moving someone to the head of the line" when dealing with potential violence. I personally have a tough time doing this, as I believe that giving in to inappropriate or threatening behavior reinforces negative behaviors. However, when dealing with someone who is clearly angry and possibly aggressive in a crowded waiting room, I want to get them out of an area where they could scare or harm others who are also seeking help.

The interviewer should adopt an honest and straightforward manner when dealing with angry and potentially violent clients. Friendly gestures, such as offering a comfortable chair or something to eat or drink (but not a hot liquid, which may be used as a weapon), can be helpful. Many patients decompress with such gestures, as offering food or drink appeals to their most basic human needs and builds trust. I continue to be amazed at how quickly an angry patient will calm down when they are offered food or drink.

A nonconfrontational but attentive and receptive manner that does not convey weakness or vulnerability is optimal. I call this an authoritative response, not to be confused with an authoritarian response. This manner calmly conveys, "I am confident, in charge, and want to help" and helps to build rapport. Some patients become angry because they feel they are not being taken seriously or treated with respect; their anger typically abates when these concerns are addressed.

It is important to avoid approaching the patient from behind or moving suddenly; it's also important to stand at least one arm's length away when talking with a patient who is escalating. In some cases, an agitated patient is aware of their impulse control problem and may welcome limit setting by the clinician. I have told patients, "I can help you with your problem, but I cannot allow you to continue threatening me or the ER staff."

A key mistake when interviewing an agitated or potentially violent patient is failing to address violence directly. The patient should be asked relevant questions such as, "Do you feel like hurting yourself or someone else?" and "Do you carry a gun or knife?" Stating the obvious, such as "You look angry," may help the patient to begin sharing emotions. If the patient becomes more agitated, it is important to speak in a conciliatory manner and offer supportive statements to diffuse the situation, such as, "You obviously have a lot of willpower and are good at controlling yourself."

Some common approaches to the combative patient are counterproductive and can lead to further escalation or a transition to violence. Arguing with, condescending to, or commanding the patient to "calm down" can have disastrous consequences. Patients often interpret such approaches as a challenge to prove themselves or validate their aggressive behavior. A threat to call security personnel also invites aggression. Other potential mistakes include

1. Criticizing or interrupting the patient,
2. Responding defensively or taking the patient's ire personally, and
3. Not clarifying what the patient wants before responding.

Never lie to a patient (e.g., "I am sure you will be out of here in no time," when this is not the case), as this could agitate the client further when they find out you lied and/or cause you—or a colleague—to have to deal with the patient's increased anger.

Take all threats seriously. It is especially important not to deny or downplay threatening behavior. To do so places the interviewer and other team members at increased risk of assault and injury. If verbal techniques are unsuccessful and escalation occurs, the clinician should excuse themselves and summon help.

Aggression/Violence. At the point in the aggression cycle when a patient has escalated to aggression, verbal techniques are not helpful. The patient is likely out of control, and their safety, as well as that of staff, is preeminent. These situations test the preparatory steps described earlier in this chapter. How soon can staff summon help? What is the escape plan for staff in a dangerous situation?

This is the stage at which physical, chemical, and mechanical restraints are often used. In the ER where I worked, we used a combination of these restraints, including a five-point restraint bed when necessary. In our system, patients could not be restrained without a physician's order, and there are specific procedures that must be followed to ensure that the rights of the patient being restrained are not violated.

Restraints of any type, or seclusion, must only be used as a last resort to avoid or limit physical harm. Only staff with training in restraint procedures should be involved in these situations; ideally, there is also a trained staff member observing the restraint procedure to provide additional oversight for staff and patient safety. Again, it is outside the scope of this text to advise in the use of, training, or description of restraints in any form.

De-escalation. The aggressive phase may last seconds, minutes, or hours, but eventually the person will begin to calm down, or de-escalate. The same signs observed when a client is escalating are often present when the client de-escalates. Thus, the same interventions can be used to help the client de-escalate. Professionals must remain aware that a patient who has been in the aggressive phase can easily return to the aggressive phase.

Resting. Resting describes the phase in which a person is not escalating, aggressive, or de-escalating. I must emphasize that people can jump from a resting phase to violence with no sign of escalation. This can sometimes happen in a person with a psychotic or other mental health disorder.

One of my coworkers was interviewing a female patient in her mid-20s several years ago when the patient jumped out of the bed, hit my coworker in the face, and knocked her to the ground. The patient then slammed my teammate's head on the ground and started to choke her. Only a quick response by an ER doctor kept my friend from sustaining greater injury. Even so, my friend suffered a concussion and understandable emotional trauma from this event. Subsequent review of the incident through coworker interviews and video surveillance revealed no observable signs of impending aggression. Furthermore, the patient did not have a diagnosed mental illness and refused to explain her actions. She was charged with assault and battery and went to jail.

Even when a person appears to be resting (not escalating or acting aggressively), clinicians should not feel overly confident in their ability to sense impending danger. The clinician should pay attention to any "gut feeling" that a dangerous situation may be developing. An uncomfortable or threatening feeling during an interview is ominous, and appropriate precautions should be taken without delay.

Assessing Threats of Future Violence

In addition to dealing with patients who are aggressive, violent, or possibly escalating toward violence, we must deal with people who could pose a threat to others in the future. While we cannot predict future violence any more than we can predict future suicidal intent, we should evaluate future violence risk. Assessing for potential future violence involves asking ourselves, and the client the following questions:

• What is the person's attitude regarding future violence?

- Does the patient have a specific person they are thinking about hurting or killing?
- What is their demeanor when they talk about the other person(s) or their plans to harm them? How detailed is their plan?
- What is their attitude about the consequences of their actions (e.g., do they care if they are hurt themselves or what could happen to them when they are caught)?
- Does the person have the capacity to carry out any threat of violence?
- Does the patient know where their intended target is? What is the patient's access to weapons?
- What is the person's history of violence? (Remember, a history of violence or aggressive behavior is a risk factor for future violence.)
- What are the person's plans for future violence?
- What is the context in which the person is making threats of violence?
- What has kept them from acting on their violent/homicidal thoughts?
- Does anyone else know of this plan? (The more secretive the plan, the more concerned I become.)

It is usually helpful to gather collateral information from people who know the client. Just as family members and friends of people who are suicidal can provide support to the client and work to keep them safe, friends and family can be used to support clients who are having problems with aggression to help develop a safety plan. When talking with people who know the client, keep in mind that many people who endorse having homicidal ideation identify a loved one or acquaintance as the person they want to harm. We have a duty to protect the potential victim if the client discloses intent to harm them.

Duty to Protect

As noted in the 1976 California State Supreme Court ruling, *Tarasoff vs. Regents of the University of California*, mental health professionals have a duty to protect individuals who have been specifically threatened with death or bodily harm by their clients. In Virginia, if the patient makes a threat of violence or expresses homicidal ideation toward a specific individual, the clinician is required to make every reasonable effort to contact the threatened individual and warn them of the client's threat. I also contact the police.

Be aware that each state has its own guidelines for what clinicians are required to report in response to a client making a threat, and it is up to each clinician to be aware of their locality's laws and practice guidelines.

Practitioners should include statements on their responsibilities about duty to protect on the informed consents that clients need to sign before treatment starts. I also repeat my responsibilities about duty to protect at the beginning of group sessions and individual sessions.

Care must be taken to divulge the minimal amount of information necessary to the threatened person to protect the rights of the client. Other than the name of the individual who made the threat, no diagnostic, medical, substance abuse, or any other patient information should be divulged to the intended victim and law enforcement. The counselor should document this contact in the client's medical record.

CASE STUDY—DALE
DUTY TO PROTECT

Dale was a middle-aged man who was brought to the ER by EMS with a primary complaint of chest pain. He was apparently having a panic attack. He admitted that he was depressed because he was under a tremendous amount of stress. Dale made suicidal and homicidal statements in front of the attending doctor, so a mental health assessment was ordered. Dale was alert, oriented, and cooperative. He was moderately agitated, even after being given Ativan, and he was very angry at his wife.

Dale stated that he had been depressed for the past two weeks. Dale said that he and his wife had separated four months prior. He said he had been seeing a lot of pictures of her on the Internet and heard things from his friends that suggested she was being unfaithful to him. He also stated that he loved his wife but wanted to kill her just the same. He had thoughts of shooting her with a semiautomatic pistol.

"I'm gonna empty an entire magazine [17 shots] one shot at a time, starting at her feet and shooting up her body until I put the last bullet in her dead, and then shoot myself under the chin with a shotgun."

Dale denied any past suicide attempts or homicide attempts. He was living alone in a trailer on his son's property and had access to multiple guns. He wife was still living in their house.

Dale denied any hallucinations and did not appear to be responding to internal stimuli. He did not appear to be delusional. Dale had a substantial history of long-term cannabis use, which he stated he would never stop. He also had a history of alcohol dependence, but he claimed that he stopped drinking four days earlier. Dale had been taking Xanax daily for the past six years. He steadfastly stated that he "will not" stop taking Xanax. He stated he last used cocaine six months earlier but added that he used it regularly years ago. He also took Percocet daily due to chronic pain. Dale had a limited awareness of his substance dependence.

I informed Dale that, given the extent of his threats, he needed to be hospitalized. Dale was unsure of whether he wanted to do this voluntarily and at one point threatened to leave the hospital because he was not receiving pain medication. I called the county crisis center, and a counselor agreed to come out to assess Dale for an involuntary admission. Following this, Dale agreed to come to the hospital voluntarily. I told him that because he had been going back and forth about going to the hospital, he would still be assessed by the crisis counselor.

At this point, Dale's wife arrived in the ER waiting room and demanded to see Dale. I went out to speak with her and told her that her husband had made specific threats against her and that I believed she was in danger. I recommended she take whatever means necessary to protect herself, including moving to a location unknown to her husband. I offered resources specific to people in her situation. I added that her husband was going to be hospitalized at least over the weekend. She was dismissive of my statements and argued that because she had been with Dale for so long, he could not possibly hurt her. Dale's wife was not allowed to see him and was asked to leave the facility by hospital security after she started threatening and screaming at me in the waiting room. I spoke with a sheriff who was providing hospital security and advised him of Dale's threats. He reported the threats to his commanding officer.

Dale's son, Cody then arrived at the hospital and stated that he was worried about his father. He noted that Dale had a conflicted history (I suspected domestic violence, but Cody did not say this outright) with his mother, and that his parents had split up after both Dale and Cody were arrested for assault two months ago. Cody noted that he had gotten rid of all his father's guns after calling EMS.

"I really don't think he would do anything to Mom," he said, "but you never know what he'll do when he gets really angry."

The officer with Dale asked how it had gone with Dale's wife (out of earshot from Dale).

"Well," I said, "different from everything I ever practiced in graduate school: Usually the person being warned is thankful." I then updated the officer on what had happened in the waiting room. Dale's wife's reactions really bothered the officer, and we were both concerned for her safety, so he called and spoke with his sergeant. The sergeant was also concerned, and she sent another officer to Dale's home address (where his wife was staying); that officer made it clear to Dale's wife that she needed to take steps to protect herself. She ultimately left to stay with her new boyfriend.

Conclusion

Violence is the most daunting mental health emergency because we as clinicians can get hurt when trying to help. Violent clients can be unpredictable, as violence can take many forms. One of the more concerning aspects of people experiencing a mental health emergency that can include violence is that clinicians and organizations often fail to anticipate and plan responses to violent clients:

One clearly explicit preventative strategy is the obligation of employers, insofar as is reasonably practical, to provide staff with the information and training necessary to ensure their safety, which should, similarly, be subjected to periodic review as a matter of routine and adapted to take account of new or changed risk situations. (McKenna & Paterson, 2006, p. 237)

Clinicians need to be vigilant to the potential for violence in any setting and with any client. Complacency or overconfidence can lead to problems. In addition, clinicians need to be mindful about caring for themselves after a violent situation.

CHAPTER 7

Medical vs. Mental Problems

Apart from a suicide attempt, most mental illnesses in and of themselves (except for anorexia nervosa) are not going to kill the patient. However, there are many signs that can appear to be due to a mental illness but actually indicate a medical emergency.

CASE STUDY—STEVEN

ZOMBIES

It was a relatively slow Friday morning at the hospital. My ER physician told me that an EMS ambulance was inbound with an adult male named Steven, who was psychotic.

"His primary care physician just called me," the doctor explained. "He's known the patient for years and says Steven called him and said some strange things. The physician is sure that Steven is psychotic, so he sent an ambulance to bring him here."

Steven arrived with the paramedics a few minutes later. He was calm and quiet as they rolled him through the ER and into a room. I went into the room with a nurse and the doctor. The doctor was her typically cheerful self.

"What's going on today?" she asked brightly.

"I burned my house down," Steven replied matter-of-factly. "Then I called my doctor, and before I knew it, these guys [gestures at the paramedics] showed up, and here I am."

"What happened?" I asked.

"Well, last Sunday, these seven zombies showed up at my house," Steven said. "Now these weren't those *Walking Dead* zombies you see on TV; these were Haitian zombies, which means they chatter a lot: They make a chattering noise, with their teeth. Anyhow, they were with me all week, talking and making all this noise. I just couldn't stand it anymore. This

---

morning, I got up, poured kerosene around the baseboards in my house, and lit a match. I went outside and called my doctor, and here I am."

While telling his story, Steven was calm, with an even voice tone and good eye contact. He was resting comfortably in an inclined hospital bed with his hands behind his head. He was fully oriented. He consented to let his blood be drawn and provided a urine specimen. Steven denied any thoughts of wanting to hurt himself or anyone else ("Well, except the zombies, of course"). Steven did not appear to be responding to internal stimuli. He did not appear anxious or depressed. He was also not surprised when the police appeared to question him about his house fire.

What could be causing these symptoms? Clearly, a psychotic disorder could be the cause, as could a depressive or bipolar disorder with psychotic features. Many chemicals of abuse could also cause these problems. The key to determining what is causing the presenting problems is to eliminate what is *not* causing the problem, a process called *ruling out*. Keep in mind that there are *many* medical problems that can cause a mental health emergency, and we won't be able to touch on them all; we will focus on the more common ones.

Signs and *symptoms* are often used interchangeably in clinical terminology; however, they have specific meanings. *Signs* can be detected by someone other than the patient (e.g., elevated heart rate or blood pressure). *Symptoms* are experienced and reported by the patient (e.g., anxiety or pain).

Medical vs. Mental

Distinguishing between medical and mental problems, or specifically, ruling out a medical problem, requires medical testing and attention to the symptom profile. Vital signs (temperature, blood oxygen level, heart rate, respirations, and blood pressure), blood work (complete blood count, blood chemistry, metabolic panel, blood alcohol level, and therapeutic medication blood levels), urinalysis (including UDS), EKG/ECG, and medical imaging (X-ray, CT scans, and occasionally magnetic resonance imaging [MRI]) are the more common tools for medically assessing patients. These diagnostics are done in addition to a physical exam by the medical provider. Attention must be paid to the signs and symptoms of the presenting problems. Most, but not all, medical problems have a short onset of signs and symptoms when compared with those of mental health problems, in which the signs and symptoms usually come on gradually. Any sudden onset of signs or symptoms requires immediate medical attention (e.g., send the patient to the ER).

Physiological Disorders

The following disorders are ones I encountered in my work in the ER over eight years. This is not intended to be an exhaustive list. However, a review of the clinical literature suggests that these illnesses, injuries, and medical disorders should be ruled out in favor of a mental illness, given the potential consequences for the patient if they receive incorrect treatment.

Urinary Tract Infections. A urinary tract infection (UTI) is detectible through a urinalysis measuring bacteria levels and blood work revealing elevated white cell counts. Physically, the person may report a sensation of burning when urinating, but this symptom may not always be present. In the elderly, a UTI can cause behaviors that are often misdiagnosed as psychotic disorders. These symptoms often flare up rapidly and occur in people without any previous history of psychosis (Morrison, 2015). Once the UTI is treated, the symptoms will often remit.

A 56-year-old female was brought to the ER by ambulance for being "unresponsive." Paramedics determined she was not in medical distress, and her unresponsiveness appeared to be of her own volition. When she arrived at the ER. she became extremely agitated, punching one staff member and biting another. She subsequently required physical, mechanical, and chemical restraints. The patient had a long-standing diagnosis of schizoaffective disorder and a history of treatment noncompliance. Subsequent medical testing revealed an elevated body temperature and elevated white blood cell count. The attending doctor determined that the patient was septic due to a UTI, and she was medically admitted. Once the UTI was treated, the patient was no longer violent; her symptoms had been caused exclusively by her sepsis.

Thyroid Dysfunction. Hyperthyroidism and hypothyroidism involve an over- or underactive thyroid, respectively. Physical signs can include weakness, weight gain or loss, changes in hair (it becomes finer), and swelling on the neck (goiter). Initial stages of thyroid problems may not include any physical signs—mental health symptoms can be the first sign of thyroid issues. Panic attacks, anxiety, depression, and even dementia and psychosis can be signs of a thyroid problem (Morrison, 2015).

Low Glucose Levels. Low blood glucose levels are a common reason people are brought to the ER with "altered mental status." Low blood sugar levels can lead to fatigue, slowed physical movements, depression, disorientation, fainting, or appearing intoxicated. Without appropriate treatment, people can enter a coma if their blood glucose becomes too l ow. I have seen patients brought to the ER by emergency medical services staff or loved ones, who assumed these patients were intoxicated or having a stroke, based on their behaviors. A simple and basic glucose test verified low blood sugar, and the appropriate treatment was provided.

Medication-Related Disorders

Extrapyramidal Symptoms. Extrapyramidal symptoms (EPSs) are the most significant side effects of antipsychotic drugs. EPSs include several movement disorders. Anticholinergic drugs are frequently prescribed to prevent the moderate and severe side effects of antipsychotic medication. EPSs can include:

- Dystonia (muscle spasms and contractions)
- Akathisia (a sense of inner restlessness)
- Parkinsonism (rigidity)
  - Neuroleptic-induced parkinsonism is more common in the elderly and in people being treated with high doses of potent neuroleptics
- Bradykinesia (slowness of movement)
- Tremors
- Tardive dyskinesia (irregular, jerky movements)

Anticholinergic Drugs. Anticholinergic medications are used to address medication- induced movement disorders. Benzotropine (Cogentin) is the most common anticholinergic drug used for treating or preventing these symptoms. Other anticholinergics include antihistamines, tricyclic medications, and medications to prevent incontinence. Anticholinergics can be abused for their mood-elevating and sedating properties.

Signs of Anticholinergic Intoxication. Two medical providers with whom I regularly worked at the hospital described the signs of anticholinergic intoxication as they were taught in medical school:

- "Red as a beet" (face is flushed)
- "Dry as a bone" (dry skin and mucous membranes)
- "Hot as a hare" (has a fever)
- "Mad as a hatter" (delirium and hallucinations)
- "Full as a flask" (cannot urinate)
- "Can't spit" (dry)
- "Can't shit" (constipated)

Tardive Dyskinesia. Tardive dyskinesia is caused by elevated levels of antipsychotic medications, particularly older (first-generation) antipsychotic medications, used for a lengthy time. Signs include involuntary, uncontrolled rhythmic movements, usually of the fingers, hands, head, or tongue. This can also include rapid, jerky movements. Tardive dyskinesia usually has a delayed effect (it rarely occurs within the first six months of treatment) but may not take as long to develop in the elderly. The involuntary movements may continue after a change or reduction in the medication dosage, and the signs often disappear when the patient is sleeping (Sadock, Sadock, & Ruiz, 2015).

Neuroleptic Malignant Syndrome. NMS is a rare but potentially fatal medical reaction that is often caused by too high a level of antipsychotic medications (neuroleptics). Signs include muscular rigidity, involuntary muscular movements, hyperpyrexia (high body temperature), autonomic instability, delirium, pulmonary/renal failure, stupor/coma, and seizures. NMS is often treated by discontinuing or decreasing the neuroleptic and utilizing benzodiazepines to treat the symptoms (Sadock, Sadock, & Ruiz, 2015).

Antidepressant Discontinuation Syndrome. Antidepressant medications are among the most commonly prescribed psychiatric medications in the United States. Antidepressant discontinuation syndrome occurs when a patient is taking a selective serotonin reuptake inhibitor (SSRI) or selective serotonin norepinephrine reuptake inhibitor (SNRI) and stops taking the medication suddenly. Abrupt cessation or major decrease in dosage from an antidepressant medication that has been taken for at least one month is necessary for this diagnosis. Symptoms include flashes of light, a sensation of electric shock, nausea, and hypersensitivity to noises or lights, anxiety, or feelings of dread. To qualify for this diagnosis, the symptoms must never have been present prior to the start of the antidepressant (Sadock, Sadock, & Ruiz, 2015). Treatment usually involves restarting the patient on an antidepressant and slowly titrating down the dosage.

Serotonin Syndrome. As the name implies, serotonin syndrome is caused by too much serotonin, one of the earliest identified neurotransmitters. Signs include diarrhea, restlessness, elevated body temperature, tremors, cognitive changes, rigidity, delirium, and autonomic nervous system instability. Serotonin syndrome can occur through the regular use of SSRIs and SNRIs in some individuals. I have encountered it in people who have intentionally overdosed on antidepressant medication in a suicide attempt. I have also encountered serotonin syndrome in people who used hallucinogenic or entactogenic plants and/or chemicals trying to get high. However, any medication can cause serotonin syndrome. The mortality rate is 10 to 15 percent, making this a mental health emergency that requires prompt identification and medical attention (Sadock, Sadock, & Ruiz, 2015).

Corticosteroid Reaction. Corticosteroids are used to treat a variety of ailments, particularly inflammation. Two common corticosteroids are Decadron and Prednisone. These steroids are different from anabolic steroids, which are based on testosterone and used to build muscle mass. Even a normal dose of corticosteroids can cause a severe reaction in some people, mimicking a manic or hypomanic episode. The symptoms typically remit when the medication is stopped.

I saw this several times in the ER; a patient would be brought in by their family, and tell the attending doctor that the patient was "crazy, bipolar, schizophrenic," or something of that nature, despite no evidence of any previous behaviors. A review of the patient's medications typically identified the culprit steroid. Once the medication was decreased or stopped, the result was a remission of the patient's problems.

Stevens-Johnson Syndrome. Stevens-Johnson syndrome is a rare disorder but worth mentioning, given the increasing numbers of people being diagnosed with bipolar disorder and subsequently receiving anticonvulsant treatment. I have encountered it at least twice in my work, and in both cases the syndrome was spotted by a doctor, one an ER physician and the other, a psychiatrist.

Stevens-Johnson syndrome is a serious skin and mucous membrane disorder that can sometimes be caused by certain medications, including lamotrigine (Lamictal), an anticonvulsant, or an injury. The problem typically starts with an upper respiratory infection, headache, fever, and gastrointestinal problems. The syndrome can then progress to a rash, which could indicate that the outer layer of skin (epidermis) is separating from the inner layer of skin. Treatment involves stopping the medication and treating the affected skin areas. If allowed to progress, Stevens-Johnson syndrome can be fatal.

Traumatic Brain Injury

There are many types of TBI. Some are obvious due to the nature of the injury, such as the result of a penetrating head wound, but the majority of TBIs are due to closed head injuries, a concussion or contusion. A *concussion* is a brief loss of consciousness following a blow to the head. A *contusion* is actual bruising of the brain, either near the impact site of the skull or on the opposite side of the skull due to the brain moving in the opposite direction of the blow and impacting on the inside of the skull (Morrison, 2015). These are likely the most common forms of TBI, and concussions are finally receiving long overdue attention.

Sports-Related Traumatic Brain Injury. Like most people who did not play college or professional sports, I had not given concussions a lot of thought. I had friends who had "had their bell rung" once or twice in high school or college, usually while playing sports, but I did not see what the big deal was. When I became a father, my wife and I insisted on our sons wearing helmets when they rode their bikes or scooters. One day, I forgot to insist and blew it big-time.

I was working in the backyard when I heard my middle son, then 7-year-old Ben, crying. I came to the front yard to find him in tears with a busted lower lip. He told me he had fallen off his scooter and had bitten his lip. He quickly calmed down. I called Claire, who was out running an errand, and told her what had happened and that Ben had stopped bleeding, so he likely did not need stitches. Claire came home a few minutes later and looked over Ben. Claire, by the way, is a pediatric trauma nurse.

"I think you're okay, kiddo," she said, and then she noticed a reddish area on the right side of Ben's forehead. "What's this?"

"Oh, I don't know, but it kinda hurts," said Ben.

"Did you hit your head there?" I asked.

"I think so," replied Ben.

"What do you mean?" Claire asked, "What do you remember?"

"I remember getting up off the ground and not much before that," said Ben.

Claire looked at me with concern, "I wonder if he got a concussion?"

Ben seemed fine. He said he was "kinda dizzy" but didn't feel bad at all. A few minutes later, he said he no longer felt dizzy. He did not report any feelings of nausea, and within a few more minutes, he was playing again.

Claire was still uncertain about the concussion, so she called the ER where she worked and spoke with a doctor. The doctor agreed there was some concern about a concussion, but in the absence of any other symptoms, it appeared that all we could do was observe Ben. He seemed fine the rest of the day.

One evening about three weeks after Ben's fall, I was on the road teaching for PESI. I was driving between Columbus and Cincinnati, when Claire called me: "We're losing our son," she sobbed. This was a surprising thing to hear, as Claire is not a dramatic person. Ben's behaviors had gotten much worse at school, and he was regularly disrupting his class. He was also complaining of headaches. Ben's teacher called Claire and expressed his concerns about Ben's behavioral problems and inability to concentrate, things with which he had not had a problem before.

Claire made an appointment with Ben's doctor, who saw him and then immediately referred him to a head trauma physical therapist. I attended the first appointment with Ben and Claire.

"Definite concussion," the physical therapist said shortly after she began examining Ben. "His right eye is tracking all over the place."

"How did we miss this?" Claire asked.

"Well, he was asymptomatic at first, and concussion problems are often delayed," she responded.

"I was starting to think he was developing ADHD," I said, "I was teaching about ADHD last week, and as I'm talking with my class, I'm thinking, 'Wow, I'm describing Ben.'"

"We see that a lot of the time," the therapist responded, "It leads to a lot of incorrect diagnoses."

With a lot of demanding work from Ben, his physical therapy (PT) team, Claire, and (to a lesser degree) me, Ben made progress. His teacher was an invaluable part of this experience, communicating with us daily. Ben began to improve. His explosive temper tantrums, something we had not seen a lot of before, were challenging but began to subside in frequency and intensity.

Neurocognitive Disorders

The most commonly seen neurocognitive disorders are delirium and dementia. These cognitive disorders include disruption of one or more of the following:

- Memory
- Language
- Orientation (person, place, time, and situation)
- Judgment
- Conducting interpersonal relationships
- Performing actions
- Problem solving

Delirium. *Delirium* is a disturbance in attention or awareness in addition to a change in baseline cognition (how the patient typically appears cognitively). Delirium can be caused by one or more factors, including, but not limited to:

- A general medical problem (e.g., a disease or infection)
- Postoperative delirium
- Seizures
- Substance intoxication (e.g., stimulants or entactogens)
- Substance withdrawal syndrome
- Head trauma
- Pain
- Shock
- Hypoxia
- Emotional stress
- Medication reactions (e.g., too many medications with anticholinergic reactions)
- Sleep deprivation

A key to diagnosing delirium is its short development time: Symptoms develop over a period of days or even a few hours (Sadock, Sadock, & Ruiz, 2015). I cannot emphasize enough: Delirium is a medical emergency. If you suspect that a patient is delirious, they require emergency medical treatment. The outcomes for delirium are straightforward: The patient improves, the patient suffers brain damage, or the patient dies.

Delirium often gets worse at the end of the day, which is sometimes called *sundowning*, a term also applied to patients with dementia. In addition to its short developmental time, disorientation along with illusions, visual hallucinations, and/or delusions are common. These signs are accompanied by emotional disturbance and a major disruption of sleep. Treating delirium typically involves treating the underlying problem. Antipsychotic medications are also sometimes used (Sadock, Sadock, & Ruiz, 2015).

Comparing Delirium and Dementia. Given that delirium and dementia are both neurocognitive disorders that have a tremendous impact on the individual, how can we tell them apart? The following table compares and contrasts these two disorders.

Feature	Delirium	Dementia
Onset	Fast	Slow
Duration	Hours to days	Years
Reversible?	Yes	No
Hallucinations?	Often	No
Memory	Globally impaired	Impaired recently, gradually expanding to include long-term memories
Speech	Incoherent	Problems remembering words, gradually worsening

CASE STUDY—STEVEN

ZOMBIES, PART 2

"Paul, come and look at this," the doctor called out. I was on the other side of the ER. I had finished my interview with Steven, and he had fallen asleep after eating part of his lunch. He had told me that he had only been able to sleep two to three hours a night for the past week, and he was exhausted.

I walked over to the doctor's workstation, which had two large computer monitors that took up a lot of space on her desk, displaying the patient's imaging results from the radiology department.

"What am I looking at?" I asked.

Adopting a teacher's tone of voice, the doctor pointed to an image that filled the screen.

"This is his brain," she said, using her finger to circle the image.

She adjusted the computer, zooming in on an area that was a lighter gray than the surrounding tissue, "And this is the tumor."

"Cancer?" I asked.

"Yep," she replied. "That particular area of the brain has a lot to do with how he processes external stimuli. I think that is the cause of his hallucinations."

"But why would the hallucinations stop just after he set the fire to 'kill the zombies'?"

"The stop in symptoms is probably temporary," she replied. "I need to transfer him to a facility that is better equipped to handle this. What is clear is that he does not belong on the psychiatric ward."

We transferred Steven to another hospital with a large, state-of-the-art oncology department. What would have happened had the doctor not scanned his head: He would have been unnecessarily placed on a behavioral health unit where he did not belong, and the appropriate treatment would have been delayed.

Other Neurological Illnesses

Brain Tumor. A brain tumor is another medical problem that can manifest as a mental health problem. A rapid onset of signs and symptoms and the absence of a prior history are typical of most medical problems that initially appear as a mental health problem (Morrison, 2015). The key to the right treatment is a thorough medical workup that includes appropriate blood work and diagnostic imagery. Assuming the patient is "just crazy" and that their symptoms are due to a mental illness is not only a disservice to our patients but bad practice.

Stroke/Brain Bleeds. People who have experienced a stroke can display a variety of mental health symptoms: Depression, mania/hypomania, anxiety, psychosis, and personality changes (Morrison, 2015). A CT scan or MRI can confirm the presence of a stroke.

Seizure Disorder. Seizures can result in the ubiquitous chief medical complaint of altered mental status, particularly during the time just after a seizure, called the *postictal phase*. During a seizure, the person typically loses control of their bladder and/or bowels and sometimes vomits. People who have experienced a seizure are often disoriented and confused. They can even be combative because of being disoriented. I have seen several patients in a postictal state who were initially assumed to have been intoxicated. As the patient is allowed to rest and recover, their symptoms diminish. If you see someone you believe is seizing, notifying emergency services immediately is imperative. Then, if possible, roll the person on their side and try to clear objects in the immediate area. Under no circumstances should you try to place anything in the patient's mouth, as this only increases their chance of choking.

Hypoxia. *Hypoxia* means that the patient's brain is not receiving sufficient oxygen. Hypoxia can lead to depressive symptoms, headaches, confusion, disorientation, and loss of consciousness, depending on its severity. In severe cases, such as with diminished breathing due to a drug overdose, the patient may need to be intubated—a tube is inserted to help them breathe. Hypoxia can also occur when the patient is asleep, a condition known as sleep apnea. Sleep apnea can be caused by a variety of things and is best diagnosed through a sleep study. Symptoms include morning headaches, insomnia, depression, problems with concentration, and irritability (Morrison, 2015).

Multiple Sclerosis. Multiple sclerosis (MS) affects about one in 1,000 people in the United States (Morrison, 2015). With MS, for reasons unknown, the myelin covering on nerve cells in the central nervous system (CNS) deteriorates and is replaced by scar tissue. Most people with MS experience episodes, often called flares or flare-ups, that last days to weeks. Because MS can impact any nerve, its symptoms vary (Morrison, 2015). Mental health symptoms can include mania/hypomania, depression, and cognitive problems—particularly issues with memory. An MRI is typically used to identify the presence of myelin deterioration.

Conclusion

We have seen that many medical problems can present with mental health symptoms, especially in an acute care or emergency setting. Therefore, it is imperative that medical conditions are ruled out before addressing mental health concerns. Likewise, it is important for clinicians to be aware of the variety of medical problems, illnesses, and injuries that can manifest as a mental illness.

CHAPTER 8

Trauma

Trauma-informed care is ubiquitous among mental health providers across the country. But what does trauma-informed care mean, and how is trauma a mental health emergency? The foundation of trauma-informed care stipulates that 1) clinicians use treatment modalities and interventions that do not further traumatize or harm a client, and 2) clinicians recognize that past negative experiences can impact how a client experiences their world (Marich, 2015). This definition infers that clinicians understand that people may experience the same traumatic event differently.

When I was in private practice 10 years ago, the practice group had a contract with a local bank that had numerous branches throughout Richmond. At that time, bank robberies were a frequent occurrence in the greater Richmond area. The bank had hired the practice to go on site and facilitate critical incident debriefing (CID) sessions any time a robbery occurred. The theory was that the bank employees who had been "held up" needed to immediately process and talk about their experience in the robbery before going home.

The goal underlying this theory was for the employees to be able to return to work the following day ready to help customers. I was not trained in CID, so I never conducted a debriefing. I remember when being asked by the practice owner if I wanted to learn CID, I responded, "What if they're not ready to talk or don't want to talk?" The owner looked at me and seemed perplexed; he was probably wondering if he had made a good decision in hiring me.

I did not realize it then, but I had stumbled onto a core principle of trauma-informed care. This was sheer happenstance, as I did not realize what I was proposing at the time. In fact, people process trauma in many ways: One size does not fit all. One of my coworkers, who regularly provided CID, observed different responses by the bank tellers who had been robbed. Some tellers were indeed ready to talk, whereas others needed time to process what had happened before they could discuss their experience. A third response by some tellers was that they did not want to talk at all and seemed to be "out of it" or even scared during the debriefing; they desperately tried to end the CID session as quickly as possible. My coworker also noted that some bank employees called out sick the day(s) following the robbery, and a few quit altogether.

Trauma-informed care considers that traumatic memories "live" in all areas of the brain, particularly in places other than the cerebral cortex. Because most "traditional" forms of therapy (e.g., psychodynamic therapies and cognitive-behavioral therapy) utilize higher levels of brain functioning, it follows that these approaches would be ineffective in dealing with traumatic symptoms (van der Kolk, 2014). The second aspect of trauma-informed care is that traumatic memories can impact how an individual sees and experiences their world, as well as how they behave, communicate, and process information.

These are key principles of trauma-informed care to consider when helping a client who is experiencing a mental health emergency. As we will see, many people with trauma histories have been diagnosed with a variety of mental health disorders. In many of these cases, the clients have then been prescribed medications that may address their symptoms but do little to address the underlying trauma. In more cases than I care to count, treating the wrong illness makes it more difficult to recognize and treat the underlying trauma.

Grief and Bereavement

Before we look at trauma as a mental health emergency, we need to first discuss bereavement. Part of understanding trauma is acknowledging what it is not. Grief, loss, and bereavement are experiences that people go through when they have lost someone or something meaningful to them. Although *bereavement, grief,* and *mourning* are often used interchangeably, I differentiate the terms: *Grief* is the subjective feeling due to a loss; *mourning* is the process by which grief is resolved; and *bereavement* is being in a state of mourning. Bereavement itself is not trauma. However, a person can experience grief and trauma at the same time, and these co-occurring experiences may even be a result of the same situation or event.

Stages of Grief. Years ago, my friend's spouse died after a lengthy illness. Several months after the funeral, a mutual acquaintance of my friend asked me, "So, what stage of grief is our friend on?" This question was not only insensitive but also demonstrated a lack of understanding about grief and the mourning process. The acquaintance's question referred to Dr. Elisabeth Kübler-Ross's well-regarded "five stages of grief" as described in her landmark text, *On Death and Dying* (1969), in which she referenced people who were terminally ill. These stages of grief—denial, anger, bargaining, depression, and acceptance—have become part of our national vernacular when attempting to understand human responses to loss. Kübler-Ross is considered by many to have brought the grieving process to the awareness of medical and mental health professionals, as well as the general public. Prior to her work and the publication of *On Death and Dying,* the grief and loss process was not considered by the medical profession when caring for patients. Furthermore, medical providers were previously discouraged from discussing death with their patients (Kübler-Ross, 1969).

Much has been written about Kübler-Ross's five stages of grief; unfortunately, quite a bit of the analysis is incorrect. The public has come to see these stages as a linear progression that a person naturally moves through when dying or faced with the death of someone close to them. For some, like my friend's friend, there are false expectations: a) people who are grieving will progress through the stages one at a time, b) each stage occurs in a "timely" manner, and c) the person will emerge from the "end" of grief whole and healthy again without a hint of sadness. Nothing could be further from the truth. Kübler-Ross makes it very clear that the five stages of grief were never meant to be a linear, one-way, or time-limited progression. Instead, the model is an attempt to show that people internalize and express their grief in various and changing ways. The grieving friend I referenced recently told me that some days he comes home and expects his wife to still be there, some days he is depressed, and still other days he feels a sense of acceptance that contrasts with the days he feels angry. Clearly, my friend has not made a linear journey through the five stages of grief as understood by our mutual acquaintance. From my perspective, however, his grief is perfectly "normal."

In my opinion, there is no wrong way to grieve. The only exceptions to this rule would be if the pain of the loss is causing the grieving person to want to hurt themselves or harm others or the grief is so intense that the person has stopped caring for their basic needs. In these cases, grief has moved into the realm of a mental health emergency. As clinicians, we must be very careful to not label "normal" grief as a mental illness. We must also be aware of the many ways in which different people and various cultures experience and express grief.

Grief is not trauma. Most people who experience a loss, even an unexpected one do not develop a traumatic response to the incident. People need time to experience the many facets of grief. There is no time limit to this process, and it never fully ends. The important thing is for people, especially clinicians, to understand this process. Moreover, it is incumbent on us to work to understand the cultures of the people with whom we work, especially when they differ from our own.

What Is Trauma?

Can we say that all losses or terrible things that happen to each of us are traumas? The short answer is "no." Each of us has bad, sometimes horrible, things happen to us—this is part of life. As M. Scott Peck (1978) noted at the beginning of his classic book, *The Road Less Traveled*, "Life is difficult" (p. 15). All major religions agree on this fact, even though they may have differing explanations as to why dreadful things happen and why life is hard. When I was in private practice, I saw this universal truth of suffering at the heart of why people had come to me for help. I found that people who were successful in their healing always integrated this truth into their lives.

Terrible things become traumas when the uniqueness/severity of the loss or harmful experience overwhelms the individual's ability to cope. Note the similarity to the definition of a *crisis* in Chapter 1. Trauma is more than a crisis because it involves not just the "thing" itself but also the body's residual reaction to it:

> An event only becomes a trauma when the overwhelming emotions interfere with proper memory processing. Afterward, traumatized patients react to reminders of the trauma with emergency responses appropriate to the original threat, but these reactions now are completely out of place—like ducking in panic under the table when a drinking glass falls on the floor or going into a rage when a child starts crying. (Levine, 2015, p. xi)

Traumatic reactions are as unique as individuals. It is not just the traumatic event itself, but the other biopsychosocial-spiritual-environmental factors, strengths, and needs that the individual possesses that determine the severity and impact of an event. Thus, one person who is involved in a car accident who has a history of family violence or instability may react differently than a peer who is in the same accident but has not experienced violence and has benefited from a stable family environment.

Therapist and author Jamie Marich (2015) determines whether something is a trauma by exploring the context of the injury: "Often, the value that a person places on what is lost determines whether something is traumatic" (p. 96). We must consider the uniqueness of the individual and their experiences when considering trauma. My practice and recommendation: If the person says the event they are talking about was traumatic to them, I don't argue, particularly in the context of a mental health emergency.

Why Is Trauma a Mental Health Emergency?

I consider trauma a mental health emergency because we must recognize trauma for what it is to be able to effectively treat it. Failing to recognize trauma and instead assuming the person has a mental health problem or diagnosable mental illness can lead to a delay in appropriate treatment or the use of inappropriate treatment. Most often, unnecessary medications are prescribed when trauma is not recognized.

Due to how trauma presents differently, it often goes unrecognized. When I worked with medical professionals in emergency medicine, I would frequently need to explain trauma to nurses, paramedics, and firefighters. I would use the example that closed injuries are usually harder to spot than open wounds, but the closed injuries can be much worse—especially because we cannot directly observe them. Marich (2012) notes that emotional and physical trauma share many characteristics.

I have used the following list she developed to educate first responders and victims of emotional trauma (reprinted here with the author's permission):

Think of Trauma as Physical and/or Emotional Wounds or Injuries

- Wounds come in all shapes and sizes
- Open wounds are visible
- Closed wounds are not
- Wounds are caused by many things
- Wounds affect individuals differently
- Wounds heal from the inside out
- Wounds usually happen fairly quickly but take a long time to heal
- Before wounds can begin to heal internally, steps must be taken to stop the initial bleeding
- Failure to receive proper treatment complicates the healing process
- Wounds can leave a variety of scars (some are permanent, some temporary; some hurt, etc.)
- The skin around a healed scar is tougher than regular skin
- No two people wound in the same way, even if they suffer the same injury

Emotional trauma works in the same way as physical trauma. Often, the cause of the trauma remains hidden, and all we can see are various signs and symptoms that something is wrong. This is because trauma and memory are intrinsically linked. We must consider how the brain stores memories and how trauma impacts the ways in which these memories express themselves. Sometimes the trauma is expressed through physical signs and symptoms as much as it is expressed through psychological symptoms.

Causes of Trauma

Before we look at the brain, trauma, and memory, let us first consider the myriad of events that can cause trauma. The following is only a partial list of the possible circumstances that can cause trauma. What else could we add to this list?

- Being the victim of, or witnessing, verbal, emotional, physical, or sexual abuse
- Being exposed to violence as a victim
- Witnessing someone being a victim of violence
- Emotional neglect or basic needs being unmet (e.g., lack of food, lack of medical care)
- Parental violence, separation, or divorce
- Family member's substance use
- Family member's death, particularly a suicide, homicide, or unexpected death
- Family member's incarceration
- Incarceration or long-term admission to a psychiatric facility
- Medical issues
- Being a primary caretaker of a family member who has medical issues
- Unstable housing; homelessness
- Deployment into a combat zone
- Being a political refugee
- Multiple relocations as a child

Levels of Safety

When faced with a traumatic situation (or even "just" a stressful one), individuals automatically engage various "levels of safety" for coping (van der Kolk, 2014). We intuitively use these coping strategies to provide us with a sense of safety. Levels of safety include social engagement, fight or flight, and freeze or fold.

Social Engagement. The first level of safety is *social engagement,* whereby one turns to the people around them for help. We may specifically ask for help or engage in activities that help us feel connected. Think of how a young child reacts when they fall and scrape their knee: They go to a parent or other caregiver and seek comfort. As adults, we do similar things. On a flight to Wisconsin last year to teach a class series, I noticed that a young adult in the row in front of me would not stop talking to the older adult next to her. It was clear from the conversation that she had not known this individual prior to boarding the flight. She talked so much, I asked myself, "Is she having pressured speech, or is she hyperverbal?" When we landed, I noticed that her rate of speech slowed considerably as we waited to disembark. Thinking about this, I wondered if she was anxious about flying and maintained a continuous conversation with her seatmate to avoid thinking about the fact that we were in a plane flying 35,000 feet off the ground. I remembered that when I was afraid of flying, this is what I used to do: Talking with my seatmates and asking random strangers what time it was, would take my mind off any turbulence we were experiencing.

Social engagement is a reflex. However, what if the people around us, who are supposed to keep us safe, either ignore our attempts at social engagement or are themselves a source of danger? Clinicians often see this in the history of adults who have been traumatized. At an early age, they turned to people for safety, but those adults were either consumed with their own issues or were indifferent to the children they were supposed to help feel safe. "If the people whom you naturally turn to for care and protection terrify or reject you, you learn to shut down and to ignore what you feel" (van der Kolk, 2014, p. 213). This creates a pattern of heightened anxiety and a quicker path to the next two levels of safety.

Fight or Flight. *Fight or flight* constitutes the second level of safety. When there is no one around to provide help or social engagement, the individual will try to either get away from the threat or fight the threat. If there is a way to get away from the threat, most people will try to disengage and move away. This may not be possible in an enclosed space or if the person threatening them is keeping them from leaving. In the first chapter, when talking about how to approach a person in crisis, I noted that it is important to provide the client with a means to get away. Thus, if their flight response is triggered, they can remove themselves and hopefully begin the process of calming down.

If the person cannot run away, their fight response is often engaged. The reason that flight and fight are listed together is that usually the inability to engage in one of these responses triggers the other. In looking back at my career, I can see now that many of the times I was assaulted by adolescents when I worked in residential treatment was that their fight-or-flight response had been engaged because I had blocked them from leaving the room. Most people do not want to engage in physical violence at all. But each of us has the capacity to do so, especially when we feel trapped and unable to escape.

Freeze or Fold. The third level of safety is the *freeze or fold* response. This reaction is triggered when there is no one who can help the individual or the people who should be providing support to the person in crisis are the ones traumatizing them and the individual cannot get away (flight) or physically attack or defend themselves from the threat (fight). For example, children and disempowered adults who are unable to fight or physically escape more powerful perpetrators will naturally freeze. In this response, a state of shock, numbing, immobility, or depersonalization can ensue.

These individuals learn that holding very still, pretending to be asleep, not breathing, or allowing their body to go slack can reduce or ward off a perpetrator's behavior. The freeze response elicits a dissociative state, thus creating analgesia and loss of memory. People who have experienced trauma that has not been resolved may "live" in this depersonalized state. Trauma-informed care considers people who experience this freeze response and recognizes that traditional forms of treatment do not address this response and its signs and symptoms. To fully understand how the body stores traumatic memories, we must understand some of the basic structures of the brain.

Trauma and Memory

The Triune Brain Model. Bessel van der Kolk (2014) and Peter Levine (2015) utilize the triune (three-part) brain model to demonstrate how traumatic memories are stored and expressed. The parts of the brain and their functions are listed below:

Brain Section	Function
Brainstem	Arousal
	Sleep/wake
	Hunger/satiation
	Chemical balance
	Voluntary and reflex movements
	Basic bodily functions: respiration, heartbeat, etc.
Limbic system	The relationship between ourselves and our environment
	Emotions
	Perceptions
Prefrontal cortex	Planning and anticipation
	Sense of time and context
	Inhibitions
	Cognition
	Analytics
	Empathy

Triune Brain and Trauma. Traumatized individuals are often stuck in survival mode: Their limbic system and brainstem remain activated, and the frontal lobes are not fully engaged. These individuals often go from fearful stimuli to a flight/fight/freeze response without being able to learn from the experience. When exposed to any reminders of the trauma, they behave as if they are being traumatized all over again:

> Traumatized people keep secreting substantial amounts of stress hormones long after the actual danger has passed … Ideally, our stress hormone system should provide a lightning-fast response to threat, but then quickly return us to equilibrium. In PTSD patients, however, the stress hormone system fails at this balancing act … Instead, the continued secretion of stress hormones is expressed as agitation and panic and, in the long term, wreaks havoc with their health. (van der Kolk, 2014, p. 30)

Thus, engaging in cognitive-behavioral therapy alone will typically not fully address how the brain is "holding" the trauma in the limbic system. Understanding a person's memories is key to understanding their trauma. "Traumatized people simultaneously remember too little and too much," according to van der Kolk (2014, p. 181).

Van der Kolk (2014) hypothesized that traumatic events seem to be recorded more easily in implicit memory; this includes behaviors that one learns from conditioning or exposure to stimuli. He further surmised that memories are stored in all areas of the brain, with more powerful, emotionally-charged memories being stored in the limbic system (mid-brain) and brainstem. Van der Kolk noted that information can be filtered and stored in different areas based on its intensity.

Because of this process, van der Kolk noted that an individual's body can remember a trauma that their conscious mind does not remember.

If everyone experiences traumatic events in their lives, why doesn't everyone develop traumatic memories or traumatic responses? According to van der Kolk, "Being able to move and *do* something to protect oneself is a critical factor in determining whether a horrible experience will leave long-lasting scars" (2014, p. 55). Also, having a support system, particularly people to whom the individual can turn for support and nurturing, can limit prolonged impacts from traumatic events (van der Kolk, 2014).

Posttraumatic Stress Disorder

Most people who experience a traumatic event do not develop the many symptoms that indicate either Acute Stress Disorder (ASD) or PTSD. Many people who experience a trauma event, have their symptoms resolve as they process the experience. Some people, however, develop ASD or PTSD. The main difference between these disorders is the length of time they last. ASD symptoms develop within three to 30 days following a traumatic event (American Psychiatric Association, 2013, pgs 271-274). Many people who develop ASD do not go on to develop PTSD.

Criteria for Posttraumatic Stress Disorder. In the *DSM-IV*, PTSD was listed as an anxiety disorder, and the symptoms had to be present for a minimum of three months. PTSD was radically reconceptualized in the *DSM-5*, which effectively broadened the diagnostic criteria. The main criteria set for PTSD are (American Psychiatric Association, 2013, pgs. 271-274):

- Exposure to actual or threatened death, severe injury, or sexual violence (does not apply to exposure to electronic media unless this exposure is work related)

- Presence of one or more intrusive symptoms associated with the traumatic events (includes dreams, intrusive thoughts, and dissociative thoughts)

- Avoidance of stimuli associated with the event

- Negative changes to mood and cognitions associated with the event (exaggerated negative beliefs about oneself and/or inability to remember an important aspect of the traumatic events)

- Major changes in arousal and reactivity associated with the traumatic events (irritability, anger outbursts, self-destructive behavior, problems concentrating, exaggerated startle response, sleep disturbance)
- Symptoms last longer than one month (if the symptoms last three to 30 days, the patient can be diagnosed with ASD)
- Functional impairment due to disturbances
- The symptoms are not attributable to another medical condition

Features of Posttraumatic Stress Disorder. Let us look at the clinical features of PTSD (Sadock, Sadock, & Ruiz, 2015; van der Kolk, 2014):

- Emotional reactions to a traumatic event are no longer part of Criterion A, namely because of the overdiagnosis of PTSD in those exposed to traumatic images in the media
- Medical events are usually not included, except sudden, catastrophic events (e.g., waking up during surgery while under general anesthesia)
- Witnessed events are also included
- People with PTSD have memories that are intrusive and involuntary
- Distressing and recurrent dreams are also common
- Sleep difficulties are common
- The person may dissociate and relive the event; this is sometimes called a "flashback"
- Flashbacks can be cued by external events or internal sensations
- The person often spends a lot of time trying to avoid thoughts and stimuli associated with the trauma
- The person may also have problems remembering the event or things that happened before the event
- The person may become quick-tempered or demonstrate poor impulse control
- They may also blame themselves for the event
- They may not be able to experience intimacy (in any form)
- They can develop a heightened startle response
- Difficulty concentrating is common
- Engaging in reckless, dangerous, or self-destructive behaviors can also occur
- In children, regression can occur (e.g., loss of speech)
- If the experience is repeated and prolonged, the person has likely developed a severe inability to start or maintain relationships
- Pseudo-hallucinations can occur: The person has an experience of hearing one's thoughts spoken in another voice or their own thoughts spoken in their voice
- Paranoia can occur
- PTSD symptoms usually begin within three months of the event, but there can be a much longer delay; this is called delayed expression

- Half of the people who meet criteria for PTSD have their symptoms resolve within three months
- Traumatic events can increase suicide risk

Trauma, Mental Health, and Medical Problems

Individuals remember, interpret, and express trauma differently; therefore, trauma signs and symptoms vary greatly in response to the many things that may cause trauma. My recommendation is to rule out the presence of trauma (and substances of abuse, which we cover in the next chapter) prior to making any mental health diagnosis. With high-risk clients, it is safe to assume that they have a traumatic history and to treat them accordingly. I believe that many people who have been diagnosed with a mental illness are really suffering from the impact of trauma. Even if the patient does not have a trauma history, approaching them in a trauma-informed manner will likely be helpful for them.

The intersection of mental illness symptoms and trauma is clear (Marich, 2015). Many people who seek psychiatric care have been abused as children or have witnessed violence in their families. More than half of severely traumatized people develop substance abuse problems. In my experience, most adults diagnosed with BPD suffered abuse as a young child, often sexual abuse.

I saw this trend daily in my work in the ER and on the inpatient behavioral health unit. In fact, I have seen this trend throughout my career. Please understand that I am not against psychiatric medication. I have seen how mood stabilizers, antipsychotic medications, and antidepressant medications have greatly improved the lives of many people with severe mental illnesses. However, I have also seen how relying on these medications alone and not assessing for the presence of trauma or providing treatment for trauma avoids addressing the client's underlying issues.

Van der Kolk (2014, p. 36) added to this with his observation:

> The theory that mental illness is caused primarily by chemical imbalances in the brain that can be corrected by specific drugs has become broadly accepted by the media and the public, as well as by the medical profession. In many places, drugs have displaced therapy and enabled patients to suppress their problems without addressing the underlying issues.

Trauma can also create symptoms consistent with medical problems. According to van der Kolk, "Somatic symptoms for which no clear physical basis can be found are ubiquitous in traumatized children and adults. They can include chronic back and neck pain, fibromyalgia, migraines, digestive problems, spastic colon/irritable bowel syndrome, chronic fatigue" (2014, p. 100). Again, this is not to say that every person who has these symptoms or disorders has a trauma history, but a history of trauma needs to be assessed in these cases, particularly when there are no apparent medical reasons for the signs and symptoms.

Recently, I was asked to interview a 19-year-old man who reportedly had a history of seizures. His seizures were atypical, in that he remembered what happened when he was seizing and was never incontinent of urine or stool. An astute neurologist, after running a full battery of tests, concluded that the young man was having pseudo seizures due to a psychological issue. The young man refused to believe this and sought out a less-capable neurologist, who prescribed him several types of anticonvulsant medications. The young man was also able to continue to receive disability payments for this disorder.

I was asked to see this patient by an ER doctor who was tired of his repeatedly coming to the ER saying he had been seizing. The patient was reluctant to speak with me but eventually agreed to do so. During our conversation, he noted that he "seized" when he was stressed. At no time did he seize when he was not under duress. I asked him about any history of trauma, and I saw his defenses go down for the first time during our conversation. He noted that in the past year, his older brother had been shot during an argument. His brother survived the shooting but wound up being imprisoned (the patient was never clear with me why this happened). The young man noted that had he been present, his brother would not have been shot and subsequently imprisoned.

This 19-year-old man could not explain why his presence would have made a difference, but he believed it to be so. He also admitted that his seizures had gotten worse since his brother's shooting. I explained to him that the medical evidence, as provided by his first neurologist and corroborated by the ER doctor, indicated that he was experiencing pseudo seizures, which are not uncommon among people who experience trauma. The patient listened carefully but said he did not wish to pursue any counseling. I could not force him to do anything he did not want to do, but I still provided him with information on appropriate trauma counselors in his area.

Common Trauma Misdiagnoses. Traumatic symptoms are often misdiagnosed as other mental health disorders (Marich, 2015). It also is possible for an individual to have an existing mental health disorder, then experience trauma and meet the criteria for ASD or PTSD as well as the existing mental health disorder. The key to determining this is a comprehensive assessment that can confirm previous clinical problems. Here are some of the mental health disorders that are commonly misdiagnosed in situations that are better explained by trauma:

- Bipolar disorders
- Anxiety disorders
- Depressive disorders
- Psychotic disorders
- Personality disorders (any of them)
- ADHD
- Autism spectrum disorder
- Conduct disorder or oppositional defiant disorder
- Intermittent explosive disorder
- Somatic symptoms and related disorders
- Neurological disorders
- Substance use or other addictive behavior disorders

An example of how a person can be misdiagnosed with one of these mental health disorders is illustrated in Brian's story. Thankfully, this story has a good ending.

CASE STUDY—BRIAN
WRONG DIAGNOSIS

Brian was from a rural county in central Virginia. He had been living with his grandmother since he was six years old due to his mother having suddenly died at that time. Brian's father had never been involved in his life, and his grandfather died when Brian was nine. Brian was 13 when I met him.

Brian had been diagnosed with ADHD when he was seven years old. I was told he was a handful, but his behaviors showed that "handful" was an understatement. Brian could not focus on much of anything. He also did not seem to care about consequences. A few days after her was admitted, we were standing outside and I watched as he picked up a fist-sized rock, looked directly at me, and then threw the rock through a window.

"Why did you do that!?!" I yelled.

"I have ADHD," Brian calmly replied, "Shit like that happens all the time."

"Okay," I replied, "but who's going to fix the window?"

"Call my grandma," he replied, "She'll pay for it."

"Don't think so," I said. The next day, I had Brian spend his free time helping a maintenance worker replace the window.

I soon came to see that Brian's behaviors were closely connected with his medication. He took Ritalin three times a day. He also took Clonidine, Trazadone, Imipramine, and two or three other medications I do not remember. He vacillated between being excited and completely sedated.

Brian's grandmother and her sister (who was also a big part of Brian's life) would come to visit Brian every visitation Sunday. They clearly loved him and often demonstrated this by bringing him gifts of food and his favorite toys. They also spoiled him. Brian was quite demanding of them, but he also loved them. He would share some of his gifts with peers who had no family visiting them. His grandmother noted that she had tried her best to raise Brian but that he was out of control. They accepted his diagnosis of ADHD, and it seemed that they allowed this to be used as an excuse for his behaviors.

The treatment plan was for Brian's behaviors to become stabilized so he could return to his home and school. The treatment program was largely based on group process, but this was very difficult for Brian, as he was the youngest person in his group.

Whereas most people completed the program in 12 months or less, at 12 months, Brian was only in the second of four phases of the program. His medications largely remained the same. After 14 months in the program, Lance (Brian's therapist) helped Brian in a way that none of us could have guessed. It occurred in group therapy, and when Brian walked out of the group room, he looked drawn and tired. He had also been crying.

"Let him rest tonight, Paul," said Lance, approaching me after group. "He's cried most of the afternoon."

"What happened?" I asked.

"I don't think he has ADHD," Lance wearily smiled, "but a lot of hurt, a lot of pain. I'll tell you tomorrow morning in the staff meeting."

Lance had been working strategically with Brian to try and understand where this kid's anger was coming from. With patience, determination, and an unwillingness to allow Brian to use any diagnosis as an excuse, he eventually helped Brian to uncover where a lot of his pain had started. We knew Brian's mother had died when he was six. What we didn't know is that Brian had found her body after she had killed herself. I don't know how she killed herself, but according to Lance, it was graphic and horrifying.

"How could any of us, let a 6-year-old kid, comprehend that?" Lance asked the staff in our meeting. "How is a kid supposed to focus his attention, learn how to read, pick up on social cues, and feel safe when this image of his mother's dead body never leaves his mind?"

Brian graduated from the program five months later after a lot more work regarding his grief and trauma. When he left the program, he was on an antidepressant and something to help him sleep but no other medications. He even smiled from time to time.

The Three-Stage Consensus Model of Trauma Treatment

How do we treat a person with trauma? There are many ways to do this, but each way requires a commitment to longer-term therapy than is typically employed when dealing with a person experiencing a mental health emergency. Our purpose is to first recognize the trauma and begin the helping process right away. According to Marich, "It is imperative to realize that clinicians can begin doing stabilization-level trauma work from the moment the client begins the assessment process" (2015, p. 132).

The three-stage consensus model of trauma treatment (van der Kolk, 2014; Levine, 2015; Marich, 2015) is widely recognized as the best approach for designing treatment to help the traumatized client.

Stage One: Stabilization
Stage Two: Working through the trauma
Stage Three: Reintegration/reconnection with society

The primary purpose of this approach is to not further traumatize the person while we are trying to help them. The model recognizes that "traumatized people have a tendency to superimpose their trauma on everything around them and have trouble deciphering whatever is going on around them" (van der Kolk, 2014, p. 17); thus, jumping right into "processing" the trauma is going to push their trauma buttons.

The three-stage consensus model recognizes that "being anchored in the present while revisiting the trauma opens the possibility of deeply knowing that the terrible events belong in the past. For that to happen, the brain's watchtower, cook, and timekeeper need to be online. Therapy won't work as long as people keep being pulled back into the past" (van der Kolk, 2014, p. 70). Therefore, the model is weighed heavily on stabilizing the client.

Stabilization. Stabilization is the only thing that I did in the ER setting. I did not do any reprocessing of trauma with the client; this is something that should only take place once the client has engaged in substantial stabilization work with a trauma-informed counselor who is also equipped to help them begin working through the trauma. Even in these cases, clinicians often jump into Stage Two without ensuring that the patient has some stabilization strategies in place. It is up to the client to decide when to move beyond Stage One (Marich, 2012). I make sure that the trauma-informed counselors to whom I refer my patients have a full understanding of the three-stage model and will take their time by following the client's lead to help the individual stabilize. Stabilization can include, but is not limited to, several interventions.

Building a Relationship. The first goal is to build rapport and relationship. In the ER setting, this means helping the client begin to learn how to stabilize themselves and to begin to understand that counselors can help them. It is important to establish personal and interpersonal safety through honest and transparent communication.

Psychoeducational Information. Providing psychoeducation about trauma can greatly help a client regain equilibrium and hope. This includes:

- How traumatic memory gets stored differently
- The impact of trauma on the brain
- The fight, flight, and freeze responses
- The internal locus of control: "What do I have control over, and what do I not have control over, and how might this have been skewed or altered by the trauma?"
- Dissociation
- The link between trauma, PTSD, substance use disorders, mental illness symptoms, and medical symptoms

Breathing. Breathing techniques can have a remarkable calming effect. In the ER and in my current practice, I spend time teaching the client/patient about the benefits of mindful breathing. When I was in graduate school and was taught about the power of breathing to self-regulate anxiety, I thought the material ridiculous. "We all breathe," I told myself. "What's the big deal?" Working with people in crisis, I quickly learned that controlling my breathing and teaching my clients how to be aware of their breathing was a valuable tool, especially with clients who were extremely anxious or panicking.

Additional Stabilization Interventions. These are the primary interventions I used in the ER setting when working with someone who had been traumatized. These early, basic interventions activate social engagement and help reduce flight, fight, and freeze responses in the client. An obvious part of the client's discharge plan should be to help them enter counseling with an appropriate trauma-informed therapist. Once a therapist has engaged a client in stabilization, that counselor may use a variety of tools to further stabilize the client before progressing onto processing the trauma. Remember that this process usually takes months, if not years, of consistent counseling. Here are additional interventions for stabilization:

- Pressure points/acupuncture
- Yoga
- Eye movement desensitization and reprocessing (EMDR)
- Guided visual imagery
- Music and sound therapies
- Dialectical behavioral therapy
- Art therapy
- Drama therapy
- Play therapy for children
- Taste and smell (gum/candy or aromatherapy)
- Blended sense exercises (including journaling)

The result of these interventions and the commitment of the counselor and client will hopefully be an individual who has learned to integrate their experiences into their lives and has an understanding that their healing is a continuous process.

Conclusion

Trauma can obviously co-occur with all the other mental health emergencies we examine. It can also occur in people who are not experiencing, or maybe have never experienced, a mental health emergency. Trauma is likely underdiagnosed, and this may explain, in part, the overdiagnosis of mental illnesses like bipolar disorder. The key to helping people who have been traumatized is to recognize the trauma in the first place and then to help them become stabilized and engaged in trauma-informed counseling with a caring, patient, and understanding clinician.

CHAPTER 9

Substance Abuse

Humans have historically used, and continue to use, a variety of substances to change their moods and emotions, experience physical sensations, and alter their levels of consciousness. A few examples of plant-based substances include alcohol (fruits or grains), cocaine (coca leaves), heroin and morphine (poppy seed pods), and marijuana (cannabis flowers and leaves). Additionally, there are countless human-made chemicals that closely resemble their plant-based and neurotransmitter cousins, including MDMA (also called Molly, Ecstasy, or "E"), ketamine (Special K or "K"), fentanyl (Apache, China White, TNT), and DXM/DM. Both naturally occurring and human-made chemicals mimic the neurological processes that occur in our brains, and they may heighten senses of pleasure, relaxation, and energy.

There are many theories as to why people become addicted to certain chemicals and behaviors; however, this text does not address these issues. The focus of this chapter is to understand how the use of certain chemicals can lead to a mental health emergency: how we recognize this and respond to the person experiencing the emergency. A big part of helping people who use drugs is understanding *what* they use and *how* chemicals impact the brain.

Our focus in this chapter is twofold: Understanding how drugs of abuse impact a person and examining the variety of substances that people use to get high. This book is not intended to be a complete text on pharmacology, neurobiology, or neurochemistry; for more detail on these topics, please see the "References" section. However, working with high-risk clients experiencing mental health emergencies requires clinicians to have a general understanding of the variety of drugs that people use and how they can lead to a mental health emergency.

All substances of abuse impact the brain, and some of these chemicals also impact other systems of the body; therefore, it is important to understand the neurobiological process of various drugs. There are two processes involved when a person uses a drug: *pharmacodynamics* (a drug's effect on the body) and *pharmacokinetics* (the body's effect on a drug).

When we consider the body's effect on a drug, we look at how the drug is absorbed, distributed, metabolized by the body. These processes are influenced by: 1) route of administration, 2) speed of transit to the brain, 3) rates of metabolism, 4) process of elimination, and 5) affinity for nerve cells and neurotransmitters. Pharmacodynamics and pharmacokinetics co-occur throughout this entire process (Inaba & Cohen, 2014).

Route of Administration and Speed of Transit to the Brain

The more rapidly a drug reaches its target receptor(s) in the brain, the greater the reinforcing potential, resulting in the message, "That felt good, do it again!" The speed at which a drug reaches the brain starts with how the drug is introduced to the body. The following descriptions of the various routes of admission start with the quickest way that a substance reaches the brain when ingested. Keep in mind that there will be variations in speed depending on the exact chemical(s) ingested and other metabolic issues (which we examine later).

Inhalation. Inhalation through the mouth is one of the quickest ways to get a substance to the brain. From the time the chemical is inhaled to when it reaches the brain takes seven to 10 seconds. Once inhaled, some of the chemical (along with the air inhaled) is absorbed into the bloodstream via the alveoli in the lungs. Blood from the alveoli goes from the lungs, through the heart, and to the brain. The quick effect of inhalation is one of the reasons that nicotine has a higher addiction potential when smoked in cigarettes or vaporizers as compared to *absorption* through the cheeks and gums via snuff or chewing tobacco. Similarly, cocaine has a higher addiction potential when smoked or freebased in powder or crack form, compared with *insufflation* via snorting powder cocaine.

Injection. Injecting a drug is a slightly slower route to the brain than inhalation through the mouth, taking anywhere from a few seconds to a few minutes, depending on whether the injection is intravenous (IV), intramuscular (IM), or subcutaneous. Once injected, the effects of the drug are felt within 15 to 30 seconds with the IV route; three to five minutes with the IM route, and three to five minutes with the subcutaneous (skin popping) route.

IV injection is the most dangerous method, as it bypasses the body's natural defenses and results in the highest level of bioavailability (the percentage of the drug that reaches a person's system remaining active). Another risk of this route of admission is that IV drug users typically develop narrowing and hardening of the veins due to repeated injections. Over time, it becomes more difficult for them to inject themselves.

Injecting into a muscle or subcutaneously is less desirable than injecting into a vein, as the effect is slower, but people who inject drugs use these routes of administration when they lack IV access. Many users develop tissue infections in the form of abscesses, which can require extensive medical care. Some injecting drug users will inject into their abscesses because the damaged tissue has a higher concentration of blood (Bourgois & Schonberg, 2009).

Mucous Membrane Absorption. Mucous membrane absorption follows injection as the next quickest means for a chemical to get to the drug user's brain. In most forms of use, mucous membrane absorption takes between 10 to 15 minutes. There are several routes people may use, including *insufflation* (snorting through the nose), *sublingual* (under the tongue), *buccal* (between gums and cheek), or *topical* (e.g., on an eyeball). Additionally, a person may insert drugs in liquid or solid form into their rectum or vagina.

Snorting through the nose via insufflation results in most of the product being trapped in folds of tissue at the back of the nose. Some of the material will travel to the lungs, and some enters the esophagus. Powdered cocaine, methamphetamine, and crushed prescription opioids and amphetamines are typically consumed in this manner. These same medications can also be used buccally by rubbing the powder into one's gums. Some medications, including Saphris and Suboxone can be used sublingually.

Some prescription and over-the-counter medications are designed to be taken as a suppository via the rectum or vagina. A trend among some people who use alcohol is to transfer alcohol into their rectum via an enema. This allows the individual to become inebriated more quickly with less alcohol. This method is often used by college students and other underage drinkers believe that consuming alcohol rectally allows them to pass a breathalyzer test. The danger of this method is that it bypasses the body's defense mechanisms for consuming too much alcohol, specifically vomiting when the body senses there is too much alcohol in the person's stomach. The person can experience alcohol poisoning, which may lead to a loss of consciousness with little warning. Alcohol, gamma hydroxybutyric acid (GHB), and other liquid chemicals can also be soaked in a tampon and inserted rectally or vaginally. Some substances can also be dropped onto the eyeball through a medicine dropper and absorbed this way.

Oral Administration. A variety of medications can only be consumed orally. This method of ingestion can take from 30 minutes to several hours until the effects are felt: The chemicals must be broken down and absorbed through the stomach or intestinal walls. One of the dangers of taking medications orally is that the person may expect the chemical to take effect quickly, and when it does not, they take more of the chemical, thinking that they did not initially consume enough to achieve the desired intoxication. The person then experiences overdose symptoms.

Skin Absorption. The slowest method of ingesting a substance is through skin contact absorption. Medications used in this manner can take up to 2 days to reach full effect.

Regardless of route, the drug will be distributed throughout the body following entrance to the bloodstream. Once in the bloodstream, the drug reaches the blood-brain barrier in 10 to 15 seconds. Some drugs readily cross this barrier, which creates an increased euphoric effect, whereas other drugs take longer. Heroin and morphine are good examples of how different drugs cross the blood-brain barrier at different speeds: Morphine takes longer to cross than heroin. As heroin crosses the blood-brain barrier quicker, it creates a rapid sense of euphoria when injected, called "the rush." Heroin is quickly biotransformed into morphine once in the brain. Morphine, while retaining the analgesic effects of heroin, takes a longer time to cross the barrier and does not create the rush that injected heroin does. (Inaba & Cohen, 2014).

Rates of Metabolism and Process of Elimination

Metabolism is the process of a drug being broken down and inactivated; the liver provides this function for many drugs. A drug's *half-life* is the amount of time it takes for half of a drug to be eliminated from the body. Generally, the slower the breakdown process, the longer the drug has an effect.

Metabolism factors vary by individual and are dependent on multiple factors, such as a person's age, ethnicity, heredity, sex, overall health, emotional state, and expectations of what the chemical will do, as well as other drugs present in the person's body. Other factors also affect an individual's metabolism, but often not all factors can be known.

Age. As people age into middle adulthood, their metabolism generally begins to slow. When this happens, the effects of drugs can become more pronounced because the person's body is not breaking the chemicals down as quickly.

Ethnicity. Ethnicity can also play a factor in metabolism levels. Some of this may be due to hereditary factors. Does an ethnic group's diet have an impact on their metabolism? What about their access to health care? How does the group typically respond to stress? These factors could all impact metabolism.

Heredity. We are becoming more aware of the role that heredity plays in substance use. There is compelling evidence of genetic predisposition toward addictive behaviors in some families. When I worked in community mental health, one of my coworkers had a young man on his caseload who could trace his family history back six generations. He found that all the men in his family were alcohol dependent as well as about half of the women. One could reasonably argue that this familial pattern had as much to do with social learning as it did with a genetic predisposition to alcoholism. Further study may reveal that *both* nature *and* nurture play a role in family systems such as this one.

Sex. Sex is another aspect of metabolism. Males and females have differing levels of specific enzymes and hormones, and these can impact metabolism. Females produce less of the enzyme alcohol dehydrogenase, which begins the process of breaking down alcohol in the stomach.

Overall Physical Health. The client's overall physical health plays a role in metabolism. People with a chronic illness often have a reduced metabolism, which increases the impact of any chemicals they use. Examples of illnesses that may impact metabolism include, but are not limited to, diabetes, heart disease, pulmonary disease, kidney disease, neuropathic disorders, and pancreatitis.

Emotional State and Expectations. A person's emotional state can also exaggerate the effects of a drug. Some drugs, particularly hallucinogens and entactogens, are highly susceptible to the physical setting of the individual and their mindset. All substances of abuse impact the user emotionally. Much of this is due to the reason *why* the person is using. Are they using to celebrate and have fun in a social setting, or are they using to try and numb themselves to physical and/or emotional pain? The person's expectation of how the substance will impact them is also important.

Presence of Other Substances. Drug *synergism*, how drugs interact and change one another in the body, can also have an impact on metabolism. For example, alcohol is relatively easily metabolized in the liver. If other medications are present, those medications are not metabolized as quickly as alcohol because the liver tends to metabolize the simpler chemical first (Erickson, 2007).

Unknown Factors. We must consider exaggerated reactions or allergies to specific chemicals. Some clients experience paradoxical reactions to a chemical. We must also consider side effects of a drug: the unintended actions created by a drug (e.g., dry mouth, drowsiness).

Affinity for Nerve Cells and Neurotransmitters. The adult human brain consists of more than 100 billion brain cells, or neurons. Each of these cells can form thousands of connections with other brain cells or nerve cells. Information is communicated electrically within the cell body and chemically from cell to cell.

Brain Function

Inaba and Cohen (2014) described how the brain can be divided into two areas: the "old brain" and the "new brain." The old brain consists of the brainstem, spinal cord, cerebellum, and midbrain (sometimes called the limbic system). These structures within the brain regulate survival functions, basic emotions, and desire/cravings; they also imprint strong memories. The old brain reacts quicker than the new brain, which consists of the cerebrum and cerebral cortex. This is the largest area of the brain by volume and is the most developed part of the human brain. Here, our reasoning, problem solving, creativity, communication, and abstract thinking occur. Because the new brain reacts slower than the old brain, the old brain can override the new brain.

Both parts of the brain create and store memory (conscious and unconscious), which is an important part of addiction. Memories exist as proteins in the brain called *dendritic spines*. It takes thousands of these spines to form a single memory, and each memory is usually interconnected with other memories. Emotionally-charged memories are the most powerful and are permanent. The memories we have of these experiences lead us to repeat them.

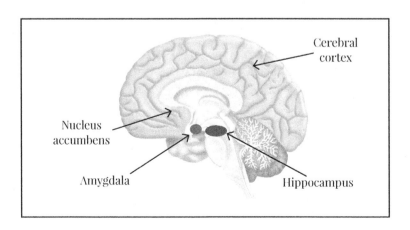

Reward System

Addictive drugs use this same reward system to reinforce maladaptive behaviors, yet they do so much faster and more powerfully than food, or even sex. Drugs provide a shortcut to the brain's reward system:

1. The chemicals flood the nucleus accumbens with dopamine: "This feels good!"
2. The hippocampus lays down memories of this rapid sense of satisfaction: "I remember how this feels."
3. The amygdala creates a conditioned response to certain stimuli: "I was at [place] with [person] doing [activity] when I got high."

The more powerful a specific drug's affinity for particular neurons, the more rapid the memory of its effects develops. This memory serves to reinforce desire, or cravings, for the drug. The more an activity is repeated, the more likely we are to remember it. Likewise, the earlier in life that a person is exposed to substances, the more chances there are for these memories to be reinforced. People who use substances can also experience *euphoric recall:* They only remember the good things about an experience.

Neurotransmitters

Neurotransmitters are the second major brain component involved in addiction. Drugs cannot create sensations or feelings that do not have a natural counterpart in the brain. One of the ways they accomplish this is to mimic or disrupt neurotransmitters and/or their receptor sites.

Norepinephrine and Epinephrine (Adrenaline). These are stimulant-like neurotransmitters that are released when the body feels a demand for quick energy. These chemicals also impact motivation, hunger, attention span, confidence, alertness, heart rate, digestion, dreaming, moods, and arousal in response to environmental situations. Many prescription medications and drugs of abuse impact norepinephrine and epinephrine (Erikson, 2007).

Dopamine. This neurotransmitter regulates sleep, working memory, muscular activity, emotions, and the addiction pathway (pleasure and reward). Too much dopamine can cause psychosis, and too little can lead to parkinsonian features (Sadock, Sadock, & Ruiz, 2015). Most stimulant drugs, including cocaine, amphetamines, methamphetamine, and caffeine, impact dopamine directly. Dopamine is thought to be the most crucial neurotransmitter involved in the pleasurable and addictive effects of drugs (Erickson, 2007).

Histamine. Histamine controls tissue inflammation, emotions, and sleep. Drugs with anticholinergic properties impact histamine. Some antihistamine medications are prescribed to produce a calming effect. Chemicals that impact histamine can be abused or used with other drugs to produce a sedating effect.

Serotonin. This was the first identified neurotransmitter. Serotonin regulates digestion, mood, body temperature regulation, sleep cycles, sexual arousal, and movement. Serotonin is present throughout the body's digestive system. Most of the newer antidepressant medications impact serotonin. Hallucinogenic and entactogenic drugs also impact serotonin.

Gamma Aminobutyric Acid (GABA). Gamma aminobutyric acid is the brain's primary inhibitory neurotransmitter and is involved in 25 to 40 percent of all synapses (Erickson, 2007). It controls impulses and muscle relaxation and generally slows down the brain. Increasing the action of GABA decreases the action of other neurotransmitters; inversely, decreasing GABA increases the action of other neurotransmitters. Alcohol, benzodiazepines, and other depressant drugs impact GABA.

Glutamic Acid (Glutamate and Glutamine). This excitatory neurotransmitter interacts with 80 percent of neurons in the brain (Erickson, 2007). It is involved with learning and sensory function and enhances the effects of dopamine.

Endorphins, Enkephalins, Dynorphins, and Opioid Peptides. These neurotransmitters are involved with pain regulation and ways the body responds to all kinds of stress. They are heavily involved in the addiction pathway, particularly with opioids.

Tachykinin (Substance P). This carries pain impulses from the peripheral nervous system to the Central Nervous System (CNS). Enkephalins and opioids can block this process (Inaba & Cohen, 2014).

Endocannabinoids (Anandamide). This neurotransmitter is postulated to be involved with mood, pain control, integration of sensory experiences with emotions, and neurological function. It functions chemically like cannabis and other cannabinoids.

Acetylcholine. This is released where nerves meet muscles, tissues, and glands. It also induces rapid eye movement sleep and impacts memory and learning. Nicotine, one of the primary psychoactive chemicals in tobacco, impacts acetylcholine.

Neural Receptor Sites and Drug Interactions

Once a neurotransmitter does its "job" by binding with a receptor site on the postsynaptic neuron, it is released back into the synaptic gap and reabsorbed by the presynaptic neuron (Inaba & Cohen, 2014). Certain drugs slow the reabsorption process, such as SSRIs. Any neurotransmitter that remains in the gap and is not reabsorbed is metabolized by enzymes.

Substances of abuse can impact receptor sites in several ways as an agonist or antagonist. An *agonist* is a drug/chemical that acts on a receptor site to mimic the effects usually created by the neurotransmitter that is naturally produced. Examples of agonists include most opioids. An *antagonist* is a drug/chemical that is capable of blocking, or reducing, the activity of an agonist (competitive and noncompetitive) at the receptor site without exerting any effect itself. Examples of antagonists include most antipsychotics, which block dopamine 2 receptors. Also, naltrexone and naloxone (Narcan) block opioid receptors.

Various drugs can alter the effects of neurotransmitters in several ways. Substances may block the release of neurotransmitters, as with heroin, or force the release of neurotransmitters, such as with cocaine and MDMA. Drugs like methamphetamine can inhibit an enzyme that helps synthesize or metabolize neurotransmitters. SSRIs and SNRIs prevent neurotransmitters from being reabsorbed, thus prolonging the opportunity to bind at the receptor sites. Drugs can also interfere with the storage of neurotransmitters or perform any combinations of these interactions.

Drug Classes and Specific Drugs of Abuse

When working with people experiencing a mental health emergency, we need to have knowledge of how drugs impact the brain and the variety of substances that people use to alter their consciousness. The following is not an exhaustive list but contains most substances that people in North America can use or abuse. Please remember that this information is current for 2018, but drug use trends change and new chemicals are developed all the time. Drug use trends are also constantly changing in specific communities all the time: What is impacting one region may not be a factor in a neighboring area, and what is a major problem in a community one year may not be the following year. The prudent clinician stays informed about the drugs that are being used in their community and how these substances impact their clients.

Opium. Opium is a naturally occurring substance and is the key ingredient for many opioids, including heroin. Synthetic or semisynthetic opioids contain chemicals that mimic opium. Opium is broken down into alkaloids: morphine, codeine, and thebaine. These alkaloids are often further refined into other chemicals or used themselves, the exception being thebaine, which is used to create other opioids. It takes 10 kg of opium to make 1 kg of morphine (Kuhn, Swartzwelder, & Wilson, 2008; Rose, 2012; Inaba & Cohen, 2014).

Opioids. *Opiates* are medicines derived from thebaine, morphine, codeine, or other opium derivatives. *Opioid* is an umbrella term for all natural and synthetic medicines that are derived from and based on opium. Opioids suppress pain in lower doses, create euphoria in moderate doses, and cause respiratory distress in high doses. People who have become dependent on opioids are often driven to inject the drug as quickly as possible because of increasing severity of withdrawal symptoms ("dope sickness"). They may no longer use opiates because they are seeking the high but rather to avoid feeling sick: Symptoms typically include nausea, vomiting, body aches, cold sweats, diarrhea, and muscle cramps. Signs and symptoms of opioid intoxication include sedation, fatigue, confusion, unconsciousness or coma, nausea, constipation, pinpoint pupils that are unresponsive to light, and slowed breathing; opioid use may lead to death.

Morphine. Morphine is the standard/benchmark opioid and is about ten times stronger than codeine. Morphine was identified and isolated from opium in 1803. One cannot understate the importance of the discovery and use of morphine. Today, morphine is administered by injection and suppository, as well as orally and sublingually.

Heroin. Heroin includes the natural products of the opium poppy and synthetic compounds derived from it. Between 15 and 21 million people between the ages of 15 and 64 use heroin worldwide (Inaba & Cohen, 2014). Whereas prescription opioid use has plateaued, heroin use has increased, due to the increasing quantity and purity of heroin (Macy, 2018). The profile of a heroin user has also changed. Heroin is increasingly used by people who have limited, or even no, previous illicit drug use. Much of this is due to the increased prescribing of opioids by medical practitioners within the past 15 years (Quinones, 2015). As more people began using powerful opioids like oxycodone, an increasing number of deaths resulted, and restrictions on prescription opioids began to take effect. Faced with a shortage of the prescription medications, the street cost of diverted prescription drugs increased. At the same time, heroin was widely available, comparatively cheaper, and stronger; therefore, it emerged as a viable alternative to prescription pills (Erickson, 2007).

Heroin is one to four times the strength of morphine (Inaba & Cohen, 2014). Once past the blood-brain barrier, heroin is quickly metabolized into morphine. The lower-grade heroin "brown sugar" or "black tar heroin" is usually injected (IV, IM, or skin-popped). This type of heroin typically comes from Mexico and Central and South America. Higher-grade heroin, which can be up to 90 percent pure, is sometimes called "China White" and can be snorted, smoked, or injected. This heroin is generally from southern or southeastern Asia.

The "rush" occurs once the heroin reaches the brain when it is IV injected, but is delayed and less intense when heroin is consumed in other ways. The rush includes feelings of warmth and pleasure, followed by an extended period of sedation, often called "nodding." The overdose potential of heroin is extremely high, especially when it is injected. As heroin made its way into all segments of society, including groups who direct content in the mainstream media, heroin use was suddenly viewed as a crisis, even though heroin has had widespread use in all areas of society for some time.

Fentanyl and Its Analogs. Fentanyl is the most powerful of all opioids, 80 to 100 times more potent than morphine (Inaba & Cohen, 2014). Fentanyl is short acting in some forms and long acting in others, so it is used to treat chronic pain and as an anesthetic in surgery. Fentanyl transdermal patches are chewed by users, or the drug is extracted physically and/or chemically from the patch. Chewing the patches, even a used patch (which still contains medication), can result in unconsciousness or death. Street versions of fentanyl are also available (e.g., "China White"). This is sometimes confused with heroin, which is also called China White in some locales. Most of the street fentanyl currently in use is illicitly manufactured.

There are dozens of fentanyl analogues, including acetyl fentanyl, Sufentanil, and Carfentanil, which is 100 times more potent than regular fentanyl. Carfentanil is not designed for human consumption but is used to sedate large animals. The extreme potency of this chemical often means that users, who are unaware of what they are using, quickly go into respiratory arrest. According to the Centers for Disease Control, 55 percent of lethal opioid overdoses from November 2016 to November 2017 involved synthetic opioid, predominately fentanyl (CDC, 2018).

Fentanyl-like Chemicals. These substances are often found with fentanyl and fentanyl analogous. 4-Fluorobutyrfentanyl (p-FBF) was created in the 1960s and found its way onto the black market in the 1980s. It is now a Schedule I drug and is sometimes sold in an intranasal spray formulary. U47700 was created by Upjohn as an analgesic in the 1970s but never commercially marketed. While not a true fentanyl analogue (but often taken with fentanyl), it is eight times more potent than morphine. U47700 is now a scheduled drug in some states.

A third fentanyl-like chemical is W-18, which is manufactured in China and smuggled to Canada where it enters the United States. There are more than 20 "W series" chemicals, but W-18 and W-15 have been seen in the illicit market. When health care workers first began seeing patients who had overdosed on W-18, this opioid-like drug would not respond to naloxone (Narcan), prompting fears that there was no way to protect users against this new opioid. The main reason that it would not respond to naloxone is that W-18 appears to bind to peripheral benzodiazepine receptors. As such, W-18 may represent the first indicator of designer benzodiazepines entering the illicit drug market. This potential area of development must be closely watched.

Prescription Opiates. Whereas all opioids have a potential for abuse, the recent trend of very potent opioids (heroin and fentanyl) has shifted attention away from other, less powerful, opioids. However, these chemicals continue to be abused. The following opioids are listed in order from weak to strong. This is not a complete list of opioids—just the ones more likely to be encountered in a mental health emergency.

- Ultram (Tramadol)
- Pentazocine (Talwin)
- Hydrocodone (Vicodin, Lortab, and Norco)
- Oxycodone (OxyContin, Percocet, Percodan, and Tylox)
- Hydromorphone (Dilaudid)
- Oxymorphone (Opana, Numorphan, and Numorphone)
- Methadone (Dolophine and Oramorph)
- Buprenorphine
- Naltrexone and naloxone

Oxycodone is responsible for many deaths in the Appalachia and other regions of the country where over-prescription and drug diversion were rampant. Part of this was due to the introduction of time-release tablets (OxyContin) that were designed to provide long-term relief from chronic pain. Doctors were told that OxyContin was not addictive, and the drug was widely prescribed. Users of the drug quickly discovered that they could misuse the drug by chewing or crushing the pills and then snorting or injecting the powder, causing an immediate high; the pills can also be burned and the fumes inhaled (Quinones, 2015).

Buprenorphine is often combined with naloxone in a medication called Suboxone. Suboxone is used for opiate detoxification in inpatient settings and medication-assisted treatment in outpatient settings (Li, Shorter, & Kosten, 2016). A primary benefit of using Suboxone as opposed to methadone is that buprenorphine causes less respiratory depression. It also has a "ceiling effect" at 32 mg, which makes overdose less likely, except when mixed with alcohol or benzodiazepines. In this formulation, should the patient try to inject the drug instead of taking it orally, they would experience withdrawal symptoms because of the naloxone.

As with other "abuse-proof" drugs, Suboxone can be abused when the tablets are crushed and insufflated. In 2014, the Food and Drug Administration (FDA) approved a Suboxone buccal film; in 2016, the FDA approved Probuphine, an implantable form of buprenorphine. There are widespread stories of abuse whereby the film is smoked or the liquid version of Suboxone is frozen and thawed, which appears to nullify the naloxone, making it easier to inject the drug (Ramsey, 2016).

Kratom (Mitragyna speciosa) is an herb that grows in tree-like plants in Southeast Asia. The leaves of this plant produce complex stimulant and opioid-like analgesic effects. In Thailand, the raw leaves are eaten or brewed into a tea. Low to moderate doses (1–5 g) produce mild, pleasant stimulant effects. Moderate to high doses (5–15 g) produce opioid-like effects but are also used for opioid withdrawal symptom management. Very high doses (>15 g) create sedating and stupor-inducing symptoms. Kratom is dose sensitive and highly variable (Boyer et al., 2008).

Kratom remains legal in most states and is also heavily marketed on the Internet. Because of this, some people diminish its abuse/dependence potential. Some use Kratom recreationally; others, for pain management effects; and still others, to wean themselves off other opioids. Chronic, high-dose use has been associated with hyperpigmentation of the cheeks, tremor, anorexia, weight loss, and psychotic symptoms (Prozialeck, Jivan, & Andurkar, 2012).

Loperamide is an antidiarrheal medication sold in nonprescription form as Imodium and in generic forms. As loperamide is a weak opioid, users must take more than 100 times the prescribed dose of 2 mg (200 mg or more) to feel any effect (Caro et al., 2017). Published research suggests that people addicted to other opioids use loperamide in an attempt to detoxify off their opioids of choice or as a replacement when they cannot obtain their opioid of choice. In addition to the obvious severe constipation associated with loperamide abuse, using this medicine in such amounts can lead to serious heart problems (Caro et al., 2017).

Naltrexone and naloxone are opioids that only have antagonistic properties. Naltrexone (Revia) is a deterrent, used to prevent relapse by limiting cravings. Naltrexone blocks the euphoric effects of opioids, cocaine, and alcohol. It is available in time-release injectable versions (Vivitrol) and implant versions.

Naloxone (Narcan) is injected or used intranasally to reverse an opiate overdose. If the unconscious person has not used an opioid, the naloxone will not have an effect. Likewise, if the naloxone is administered orally, it has no effect, which is why a person can orally consume Suboxone and not experience the withdrawal effects of the naloxone.

As the opioid epidemic has reached all areas of our society, many communities are providing Narcan to police officers and the public to help prevent overdose deaths from heroin and other opioids. What nonmedical personnel must understand is that using Narcan to help someone who has overdosed on an opioid is only the first step in helping them. The initial Narcan dose typically lasts about 20 to 30 minutes. Once it wears off, the opioids that remain in the patient's system bind with their appropriate opioid receptors again, and the patient can lapse into unconsciousness. It is imperative that the individual receive emergency medical attention immediately! Narcan is designed to buy time for the patient to get to an ED—it is not a lasting solution to the overdose.

Opioid Withdrawal Symptoms. Having witnessed many people experiencing opioid withdrawal symptoms, the best description I can give to those who have never witnessed this process is to imagine: a) the worst case of food poisoning they have heard about b) plus the worst influenza case they have heard about and c) multiply the intensity by a factor of three and have the experience last seven to 10 days. Despite the severity of symptoms most heavy opioid users experience, not everyone experiences the same symptoms or severity of symptoms. I have met heavy, long-term opioid users who stopped using and experienced little discomfort.

The most common opioid withdrawal signs include mental and physical symptoms. Mental symptoms may consist of cravings, irritability, insomnia, cognitive difficulties, depression, anxiety, and anorexia (complete loss of appetite). Physical symptoms include:

- Nausea, vomiting, stomach cramps, diarrhea
- Muscle cramping, aches, and pains
- Bone aches and pains
- Fever
- Hot and cold flashes, chills or inability to feel warm enough
- Diaphoresis (sweating)
- Lacrimation (watery eyes), rhinorrhea (runny nose), and piloerection (skin hairs standing on end)
- Dilated pupils
- Yawning

Opioid withdrawal symptoms appear within six to eight hours of the last dose. Symptoms typically peak in intensity on the second or third day and dissipate by the seventh to tenth day. The withdrawal syndrome is much longer with methadone: Withdrawal can last at least three weeks after the last use if the patient was using a large amount and/or over an extended period. Post-acute opioid withdrawal symptoms continue for months and can include depression, anxiety, problems concentrating, sleep problems, difficulty handling stressful situations, and cravings.

Stimulants. Stimulants are the most widely used psychoactive substances in the world and include nicotine (e.g., tobacco) and caffeine (e.g., tea, coffee) (Inaba & Cohen, 2014). These chemicals typically impact epinephrine (physical energy), norepinephrine (confidence, feelings of well-being, motivation), serotonin (mood), and dopamine (keys the reward system). As the body must rest at some point, a person abusing stimulants inevitably becomes physically, mentally, and emotionally exhausted no matter how much they use. Weight loss is a side effect of most stimulants—many dietary aids contain stimulants of varying intensity.

Tolerance to stimulants can develop quickly, as can downregulation of serotonin and dopamine receptor sites in the nucleus accumbens (Inaba & Cohen, 2014). Downregulation means that the brain decreases available receptor sites for serotonin and dopamine, which increases the person's tolerance to the stimulant they have been using. When the person stops using the drug, their brain requires a lot of time to re-engage those receptor sites, a process that can take years (Erickson, 2007). Stimulant intoxication signs can be physical, behavioral, and cognitive. Physical signs include dilated pupils, fast heart rate (tachycardia), and fever. Behavioral and cognitive signs include increased activity, aggression, panic, paranoia, and psychosis.

Cocaine. Cocaine, or "coke," is the strongest naturally occurring stimulant. It is derived from the coca plant, which grows on the eastern slopes of the Andes Mountains in South America. Coca also forms an important part of the spiritual lives of the communities where it grows (Wainwright, 2016). The coca leaves are usually chewed, sometimes with the addition of crushed limestone or seashells to aid in absorption (Streatfield, 2001). When Cocaine is mixed & injected with herion, it is called a speedball.

Cocaethylene (Cocaine + Alcohol). Some of the earlier forms of cocaine included mixing it with wine. Vin Mariani, a "medicinal tonic" that contained lesser amounts of cocaine than other wines, was one of the best-known examples (Inaba & Cohen, 2014). Cocaethylene's effects are like cocaine, but the duration of the high is lengthened and the high is not as strong as with cocaine alone. The average half-life of cocaethylene is three times that of cocaine. Adding alcohol to cocaine increases the toxicity of cocaine, especially its ability to cause cardiac conduction abnormalities (Streatfield, 2001).

Cocaine Hydrochloride Salt. This powdered form of cocaine is the most usual form used in the United States. It can be injected intravenously or insufflated (snorted). Powder cocaine that is injected reaches the brain in seconds, whereas, snorted cocaine takes several minutes to reach its full effect.

Freebase. This smokable form of cocaine is made by cooking cocaine hydrochloride with ether or sodium hydroxide, which removes the hydrochloride. A major problem with this method is that ether and other compounds that are used to remove the alkaloid from the cocaine are flammable, putting the user at risk of burns. Smoked cocaine reaches the brain in seconds.

Crack. This smokable cocaine is made by cooking cocaine hydrochloride with baking soda or sodium bicarbonate. The risk of fire is lower than with freebasing cocaine, although burns to the user's hands or face are not uncommon.

Oxidado. Oxidado is a cocaine paste that is smoked. This form of cocaine is less common in the United States compared with the other three methods of use. Usually found in Latin American countries, it is often smoked in tobacco or cannabis cigarettes.

Cocaine Intoxication and Withdrawal. Signs of cocaine intoxication can be observed in a person's physical, cognitive, and behavioral presentations. Physical signs of cocaine intoxication may include dilated pupils, rapid or irregular heartbeat, epistaxis (nosebleeds), dry mouth, and weight loss. Cognitive signs may include increased confidence, excitement, euphoria, and/or anxiety. Behavioral signs may include excessive talking and reduced appetite. Overdose symptoms include a rapid heartbeat, hyperventilation, sweaty skin, and feelings of impending death. Death by overdose is rare when compared with overdose on depressant chemicals like alcohol or opioids. With cocaine overdoses, the primary concern is the drug's cardiotoxicity.

Methamphetamine. Methamphetamine, or "meth," is typically two to three times stronger than amphetamine and lasts longer. It can be taken orally, insufflated injected, or smoked. Phenylacetone, or phenyl-2-propanone (P2P), and ephedrine/pseudoephedrine are precursor chemicals to making methamphetamine products. Most meth is now produced in "super-labs" found in other countries and shipped to the United States, but some methamphetamine users continue to produce their own drug (Inaba & Cohen, 2014). Meth production labs are environmental disasters and result in injuries and deaths each year due to fire and/or explosions.

Differences Between Methamphetamine and Cocaine. In places where methamphetamine becomes popular, it generally does so as a replacement for cocaine (Weisheit & White, 2009). The two drugs, while both powerful stimulants, have differences.

Differences Between Methamphetamine and Cocaine	
Methamphetamine	**Cocaine**
Human-made	Plant-derived
Less-intense rush than cocaine	More-intense rush than methamphetamine
Smoking or shooting produces a longer-lasting high	Smoking or shooting produces a brief, intense high
50 percent of the drug is eliminated from the body in 12 hours	50 percent of the drug is eliminated from the body in 1 hour
Inhibits enzymes that metabolize norepinephrine and epinephrine	Forces a release of dopamine and norepinephrine

Methamphetamine Intoxication and Withdrawal. Methamphetamine tolerance often develops quickly. Signs of methamphetamine intoxication (also review the symptoms of cocaine intoxication, which are similar) include physical and behavioral symptoms. Symptoms include dilated pupils, hyperactivity, lack of interest in food or sleep, aggression and violence, increased sex drive, and psychosis (especially with paranoia).

Acute methamphetamine withdrawal symptoms usually peak within two to four days, but depression, anxiety, and irritability can continue for months, and cravings can continue for months or years after use ceases. There are few medical risks associated with meth withdrawal, and antidepressants may be used to address withdrawal-related depressive symptoms (Weisheit & White, 2009). Methamphetamine withdrawal includes the following physical and mental/behavioral symptoms:

- Anhedonia
- Anxiety
- Depressed mood
- Irritability
- Cravings
- Fatigue
- Insomnia or hypersomnia

- Psychomotor retardation at first, then agitation
- Paranoia
- Headaches
- Increase in appetite
- Apathy
- Social withdrawal

Amphetamines. Amphetamines are not as powerful as methamphetamine and are often used to treat medical and psychiatric issues. Prescription amphetamines include methylphenidate (Ritalin, Concerta) and amphetamine (Adderall, Vyvanse). These medications are Schedule II drugs, which require a separate prescription for each refill. They are also two of the most popular chemicals for the treatment of ADHD, and they may also be used to treat some sleeping disorders. They can be abused by crushing them and then snorting the powder or dissolving the crushed pills in water and injecting the mixture. Some parents have trained their kids in the symptoms of ADHD to get prescriptions for these drugs for themselves. Many high school and college students not diagnosed with ADHD use these drugs to help with concentration while studying and taking tests (Kuhn, Swartzwelder, & Wilson, 2008).

Amphetamine Psychosis. Amphetamine psychosis typically appears after large doses or chronic use of stimulants, although, in rare cases, people may become psychotic after a relatively small dose. The amphetamines overexcite the brain's fear centers. Delusions, paranoia, fears about persecution, hyperactivity, and panic are reported as the most common features. Onset of amphetamine psychosis can be from 2 to 48 hours after the initial dose. Psychotic symptoms generally disappear as abstinence continues and rarely persist beyond 24 to 48 hours after the cessation of drug use.

Hallucinations are frequently reported in chronic amphetamine users, with more than 80 percent of users reporting hallucinations, typically visual or auditory. Tactile hallucinations can also be present, such as the feeling that something is crawling on or under the skin. To the person experiencing them, these hallucinations are real, and this can lead to violence as they react to the hallucinations. Delusions are also reported, along with panic symptoms and extreme fearfulness. This also can lead to violence at times (Sadock, Sadock, & Ruiz, 2015). Amphetamine psychosis closely resembles paranoid schizophrenia. Clients experiencing this type of psychosis may also demonstrate stereotyped, repetitive behaviors (e.g., "tweaking"), such as habitual scratching.

Cathinone and Methcathinone Derivatives. Cathinone is derived from the Khat (or Qat, pronounced "cot") plant from Africa and the Middle East. Leaves of this plant are chewed, made into a paste, or brewed into tea. Cathinone can also be extracted from the plant, purified, and snorted or injected. Khat is more potent than caffeine, and its stimulant effects are similar to, but less powerful than, those of cocaine (Inaba & Cohen, 2014).

Bath Salts. Methcathinone and mephedrone are synthetic and more potent forms of cathinone. Both chemicals can be taken like cathinone or can be further developed into methylenedioxypyrovalerone, otherwise known as bath salts. This intoxicant has nothing in common with the Epsom salts that people use in their baths. These chemicals were named "bath salts" by producers to avoid having to follow Food and Drug Administration (FDA) rules on listing the ingredients of any substance that is consumed. By stating on the packets that the chemicals are not intended for human consumption, producers can avoid labeling their product as a drug. Of course, people in the know are aware that the product they are purchasing at a convenience store or "head shop" is manufactured precisely to be consumed as an intoxicant drug. Bath salts are sold in powder, tablet, and capsule form, with an average dose of 5 to 20 mg (Winstock et al., 2011).

Methylenedioxypyrovalerone is four times as potent as methylphenidate (Ritalin). Bath salts also have entactogenic and hallucinogenic properties, which appear to precipitate psychosis more frequently than other amphetamines because of their faster and stronger impact on the dopamine system. Effects are typical for most amphetamines but coming down from bath salt use is very unpleasant, and tolerance can build quickly. Most intoxicant effects resolve in three to four hours, with milder effects lasting a total of six to eight hours (Ross et al., 2012; Rose, 2016).

Flakka. Alpha-pyrrolidinovalerophenone, or flakka, is another synthetic cathinone that emerged in Florida and other states in 2014 and 2015. It is manufactured in China, shipped to the United States in bulk, and sold relatively cheaply here—one dose costs as little as $5. Like bath salts, this cathinone can be insufflated but it is mainly orally ingested. It cannot be smoked, but it is water soluble, so it could be injected (Rose, 2016).

Cannabinoids. The cannabinoid class of drugs includes cannabis (marijuana) and chemicals derived from it, as well as synthetic products meant to mimic cannabis. Evidence of humankind's use of cannabis has been found in many ancient civilizations, and it is the most abused illegal drug in the world (Lee, 2012): There are 10 times the number of cannabis users than there are heroin and cocaine users.

Cannabis Plant. There are two primary types of marijuana: *Cannabis sativa* and *Cannabis indica*. *Cannabis sativa* grows in tropical/semitropical regions or indoors and is a tall plant that tends to have more tetrahydrocannabinol (THC), the primary psychoactive ingredient in cannabis. *Cannabis indica* grows in more temperate climates and is a smaller, bushy plant that tends to have less THC and more cannabidiol. Cannabidiol (CBD) is not psychoactive and is more relaxing than THC; research is ongoing as to possible medical uses for this chemical (Lee, 2012).

Marijuana has become more refined and bioengineered over the past 25 years. Selective breeding and development of new and more potent strains of marijuana means that THC levels have increased. Different grades of marijuana, based on THC content, have been developed:

- Low grade: Marijuana consists of the leaves of both sexes of the plant. THC content is 1 percent or lower

- Medium grade: Marijuana consists of the dried flowering tops of the fertilized female plant. The flower stops secreting THC-containing resin once fertilized. THC content is 1-7 percent

- High grade: This marijuana is also called *Sinsemilla*, or without seed, to reference the growing method and its results. It consists of the flowering tops of female plants raised in isolation from male plants to prevent pollination. The flowers grow in thick clusters (buds), and THC content may be 7 to 8 percent or higher

Hash Oil. In addition to using cannabis in its original plant form, hash oil can be isolated as a natural cannabis by-product and is sometimes called "amber," "shatter," or "shattered glass." To make hash oil, cannabinoids are extracted from plant material using solvents (e.g., the plants are boiled in alcohol, or pressurized butane or propane is used). This produces a concentrated viscous liquid that is often dried to form a solid, glassy material. Although currently, hash oil is more commonly vaporized, it was traditionally mixed with marijuana or tobacco and smoked. The use of hash oil was historically more common in the Middle East but is now seeing more widespread use in the United States with the growing popularity of butane hash oil. The THC content can be from 20 to 70 percent in hash oil, creating more pronounced psychiatric symptoms than with other forms of cannabis (Inaba & Cohen, 2014).

How Dangerous Is Cannabis? Marijuana's benefits and risks have both been overstated. Cannabis is not as dangerous a drug as cocaine and heroin: To date, there is no evidence of anyone ever dying of a marijuana overdose. Tolerance to cannabis occurs rapidly, but many new smokers at first have higher sensitivity to THC (Inaba & Cohen, 2014).

Although many people who smoke cannabis also smoke tobacco cigarettes, this trend is shifting. More people are smoking or vaporizing cannabis, and fewer people are smoking tobacco. Cannabis dependence, or cannabis use disorder (moderate and severe), was once thought unlikely but is a real condition, as heavy cannabis users report tolerance and withdrawal symptoms. Cannabis users, particularly those using cannabidiol products, report a beneficial reduction of chronic pain, chemotherapy-induced nausea and vomiting, anorexia, glaucoma, and many other medical problems (National Academies of Sciences, Engineering, and Medicine, 2017). However, cannabis use can cause pregnancy complications and problems with cognition and academic achievement and may lead to the use of other substances (National Academies of Sciences, Engineering, and Medicine, 2017). As such, cannabis requires additional study into its risks and benefits.

There are challenges in determining the risks of recurrent cannabis use compared with tobacco use. What is known is that because marijuana smoke is held in the lungs longer than tobacco smoke, chronic marijuana smokers can develop acute and chronic bronchitis (National Academies of Sciences, Engineering, and Medicine, 2017). Research is ongoing as to whether marijuana causes cancer. Some studies suggest that it helps to fight some forms of cancer, and there is agreement that it helps people cope with chemotherapy side effects, including nausea (Lee, 2012).

Whereas cannabis does not pose the immediate dangers of many of the other drugs we examine in this chapter, including alcohol, it is often a co-occurring and/or contributing factor for people experiencing a mental health emergency. The link between regular cannabis use and mental illness, particularly psychotic disorders such as schizophrenia, is well documented; however, this research is still inconclusive and requires further study (Roffman & Stephens, 2006). Cannabis appears to interfere with the efficacy of antipsychotic medications and may precipitate psychosis in people who are predisposed to a psychiatric disorder (Lynch, Rabin, & George, 2012; National Academies of Sciences, Engineering, and Medicine, 2017). Also, many people are misdiagnosed with schizophrenia due to their chronic cannabis use. Given the increased number of people using cannabis, if cannabis were a direct cause of schizophrenia, we should see an increase in its incidence. No such increase exists, which suggests that more research is needed to examine the cannabis-psychosis link.

Cannabis Intoxication. Cannabis intoxication causes cognitive, behavioral, and physical symptoms. Physical signs include dilated pupils, bloodshot eyes, problems tracking with eyes, dry mouth, increased heart rate, and/or deep body relaxation. Another physiological response may be cyclical vomiting syndrome, which typically appears only in people who have used heavily for more than a few months. Cognitive and behavioral symptoms of cannabis intoxication include euphoria followed by relaxation, laughing/giddiness, slowed thinking, paranoia in some case (may increase with long-term use), and/or possible hallucinations in high doses or in susceptible individuals.

Cannabis can be smoked or orally ingested. When cannabis is eaten, the effects are stronger and longer, since the cannabis is metabolized by the liver into other, more potent chemicals (Inaba & Cohen, 2014). The circulatory system then takes the chemicals to the brain, which contains receptor sites for endocannabinoids that help regulate mood, appetite, sleep, and many other functions.

Cannabis Withdrawal. Cannabis withdrawal is a longer process than withdrawal from stimulants or opioids. Long-term users report an absence of symptoms when they first stop using. This is because cannabinoids are stored in body fat, which means they remain present in the body longer than most other drugs. Recent studies have suggested that heavy cannabis users can develop physiological and psychological dependence on cannabis, but more study is necessary (National Academies of Sciences, Engineering, and Medicine, 2017). Most heavy users do not experience all signs but may experience the following:

- Restlessness, hyperactivity, and/or sweating
- Irritability, anxiety, and/or anger
- Stomach pain, nausea, and/or loss of appetite
- Insomnia
- Cravings
- Inability to concentrate

- Depression

Most acute cannabis withdrawal symptoms usually end within seven to 10 days of cessation. However, mood disturbance, anxiety, and abject boredom, as well as problems with concentrating can continue for months. Medications for these symptoms are typically not used.

Synthetic Cannabis (Cannabimimetics). Cannabimimetics are various synthetic chemicals that mimic THC but bind more readily to endocannabinoid receptors (specifically the CB-1 receptor), thereby creating a stronger response. Some have names that were created for sales purposes on the commercial market, like "Spice" and "K2." Other names simply identify the chemical compounds, such as JWH-018 (1-pentyl-3-(1-naphthoyl) indole) and the other 200-plus compounds in the JWH series (National Academies of Sciences, Engineering, and Medicine, 2017).

Once easily obtained as incense or potpourri at "head shops" and even convenience stores, synthetic cannabis is now illegal in many states (Inaba & Cohen, 2014). Synthetic cannabis typically does not show up on drug screens for THC. These chemicals are typically dissolved and applied to inert plant material, which is dried, crushed, and smoked. "Spice" tends to create sensations like those caused by marijuana but is shown to create more anxiety, aggression, elevated heart rates, vomiting, psychosis, paranoia, and excited delirium, all of which are uncommon with marijuana use (Wainwright, 2016).

Psychedelic Drugs. Psychedelic drugs comprise several classes of plants and chemicals that alter perception and/or mood. Psychedelics are three overlapping classes of drugs: entactogens, hallucinogens, and dissociates. Psychedelics can also be divided into two classes based on their chemical makeup: phenethylamines and tryptamines. Phenethylamines are drugs found in all three classes that are chemically like the neurotransmitter dopamine. Tryptamines are drugs also found in all three classes that are chemically like the neurotransmitter serotonin. (Shulgin & Shulgin, 2011).

Psychedelic drug users are heavily influenced by their environment and mindset. The person's mindset, or "set," includes their emotional well-being and expectations of the substance. The physical environment or setting in which the person takes the drug influences outcomes as well. Set and setting are important for many drugs of abuse but are extremely important for psychedelics.

If a person is not anxious or depressed and has realistic expectations for what to expect from a substance, they will typically have a neutral to positive experience provided they are in a place where they feel safe. A person who is angry, anxious, depressed, or stressed in another way or is using the chemical in a setting that does not feel safe, will likely experience a neutral to negative reaction to the plant or chemical they are using (Shulgin & Shulgin, 2011).

Please keep in mind that many psychedelic chemicals have properties that fall in more than one category, sometimes depending on the dosage. For example, ketamine is primarily a dissociate but also has hallucinogenic properties. Any of the hallucinogenic plants or chemicals can also have entactogenic effects.

Entactogens. Entactogens are a wide variety of drugs that change mood and perception. The most well-known of these chemicals is methylenedioxymethamphetamine (MDMA), commonly called Ecstasy or Molly. Entactogens increase empathic response, and MDMA and other entactogens were used as therapy aids for years before many were classified as Schedule I drugs by the Drug Enforcement Administration (Shulgin & Shulgin, 2011; Shulgin & Shulgin, 2014). Entactogens are usually taken in social settings. Reactions to some of these chemicals are similar to those with dissociates or hallucinogens at regular doses, but in higher doses, many of these drugs act like stimulants. These "designer drugs" are completely human-made but mimic plants like peyote.

Methylenedioxymethamphetamine. The experiential process of MDMA use often follows a pattern: "coming on" (30 minutes), "plateau" (30–80 minutes), "coming down" (3–6 hours), and "afterglow" (the day after). The level of dosage may impact a user's experience and can be categorized as a low dose (50–75 mg), moderate dose (125–160 mg), or high dose (180–200 mg) (Kuhn, Swartzwelder, & Wilson, 2008). Behavioral and cognitive signs of MDMA intoxication may include reported feelings of self-awareness, acceptance, agitation, and/or anxiety. Physical signs of intoxication include the following:

- Dilated pupils
- Nystagmus (eye tremors, a common reaction to many psychedelics)
- Confusion
- Headaches and/or nausea
- Increased sex drive
- Heightening of pleasure senses
- Increased physical energy
- Grinding and clenching of teeth (the main reason that some people who use MDMA put pacifiers in their mouths)
- Sweating

Methylenedioxymethamphetamine acts on serotonin rather than on dopamine (compared with stimulants). It is often taken with other drugs (e.g., alcohol, LSD, DXM, Ritalin, opioids, Viagra), and pure MDMA is rare, as there are usually several adulterants present. MDMA cannot be taken regularly, as it quickly loses its effectiveness if taken on a regular basis (the brain must take time to replenish serotonin). Thus, entactogens do not have a withdrawal syndrome, except for latent feelings of depression (Inaba & Cohen, 2014).

Other Entactogens. There are many other entactogens that are less well-known than DMA. There is also a specific subset of entactogens called 2C phenethylamines: The *2C* stands for the two carbon atoms that are part of the molecular compound. There are 27 known 2C compounds, the common ones being 2C-B ("Nexus," which was produced by altering mescaline), 2C-I ("Bromo"), 2C-T-2, and 2C-T-7 ("T7") (Shulgin & Shulgin, 2011). As with similar substances, lower doses are more entactogenic, with higher doses acting more as a stimulant or hallucinogen than an entactogen.

The NBOMe series were chemically developed from the 2C series and include 25I ("N-bomb" or "Smiles"). These chemicals are far more potent than their 2C parents, with typical doses in the microgram range. They appear as a white powder but can be darker due to impurities. They can be taken orally, sublingually, or by insufflation (Wainwright, 2016).

Hallucinogens. Hallucinogenic plants and chemicals present the widest variety of effects of any drug class. We know less about hallucinogens and how they impact the brain than we do most other drugs. These are also some of the oldest chemicals used by humans, with histories dating to the dawn of civilization (Inaba & Cohen, 2014). Hallucinogenic compounds can create perceptual disturbances that approximate auditory, visual, and tactile hallucinations. They can also provide increased insight and "internal discussions." At the same time, hallucinogens can impair judgment and in some cases cause the user to experience delusions (Ott, 1993).

Lysergic Acid Diethylamide (LSD). Is an extremely potent drug: Doses are measured in the microgram range, usually 150 to 300 mcg. Effects start after about 20 minutes, peak at two to four hours, and can last six to 12 hours. LSD is orally ingested as a clear liquid or via a medium such as blotter paper or sugar cubes to which the LSD liquid has been applied. Tolerance develops very quickly but disappears days after cessation of use. "Bad trips" are often a panic reaction to the drug and are described as nightmarish. Withdrawal is mental and emotional, not physical (Lee & Shlain, 1985; Hofmann, 2009). Signs and symptoms of LSD intoxication include the following:

- Visual hallucinations
- Dilated pupils
- Overloaded senses
- Anxiety, possible paranoia
- Abnormal laughter
- Nausea
- Dizziness
- Numbness
- Impaired reasoning and loss of judgment
- Difficulty with verbal expression (e.g., single-word answers and non sequiturs)

Lysergic Acid Hydroxyethylamide. Lysergic acid hydroxyethylamide (LSA) is an analogue of LSD and has about one tenth the potency of LSD. It is found naturally in the seeds of *Ipomoea Violacea* (morning glory) and *Argyreia nervosa* (Hawaiian baby woodrose). Commercial morning glory seeds are coated with a toxin that causes vomiting to prevent ingestion (Thies, 2009). Seeds are eaten whole, crushed, or consumed in an extract. LSA causes more nausea, even without the toxic coating on commercial seeds, than LSD does (Schultes, Hormann, & Ratsch, 2001).

Dimethyltryptamine. DMT is found in many plant seeds, vines, tree bark, and other plant materials or is chemically synthesized. Chemically, it is the most basic psychedelic drug, and it probably exists as a neurotransmitter and interacts with the pineal gland (Inaba & Cohen, 2014). DMT is smoked (it smells like burnt plastic and is often added to cannabis), sniffed, or injected (IV), which produces a short (30 minutes or less), intense hallucinogenic trip (a.k.a. "business man's high") (Strassman, 2001).

Ayahuasca tea, or *yagé*, contains harmaline (a monoamine oxidase inhibitor) and DMT: The harmaline allows the user to orally consume the DMT. Even then, drinking *yagé* typically causes intense vomiting prior to the hallucinogenic effects (Ott, 1993; Schultes, Hormann, & Ratsch, 2001). 5-MeO-DMT is a venom from a desert toad that is similar to DMT and is usually dried and smoked in a cigarette (Inaba & Cohen, 2014).

Psilocybin and Psilocin. Psilocybin and psilocin are chemicals found in a variety of mushrooms (which are orally ingested) that produce hallucinogenic symptoms. Psilocybin and psilocin effects last about 6 hours, with a rapid onset, and produce vivid colors and other visual effects. Users often feel that they have left their bodies to commune with spirits, aliens, or "others" who may guide them (Ott, 1993; Schultes, Hormann, & Ratsch, 2001; Kuhn, Swartzwelder, & Wilson, 2008). Signs of psilocybin/psilocin intoxication include the following:

- Dilated pupils
- Warm skin
- Excessive sweating
- Body odor
- Impaired coordination
- Disorientation
- Hallucinations
- Mood and behavior changes

Amanita Muscaria (Fly Agaric). *Amanita Muscaria* comes from a mushroom that grows wild in Siberia and North America. This fungus has been highly valued for centuries. Its hallucinogenic effects appear to come from ibotenic acid and muscimol, which are similar to GABA. The mushrooms are boiled and the resulting liquid consumed, with the effects taking two to three hours to peak and lasting for about six hours. Because the active ingredients are not broken down prior to excretion, the urine from people who have consumed *Amanita Muscaria* can be drunk and produce the same hallucinations (Ott, 1993; Schultes, Hormann, & Ratsch, 2001).

Salvia Divinorium. *Salvia Divinorium* is a mint plant grown in Mexico. It creates hallucinations and some dissociative thoughts. *Salvia Divinorium* is used as a replacement for cannabis by people who must submit to regular urine drug screens because salvia does not appear in the testing results. Possession of *Salvia Divinorium* is now illegal in some states.

The *Salvia Divinorium* plant is smoked and produces symptoms similar to those with ketamine. The leaves can also be chewed or brewed into a tea, but the material must be absorbed through gum tissue, as stomach acid neutralizes it. The effects usually last for less than one hour and typically consist of a modified perception of reality (Schultes, Hormann, & Ratsch, 2001; Inaba & Cohen, 2014).

Mescaline. Mescaline (3,4,5-trimethoxyphenethylamine) is a chemical derived from peyote or San Pedro cacti or made synthetically. Peyote is a small cactus, the top of which (button) is cut, dried, and eaten or boiled and made into a tea. The effective dose is 400 mg (7–8 buttons). The effects are like those with LSD. In fact, many people who think that they have taken mescaline actually received LSD (Siegel, 2005). The experience lasts 12 to 15 hours; it starts slowly and typically involves vomiting before onset of colorful visions and hallucinations.

Nutmeg. Nutmeg and mace, both spices, come from the same tree. The hallucinogenic effects of nutmeg (and probably also mace) require consumption of an extraordinary amount, near-toxic levels: 1 gram of nutmeg per 10 pounds of body weight. Hallucinations last for about 24 hours, following a slow onset of several hours. Dissociative effects can last for several days afterward, along with feeling physically ill, mainly being nauseous (Kuhn, Swartzwelder, & Wilson, 2008; Thies, 2009).

Dissociates. Many of these drugs are structurally similar to most of the hallucinogenic drugs and nearly all the entactogens (there is a lot of overlap). Dissociates create a feeling that the user is outside of their body and/or in a different reality.

Phencyclidine. PCP and many analogues were developed by Parke-Davis Research Laboratories, as an anesthetic in 1956; however, these drugs were found to have many negative effects. PCP comes in a variety of forms (liquid, tablet, powdered) and has stimulant, depressant, hallucinogenic, anesthetic, and analgesic properties. PCP can be smoked, insufflated, swallowed, or injected. PCP is often smoked in tobacco cigarettes or marijuana. A low dose lasts about two hours, a moderate dose up to six hours, and a heavy dose for much longer. Some people can develop psychotic reactions that can last for several days after the drug is no longer detectible in their system (Kuhn, Swartzwelder, & Wilson, 2008; Inaba & Cohen, 2014). Signs of PCP intoxication include the following:

- Perspiring heavily
- Staring blankly
- Agitation, excitement
- Memory loss
- Chemical odor on the person
- Incomplete/slurred verbal responses
- Increased pain tolerance
- No communication
- Disorientation
- Depersonalization
- Muscle rigidity
- Psychosis

Dextromethorphan. DXM/DM is the active ingredient in many over-the-counter cough suppressants. An opioid, DXM/DM works on suppressing the cough reflex as opposed to dampening pain. Pure DXM is a powder made up of white to slightly yellow crystals. There are numerous websites that describe ways to chemically separate DXM from the other ingredients in over-the-counter products. DXM has few to no psychotropic effects in the doses used medically. Alteration of consciousness usually occurs following ingestion of 7 to 50 times the therapeutic dose over a brief time (Kuhn, Swartzwelder, & Wilson, 2008; Theis, 2009).

This drug is often used by adolescents and young adults who must provide UDSs and wish to get high without testing positive (although high doses of DXM can test positive for PCP on some tests). Most DXM users state that the "trip" lasts approximately five to six hours from beginning to end. Often, users will "dose," or take the DXM in stages by starting with four to 12 tabs of Coricidin (or a comparable medication), and then taking more tabs several hours later. This can lead to heart and kidney problems, including kidney failure. Users also report an "afterglow" that lasts 24 to 48 hours after they have come down. Signs of DXM intoxication include the following:

- Decreased appetite
- Dilated pupils
- Loss of control
- Slurred speech
- Fever, sweating
- Dissociation
- Panic reactions
- Rash
- Nausea, vomiting

Ketamine. Ketamine is one tenth the strength of PCP and was developed for the same purpose as an anesthetic, but it is not as strong or long lasting. Ketamine often comes as a white powder that is snorted, eaten, injected, or smoked; it can also be used in liquid form. Used through insufflation and injection, there is a quick onset and termination; trips are short-lived (1–2 hours). In higher doses, ketamine works as an anesthetic and very high doses can cause delirium and depression. People who use ketamine recreationally favor it in low doses to create a variety of hallucination and dissociations. Most notably, users report a sense of leaving their body, journeying out into the universe, and even losing a sense of time. Ketamine users also report detailed near-death experiences (Morgan & Curran, 2011). People who use higher doses to try and alter their consciousness report feelings of floating in space, temporary schizophrenia, and sensory isolation—often called "falling down the K-hole" (Jansen, 2004).

Ketamine is one of the most "split" drugs ever—it produces quite disparate effects. It wakes people up and also puts them to sleep. It is addictive but can be used to treat addiction. Ketamine is a proconvulsant and an anticonvulsant. Ketamine is used as an animal tranquilizer and as an anesthetic in children and the elderly. Patients rarely die due to overdose because they are usually able to maintain an airway. Frequent ketamine users sometimes report "K-cramps," intense abdominal pains, and it is not certain why this occurs (Inaba & Cohen, 2014). Tolerance to ketamine via abuse can develop rapidly. There is also concern about dependence, but this is hard to gauge at this point, as a specific withdrawal profile has not been described (Morgan & Curran, 2011).

Sedatives and Depressants. Signs of sedative and depressant intoxication, including alcohol, may consist of the following:

- Lowered inhibitions
- Mild euphoria
- Depression, sedation, and relaxation
- Memory loss
- Drowsiness, sleep induction
- Reduced coordination and speech

Alcohol. Alcohol is the number one drug that brings people to emergency departments in the United States; 30 percent of all inpatient hospital beds are occupied by a patient who is sick due to their current or past alcohol abuse (Inaba & Cohen, 2014). Newer ways of using alcohol, including vaporizing it or using an alcohol enema, get alcohol to the brain very quickly while bypassing the body's natural defenses in the gastrointestinal track.

The classic formula for alcohol equivalency is 12 oz. of beer = 10 oz. of wine cooler = 7 oz. of malt liquor = 5 oz. of wine = 1.5 oz. of liquor. This formulary has changed somewhat with the increasing popularity of craft beers, many of which contain more alcohol than most mass-produced beers.

Alcohol is more easily metabolized by the liver compared with other substances (e.g., benzodiazepines); therefore, if a person uses another drug in addition to alcohol, the liver will first break down the alcohol while passing the other drug into the bloodstream with minimal or no change (Erickson, 2007).

Alcohol Withdrawal and Detoxification. Alcohol withdrawal symptoms begin four to 10 hours after the last drink was consumed. In mild forms of withdrawal, the symptoms resolve after 48 hours. Tremulousness is the earliest symptom, and for many alcoholics, this indicates the need to drink again to avoid more pronounced symptoms. Tremors appear within hours after drinking stops and peaks in one to two days but can persist for weeks. In more severe forms, auditory hallucinations that feel very real to the person can occur within 24 hours of cessation (Erickson, 2007; Inaba & Cohen, 2014).

Between six to 48 hours after stopping alcohol use, 3 to 4 percent of untreated patients who have been drinking regularly and heavily will have a seizure. About 30 to 40 percent of patients who have a seizure will progress to delirium tremens (DTs; alcohol withdrawal delirium) if they are left untreated. DTs are fatal in up to 25 percent of people who are not treated. They can precede or follow a seizure. Repeated withdrawal episodes seem to "kindle" more serious withdrawal episodes (Corliss, 2010; Erickson, 2007).

Many alcoholics and other substance-dependent individuals erroneously believe that getting "clean and sober" (detoxing) is the only thing needed to be free of their addiction.

Sobriety and recovery take a long time and present with long-lasting symptoms. Post-acute alcohol withdrawal symptoms can occur in long-term alcohol users who have detoxified and experienced some sobriety (several weeks to months) and may include the following:

- Cognitive impairment (difficulty concentrating, impairment in abstract reasoning, and repetitive thinking)
- Memory impairment (especially in short-term memory; difficulty learning additional information)
- Emotional overreaction, irritability, and mood instability
- Sleep disturbances
- Fatigue
- Hypersensitivity to stress
- Emotional numbness and difficulty in experiencing pleasure

Benzodiazepines. Benzodiazepines are used to treat anxiety, as sedatives, to help with sleep, to treat seizures, and as muscle relaxants. Benzodiazepines are also used to help detoxify people from alcohol and to control seizures. Benzodiazepine intoxication signs are similar to those of alcohol intoxication. The following are the most common benzodiazepines:

- Xanax (alprazolam)
- Valium (diazepam)
- Ativan (lorazepam)
- Klonopin (clonazepam)
- Librium (chlordiazepoxide)
- Restoril (temazepam)

Clonazepam and diazepam are longer-acting benzodiazepines, whereas Xanax and lorazepam are shorter-acting medications. While not technically benzodiazepines, newer drugs that are marketed as sleep aids are also common and include Ambien (zolpidem), Lyrica (pregabalin), Rozerem (ramelteon), Sonata (zaleplon), Imovane (zopiclone), and Lunesta (eszopiclone). These medications are commonly called "Z-hyponotics." (Inaba & Cohen, 2014).

Flunitrazepam (Rohypnol). Rohypnol (also known as "roofies") is illegal in the United States but is available in other countries, particularly Mexico. It is similar in many ways to GHB but is a benzodiazepine with faster onset, longer duration of action, and stronger effects at lower doses. It has five times the potency of Valium. Rohypnol is a clear liquid and is ingested orally. Due to its being used as a "rape drug" Rohypnol has been reformulated so that it releases a blue dye when it is added to a liquid. Overdoses (along with those of other benzodiazepines) can be treated with Flumazenil, a GABA receptor antagonist (Inaba & Cohen, 2014).

Barbiturates. Barbiturates are like benzodiazepines but generally stronger and more sedating. They initially produce a stimulatory effect followed by sedation, much like alcohol. Barbiturates are infrequently seen on the street, and in most clinical settings they have been replaced by benzodiazepines. It is very dangerous to suddenly stop barbiturate use, as this can lead to seizures. Examples of barbiturates include Tunial, Luminal (phenobarbital), Nembutal (pentobarbital, a.k.a. "yellow jackets"), and Secobarbital (a.k.a. "reds") (Inaba & Cohen, 2014).

Depressant Withdrawal. The onset of withdrawal signs depends on the potency of the drug from which the person is withdrawing. A short-acting benzodiazepine may produce symptoms within six to eight hours, but the withdrawal symptoms of a longer-acting sedative may not develop for more than a week. Severe withdrawal is most likely to occur when a substance has been used at high doses for prolonged periods. Withdrawal may progress to delirium, usually within one week of last use. Long-acting barbiturates or benzodiazepines may be used in withdrawal substitution therapy. Signs for depressant (alcohol, benzodiazepine, or barbiturate) withdrawal include the following:

- Nausea/vomiting
- Cravings
- Malaise and weakness
- Tachycardia
- Sweating
- Depression
- Delirium, including hallucinations
- Anxiety rebound and agitation
- Irritability
- Orthostatic hypotension
- Tremors
- Insomnia
- Possible seizures
- Depersonalization
- Possible high fever

Gamma Hydroxybutyric Acid. Gamma hydroxybutyric acid is a "club drug," sometimes called "Georgia Home Boy" or "Grievous Bodily Harm," that has depressant properties. It is sold as a clear liquid, powder, tablet, or capsule. Positive symptoms reported by users include euphoria, happiness, increased sexuality and well-being, heightened sense of touch, relaxation, and disinhibition. GHB is sometimes used in the place of alcohol because the user can quickly become intoxicated, but the effects resolve in four hours with no hangover symptoms. Users also report that GHB has none of the aftereffects of other depressants. Symptoms of GHB use are like those of benzodiazepines, but the mechanism of action appears to be different. GHB is also a neurotransmitter and has long been used to help build muscle. It is also used in prescription form, Xyrem, as a sleep aid (Porrata, 2005).

Dosing of GHB is extremely difficult and has a steep curve, placing users at a substantial risk of unintentional overdose. GHB and Rohypnol (flunitrazepam) are used as rape drugs. I have worked with several individuals in my career who suspected that their rapes were facilitated by GHB or a similar chemical. One reported that she remained conscious throughout the assault, but she was unable to move or defend herself. Another young woman said that she woke up one morning and realized that she had been assaulted but had no memory of anything the previous evening. Because GHB is metabolized into water and carbon dioxide without residual metabolites, detection is difficult, and then it can be detected only within 12 hours of use (Miotto et al., 2001). Signs of GHB intoxication include the following:

- Nausea and/or vomiting
- Dizziness
- Fatigue
- Confusion

- Tremors
- Agitation
- Headache

- Euphoria
- Impaired memory, judgment, and/or coordination

GHB Withdrawal. Withdrawal symptoms reported after taking GHB include the following (Miotto et al., 2001):

- Insomnia
- Tremor
- Increased heart rate
- Confusion
- Nausea and vomiting

Gamma-butyrolactone (GBL), 1,4-butanediol (BD), and gamma hydroxyvalerate (GHV) are precursor chemicals (pro-drugs) that are sometimes used as substitutes for GHB. Ingredients for these chemicals can be found on the Internet and in paint strippers, drain cleaners, and nail polish removers.

Inhalants. The inhalant drug class is the only one that is defined by its method of use and includes diverse substances that readily vaporize. Inhalants are sometimes referred to as "volatile solvents," but this does not take into account the many things that people inhale that are *not* solvents. The peak age of inhalant abuse is 14 to 15 years, and use typically declines by age 19 (Inaba & Cohen, 2014). Cohort groups can vary widely. In one eighth-grade sample group, 20 percent of students may have used inhalants, or "huffed," but among the following year's eighth graders (even at the same school), far fewer may have huffed (National Institute on Drug Abuse, 1992; Williams & Storck, 2007).

Types of Inhalants. Solvents are typically used for huffing by teenagers. Adults who huff solvents usually started when they were teens. Solvents are quickly absorbed into the bloodstream and impact the CNS much like depressants. Most solvents are lipophilic, which means they are stored in fatty tissue in the body and are eliminated much more slowly than most other drugs (National Institute on Drug Abuse, 1992). In a very real sense, inhalants are poisons, not drugs. A variety of chemicals can be used as inhalants:

- Solvents and aerosols: Toluene is the most-abused solvent and is usually in other chemicals including many of the following listed
- Gasoline and fuel additives: More deaths occur from inhalation of gasoline when compared with other inhalants. Fuel additives like STP are common products used
- Airplane glue and rubber cement
- Spray paints, paint thinner, and paint stripper
- Hairspray, deodorants, and air fresheners
- Lighter fuel and fuel gas
- Air dusters (computer cleaner), known as "dusting"
- Correction fluid; writing markers

- Nail polish removers
- Coolants (e.g., Freon)
- Air-freshener aerosols

Inhalant Intoxication. Effects begin in 10 seconds, last three to five minutes, and are like those seen with many depressants, especially alcohol. Signs of inhalant intoxication include the following:

- Stimulation and/or euphoria
- Loss of inhibition
- Headache
- Nausea and/or vomiting
- Slurred speech
- Dizziness
- Dilated pupils
- Loss of coordination
- Wheezing
- Memory impairment
- Muscle weakness
- Unsteady gait
- Tremor
- Fatigue
- Stupor or coma
- Hallucinations
- Smell of chemicals

Sudden Sniffing Death. Sudden sniffing death (SSD) syndrome is the leading cause of death related to inhalant abuse. It can occur when a person who has used inhalants is startled or scared, leading to a heart arrhythmia, which in turn can lead to cardiac arrest. SSD can occur in the hours after use. It is caused by the action of some solvents in inhibiting the heart's ability to handle an adrenaline surge and is probably due to the solvent's tendency to disrupt the electric action of the heart (National Institute on Drug Abuse, 1992).

The following prescription drugs are also frequently abused.

Quetiapine (Seroquel). Seroquel is an atypical (second-generation) antipsychotic that is used to resolve or diminish symptoms of psychosis and as an adjunctive treatment for depression. Seroquel is often used off label as a sleep aid. It is the only atypical antipsychotic that has abuse potential, due to its calming and sedating effects (Malekshahi et al., 2015). Seroquel is usually combined with a benzodiazepine or diphenhydramine (an antihistamine), which results in an effect that is approximate to a heroin high. Seroquel is also crushed and insufflated or dissolved in water and injected. Seroquel has several side effects, particularly when abused:

- Sedation
- Dystonia (stiff muscles)
- Muscle spasms
- Akathisia or parkinsonism (abnormal movements)

Much of the research on Seroquel abuse comes from prison populations, where the drug has a history of being abused (Erdogan, 2010). The immediate-release Seroquel formulary is more often abused than other forms of the drug. Seroquel has been removed from many prison formularies and should be avoided in patients with a substance abuse history.

Gabapentin (Neurontin). Neurontin is used to treat seizures, diabetic neuropathy, fibromyalgia, and neuropathic pain. When abused, gabapentin is often obtained illicitly or via prescription diversion. Doses for abusing gabapentin usually exceed 2,000 mg, and in some cases the doses are higher than 5,000 mg. Like Seroquel, gabapentin can also be abused by crushing and snorting it or injecting it (Webb, 2011). Signs of gabapentin intoxication include the following:

- Euphoria
- Relaxation
- Ataxia (lack of coordination of voluntary muscle movement)
- Nystagmus (involuntary eye movement)
- Slurred speech
- Upset stomach
- Double vision
- Hypotension

Neurontin has the following withdrawal signs:

- Disorientation, confusion
- Tachycardia
- Excessive sweating
- Tremors
- Agitation

Diphenhydramine (Benadryl) and Hydroxyzine (Vistaril). These are both antihistamine medications with anticholinergic properties. Both are typically used to treat allergies, including skin rash, itching, and hives. These medications are sometimes used off label to treat anxiety. Abuse or overuse of these medications cause sedation and drowsiness. In the case of Benadryl, using high doses causes dramatic visual hallucinations.

Promethazine (Phenergan). Phenergan is an anti-nausea medication that causes drowsiness and sedation. It is sometimes mixed with cough syrup containing codeine and called "purple drank."

Urine Drug Screens and Assessments

A UDS is the cheapest and easiest to use form of drug testing. A UDS should be used when assessing a person experiencing a mental health emergency to discover if any detectable drugs are in their body. Blood assays are typically used to determine blood alcohol level (BAL), as they are more accurate than a breathalyzer. Be aware that many drugs of abuse, including multiple synthetic opioids, are not detectable with some standard drug screens. Most onsite testing involves quick-result immunoassay, which gives a general indication of detectable metabolites in the person's urine (American Society of Addiction Medicine, 2017). The results of these tests are not admissible in court (Cary, 2012).

From a therapeutic standpoint, a UDS can be used to verify the client's honesty and provide opportunities for more effective treatment. I may utilize the UDS results to address a client's incongruence between report and behavior. For example, "I am glad that you consistently keep your appointments with me and are working hard. However, your UDS indicated that you have recently used cocaine, and you told me last week and today that you stopped using weeks ago. Remember, I am not the police, so the results stay here, but if I am to help you, I need to know more about what is going on, and I need you to be honest with me."

A UDS has limited value if the person is not directly observed giving the sample, but this may not be possible in many clinical settings. Therefore, while having some value, field tests can only suggest the need for additional testing. I have also observed many ways that people have attempted to provide a "false negative" sample, primarily when I was working in a drug court program. Participants would adulterate the sample by adding a foreign substance (e.g., dishwashing soap or bleach) or provide another person's urine. One participant even wore a false penis device complete with freeze-dried urine that he purchased online.

Assessment and Disposition for High-Risk Clients Who Use Substances

It is important for clinicians to know about the resources available in their communities for their clients who have substance use disorders. It is especially important when faced with a mental health emergency that the use of substances be confirmed as quickly as possible. Some clients will require longer-term care, but the immediate intervention is the most important in an emergency. Read the case study of Jack and consider how you would respond by answering the questions that follow.

CASE STUDY—JACK

SUBSTANCE ABUSE

Jack was a 69-year-old man who was brought to the ER by EMS after a passerby saw him fall. Jack had been drinking and reeked of alcohol, although he stated that his last drink had been 48 hours earlier. His BAL was .223. Jack had a long history of presenting to the ER in an intoxicated state.

A mental health assessment was requested because Jack told EMS and the attending doctor that he was seeing lizards and dinosaurs. Jack was willing to speak with me, although he was having difficulty breathing. He stated that his father and grandfather were moonshiners and that he was given grain alcohol at an early age. He eventually left home and started hanging out with criminals, who got him to sell drugs. Jack said that he joined the army at 19 to get away from "the wrong crowd."

Jack became tearful when talking about his time in Vietnam, where he was a machine gun operator on a troop transport helicopter. He talked about shooting people in the fields as he flew over them and feeling great remorse for this. Jack said he was discharged from the army after he was wounded in his left eye by shrapnel. He also stated that this wound damaged his brain. Jack added that he did not start drinking or smoking tobacco heavily until he was 39. He did not know why he started using at that time.

Jack was homeless and lived in a wooded area in the city. He admitted that he had thoughts of dying but that he did not have "the guts" to kill himself. He stated that he went to Mass every day to ask to be forgiven, but he did not think he would be forgiven for the people he killed. He stated that he sees lizards and dinosaurs every so often, and he does not connect this with his use of alcohol or with any withdrawal signs. He said that he hears voices and further questioning revealed that these voices were the people whom he says he killed.

SUBSTANCE ABUSE

What is the most concerning need now?

What would you do first?

What is the differential diagnosis for Jack?

Once he is stabilized, what services could you help Jack obtain?

OVERDOSE

Percy was a young man in his late 20s who came to the outpatient clinic where I worked. While waiting to register as a new patient, he slumped over in his chair. EMS were called immediately. Percy's airway was not obstructed: He was breathing and had a pulse. EMS staff discovered that his pupils were pinpoint and unresponsive to light. They administered a) _____ for a potential b) _____ overdose and took him to the hospital.

Percy remained in the hospital for a day, and he was then discharged back for follow-up care at the clinic. During his initial assessment, he denied any suicidal or homicidal ideation, and he did not demonstrate psychotic symptoms.

He admitted to being an intravenous (IV) heroin user for the past three years. He also used cocaine occasionally, injecting it with his heroin. (This is called a c] _____). Last year, Percy entered a long-term treatment program that included the medication d) _____ (or e] _____) to help him manage his opioid recovery. He was able to stay in this program for about three months, but after testing positive for benzodiazepines, he was terminated from the program. Shortly after, he resumed his heroin use.

Percy also used alcohol, nicotine, cannabis (which is also called f] _____), and Xanax (which is a g] _____ [type of drug]), but he stated that his drug of choice was heroin. He had been to the hospital twice for overdosing on heroin. He minimized his cocaine use.

Percy had not always struggled with addiction. He had completed high school and dropped out of college at the end of his freshman year. He reported that he dropped out because his father died of a sudden heart attack, and he had to move home to help his mother care for his two younger brothers, as his mother had a chronic mental illness. Percy had planned on becoming an architect but wound up having to work two tedious jobs to help support his family. Percy had consumed a lot of alcohol in high school and college, and he began to drink more after work and started using cannabis with his coworkers.

Within two years, Percy had "moved on" (in his words) to harder drugs. His mother's mental illness had gotten better through improved medication management and social support. His two younger brothers had graduated high school and moved out on their own, thus freeing Percy from "being tied" (his words again) to his family.

Although Percy was free of his responsibilities, he found he had less control over his drug use. He was fired from his jobs because of his use of substances, and he soon found it difficult to maintain employment for more than a month due to his addiction. Not long after this, his mother asked him to leave her home after she found his works (which is a name for h] _____).

Percy drifted from friend to friend during this time. He would work menial jobs when he could find them, but his drug use was the most important thing to him. He started a relationship with a fellow drug user, who became pregnant shortly after. Not wanting to give birth to a drug-addicted child, Percy's partner entered a recovery program and maintained her sobriety. She soon discovered that she could not maintain her recovery while still in a relationship with Percy. She offered him a choice: enter recovery himself or lose her. Percy did not take long to choose drugs over his partner. Due to these circumstances, Percy has an 18-month-old son with whom he has had little contact. He does not seem too bothered by this. He admitted that his use is out of control, and he believed that he would never be able to stop using.

Answers to the "fill-in-the-blanks" in the case study are at the end of this chapter.

Drug Quiz

1. What substance of abuse kills the most people each year? _____

2. What substance of abuse has the highest addiction potential? _____

3. What substance of abuse brings more people to an ER than any other? _____

4. What is the most widely used illegal drug? _____

5. What is the quickest way to get a drug to the brain? _____

6. What are two of the suspected reasons for the increase in heroin use in the United States? _____, _____

7. What are five ways that a drug can be introduced into the body: _____, _____, _____, _____, _____

8. Heroin is this type of drug: _____

9. Cocaine is this type of drug: _____

10. What is the biggest risk for a person who has used alcohol or other depressants for a long time and then suddenly stops using? _____

11. _____ is the name of a drug used to reverse an opioid overdose.

12. _____ is the most crucial neurotransmitter involved in the pleasurable and addictive effects of drugs.

13. Three signs of stimulant abuse are: _____, _____, & _____

Quiz answers can be found at the end of the chapter.

Conclusion

Substance use disorder is a chronic, insidious disease that takes the lives of many people each year. Drug use, intoxication, and withdrawal must be considered in any mental health emergency. Although the substance itself may not be the only cause of the crisis, substance use is likely contributing to the crisis and will have an impact on any interventions. Knowledge of area resources, such as detoxification units, inpatient treatment centers, and intensive outpatient treatment programs, and services for people with comorbid disorders is a must for clinicians. Also, providing clients with information on local Alcoholics Anonymous, Narcotics Anonymous, and other support groups could greatly benefit them.

Answers

Drug Quiz

1. Tobacco/nicotine
2. Tobacco/nicotine
3. Alcohol
4. Cannabis/marijuana
5. Inhalation through the mouth
6. The heroin supply is plentiful, heroin price is low, prescription opioids were over-prescribed, and if the prescriptions are later stopped, the patient is now dependent and can turn to heroin (which is cheaper to purchase illicitly when compared to diverted prescription opioids)
7. Inhalation through the mouth (smoking and huffing); insufflation through the nose; introduction buccally or in the rectum, vagina, or eye; IV injection; subcutaneous injection; IM injection; and contact absorption
8. Opiate/opioid
9. Stimulant
10. Withdrawal seizure, possible delirium
11. Naloxone/Narcan
12. Dopamine
13. Increased energy, dilated pupils, tachycardia, fever (possible panic, aggression, paranoia, or psychosis)

Overdose Case Study

a. Naloxone (Narcan)
b. Opiate/heroin/opioid
c. Speedball
d. Methadone
e. Buprenorphine/Suboxone/Subutex
f. Marijuana
g. Benzodiazepine
h. Syringe, spoon, lighter/matches, tourniquet—items a person uses to prepare and inject IV drugs

CHAPTER 10

Our Response and Caring for Ourselves

As we "walk" with high-risk clients through their crises or mental health emergencies, it is unavoidable that their experiences will have an impact on us. We may call it burnout, compassion fatigue, or vicarious traumatization; as helpers, we often feel this is something we must deal with and move on. More recently, professional associations have begun to see the need and relevance for clinicians to understand how their work impacts their mental and physical health. Working in professions that help people who are experiencing mental health emergencies is recognized as risky and, in some cases, hazardous (Needham, 2006).

Practitioners experience a variety of responses to the stress incurred while working with people in crisis. In extreme cases, specifically involving assault and injury by a patient, clinicians may experience anxiety, other emotional/psychological responses, and/or somatic symptoms. Whereas the actual rate of PTSD in mental health practitioners is not known, clinicians are at risk for developing PTSD in serious cases of assault. The reason that the rate of PTSD among clinicians is unknown is probably because clinicians don't always report assaults; therefore, the mechanism to alert for symptoms of PTSD is not consistent, a theory supported by Needham (2006), who stated that "a basic problem regarding psychological responses to patient violence is the under-reporting of violent incidents. One possible explanation for under-reporting is shame, guilt, denial, or fear of repercussion with administration" (p. 307).

When we consider risk exposure to include incidents beyond violence, such as the types of mental health emergencies examined in this book, there are likely many more negative responses than those mentioned previously. When we help a client through a mental health emergency, it is important to ask ourselves the following:

- How does (or did) this mental health emergency impact me?
- What are some ways that I can "carry" another person's trauma, or crisis, when I listen to their stories and "walk" with them?
- What can I do to avoid burning out?

Burnout: A Brief Explanation of a Frequently Used Word

The *APA Dictionary of Clinical Psychology* (2013, p. 88) defines *burnout* as:

Physical, emotional, or mental exhaustion, especially in one's job or career, accompanied by decreased motivation, lowered performance, and negative attitude towards oneself and others. It results from performing at a high level until stress and tension, especially from extreme and prolonged physical and mental exhaustion or an overburdening workload, take their toll. The word was first used in this sense in 1975 by U.S. psychologist Herbert J. Freudenberger (1926–1999) in referring to workers in clinics with heavy caseloads.

Signs and Symptoms of Burnout

Early in my career, I came face to face with clinicians who were burned out. I remembered thinking, "Does this clinician even like people?" I mention this when I teach groups or classes about high-risk clients, and I always receive knowing nods from participants. We have all encountered peers who are so burned out or traumatized that they didn't seem to like people anymore. The following is a list of some of the signs and symptoms of burnout:

- Feeling helpless or hopeless (for clinicians this could manifest as feeling that one is not making a difference)
- Diminished creativity
- Chronic exhaustion
- An increase in physical illnesses or complaints
- An inability to listen or empathize with others
- Increasing feelings of anger
- Cynicism
- Increasing use of substances in an effort to numb onself

Doing Something

What we do know about dealing with trauma is that doing something is better than doing nothing. As clinicians, we must remember that caring for ourselves is as important as caring for our clients. The following are a few things that my peers and I do to help us unwind, cope with other people's trauma, relax, or recharge ourselves.

Exercise. Physical activity is important for comprehensive physical and mental health. Exercise doesn't have to be strenuous to be effective. Walking, swimming, and biking are just some ways that a person can get their heart rate up and improve their cardiovascular health, which also promotes emotional health. Some of my colleagues prefer martial arts, hiking, dancing, aerobics or spinning classes, or boot-camp workouts. A few of my peers and I have also discovered adventure/obstacle racing as an outlet.

Yoga. Several of my current and former supervisees have been long-term practitioners of yoga, and a few other supervisees have recently discovered the benefits of practicing yoga and meditation (either together or separately). One of my former supervisees has combined yoga with group therapy to help her clients impacted by trauma develop mindfulness.

Artistic Expression. Like exercise, artistic expression can take a variety of forms, including painting, sculpting, music, drawing, and photography. These are a few creative outlets people use to express themselves outside of work. Many years ago, I planted a vegetable garden because I like tomatoes. A few years ago, I came home from work, and instead of going inside, I first went to the garden. I liked seeing how the plants grew. It had been a particularly tough day, and I noted that I rarely saw short-term growth in my clinical work, but that I liked to see the changes in the plants—actual "fruits" of hard work.

Being a Part of a Spiritual Community, Journaling, and Grounding/Centering— Reminding Ourselves Every Day Why We Do What We Do. Many of these activities can help improve well-being and prevent burnout. It's important to find the techniques that work best for you, as each of us is different.

What Works for You?

What are three things that you do to take care of yourself?

What is at least one thing you would like to do to take care of yourself that you are not doing right now?

What are three steps you can take to make the one thing you would like to do a reality in the next six months?

Debriefing

Older intervention strategies for addressing crisis situations encouraged people to talk about a traumatic experience as soon as possible following the event. We now recognize that people process crisis situations and trauma differently: Some people may need to debrief immediately, while others may need a lot more time.

As I was writing this book, my former teammates in the ER faced a situation uncommon for them. A 5-month-old baby was brought in by his father because he had not eaten since the previous day. The baby had been born premature and had to be on supplemental oxygen. When examining the baby, the doctor noticed an odd twitching movement. The baby's father said that this twitching had been happening since the baby had stopped eating. The doctor quickly determined that the baby was having seizures. A CT scan of the baby's head showed an accumulation of fluid and skull fractures. Another CT of the baby's body showed that his ribs had been broken and were in various stages of healing. The radiologist concluded that the child had likely been abused more than once. The baby was stabilized and sent to a specialty hospital for children.

Several of the nurses worked nonstop with this baby. I offered to help them debrief if they wanted to. One of the nurses, who had a young son of her own, took me up on my offer and said she could not imagine how someone could hurt a child. Another nurse, who had been in the military and deployed overseas, voiced her appreciation of the offer for debriefing but said that she had a close group of other veterans with whom she met and would talk with them. Other staff persons had a variety of responses, with some wanting to talk right away and others saying they wanted to wait.

Debriefing should not be forced, but neither should the need for debriefing be ignored. The team in the ER had gotten used to treating people with gunshot wounds and traditionally would debrief following these incidents. Because we almost never treated infants, the situation with the abused baby was an extreme outlier for the team. The horrendous situation needed to be addressed. The key is for professionals to have the opportunity to debrief a crisis on *their* time (which may require flexibility from their agency) and in a nonthreatening manner.

Peer Supervision

Peer supervision is also very important, especially for "seasoned" clinicians. I point out to my graduating students that they will soon earn a piece of paper that proclaims that they have earned a Master of Social Work, but their education does not stop once they receive their degree. I emphasize that quality clinicians are lifelong learners.

This brings up an interesting point that one of my new supervisees made recently: Where is the line between supervision and counseling? To be clear, good supervision cannot take the place of counseling. Most clinicians I know, including myself, have been in counseling at some point in our careers to address personal issues that may or may not have been caused by or revealed in our clinical work. At the same time, if we consider that all clinical work is an exchange between two individuals, and that both individuals can be impacted (positively and negatively) by this exchange, it stands to reason that part of supervision should include attention to countertransference issues that have (or are) occurring in the clinical relationship. I think supervision, regardless of the level of experience of the clinician being supervised, must take all thoughts, emotional responses, and behavioral reactions of the clinician into account.

Documentation

In several of the jobs I have had, one of my tasks has been to audit charts for compliance. One of the common things I have seen in several settings is a lack of detailed documentation of a crisis incident. Surprisingly, colleagues who typically did an excellent job documenting their scheduled individual, family, and group therapy sessions had problems documenting crisis situations. Why would this be?

For some clinicians, it may be difficult to go over something stressful or traumatic that just happened. In a few cases, the clinician may be traumatized themselves and find it difficult to access their memories of the traumatic event. For others, there may be a desire to record what happened as quickly as possible so they can move on. Still others have been taught to write down as little information as possible with the concern that their notes could be used against them in legal proceedings. I know that this school of thought continues to be taught, and while I see the reasoning behind it, I disagree with it.

Consider that memories are fallible. As such, recording the events as they occurred is the best way to preserve the information as it happened. I was taught the following maxim: "If you didn't write it down, it never happened." Memories fade, perspectives change, and facts can become distorted over time. Therefore, I encourage my supervisees, students, and peers to make detailed clinical notes. If nothing else, detailed notes have helped me to guide therapy more effectively from session to session.

Solid documentation also serves as a protection (but not a guarantee) against future litigation. Using proper documentation, the competent clinician should be able to show the court what transpired, how they responded as a professional, and why they chose their response (e.g., use of "best practices," theoretical base, or knowledge base). The key is to record in detail all aspects of the crisis, including any known precipitating events, interventions, and outcomes. It is important to stick to the facts: Do not presuppose or assume anything. See documentation as a necessary means to protect yourself, the people you serve, and your organization. Always follow local, state, and federal guidelines regarding the protection and storage of all electronic and paper documentation.

Conclusion

One of the key aspects of a crisis or mental health emergency is the uniqueness of each event. My purpose with this book was to try and encompass as many situations as possible while presenting the information through real stories of people in crisis. My hope is that you are not faced with mental health emergencies on a frequent basis, although for some of us, working with high-risk clients is what we do. Whether your daily work is with people in acute crisis or you work with people who generally are not in crisis, your work, your clients, your relationship with your clients, and YOU are important.

At the end of each class I teach at Virginia Commonwealth University, I offer the following pieces of unsolicited advice, and I also try to remind myself of these things on a regular basis. What we do as clinicians is important, but how we live our lives as individuals is more important. May you continue to grow as a clinician and as a uniquely created individual who has chosen to serve others. The following sentiments provide good guidance for helping others and caring for yourself:

- Life is unfair.
- Life is hard.
- Your clients don't care what you believe, what you like, for whom you voted, or your feelings. They want to know, "How can you help me?"
- If you take credit for when your clients do well, be prepared to accept the blame when they fail. I recommend you do neither.
- We are here to empower people, not live their lives for them.
- The ends NEVER justify the means: Always do the right thing.
- Be loyal to the truth, not to a person.
- Help other clinicians, as clinicians have helped or will help you.
- Be safe!
- Be nice.
- Be humble.
- Don't refer a client to services to which you would not refer one of your family members or friends.
- Work hard and then go home: Maintain a life outside of your job.
- Our profession is founded on a belief in something greater than ourselves. Strive to determine what that something is for you.
- Do not stop learning.
- Remember, we are the "good guys" ("good ladies," "good people ...").
- Smile.
- Laugh.
- Watch the sunrise as often as you can.

References

For your convenience, purchasers can download and print worksheets and handouts from www.pesi.com/HighRisk

Akhgari, M., Afshar, E., & Jokar, F. (2016). Street level heroin, an overview on its components and adulterants. In V. Preedy (Ed.), *Neuropathology of drug addiction and substance misuse* (Vol. 1) (pp. 867–877). Cambridge, MA: Academic Press.

American Foundation for Suicide Prevention. (2018). *Suicide statistics for 2016.* Retrieved from http://afsp.org/about-suicide/suicide-statistics/

American Psychiatric Association. (2000). *Diagnostic and statistical manual of mental disorders,* (4th ed.), *text revision.* Washington, DC: American Psychiatric Association.

American Psychiatric Association. (2013). *Diagnostic and statistical manual of mental disorders,* (5th ed.). Washington, DC: American Psychiatric Association.

American Psychiatric Association. (2013). *APA dictionary of clinical psychology.* Washington, DC: American Psychiatric Association.

American Society of Addiction Medicine. (2017). *Consensus statement: Appropriate use of drug testing in clinical addiction medicine.* Retrieved from https://www.asam.org/quality-practice/guidelines-and-consensus-documents/drug-testing

Anderson, C. E., & Loomis, G. A. (2003). Recognition and prevention of inhalant abuse. *American Family Physician, 68*(5), 869–874.

Anderson, S. (2009). *Substance use disorders in lesbian, gay, bisexual & transgender clients: Assessment & treatment.* New York: Columbia University Press.

Andrabi, S., Greene, S., Moukaddam, N., & Li, B. (2015). New drugs of abuse and withdrawal syndromes. *Emergency Medicine Clinics of North America, 33*(4), 779–795.

Arnaout, B., & Petrakis, I. L. (2008). Diagnosing co-morbid drug use in patients with alcohol use disorders. *Alcohol Research and Health, 31*(2), 148–154.

Asher, J. (2007). *Thirteen reasons why.* New York: Penguin Publishing.

Associated Press. (2016). Middle-aged whites are third of U.S. suicides. *Richmond Times-Dispatch.* April 23, A2.

Bohan, M. E. (2009). Addicting drugs: Newer drugs of abuse and popular drug combinations. Presentation on April 17, 2009, at the Virginia State Drug Court Conference, Williamsburg, VA.

Bostwick, J. M. (2015). When suicide is not suicide: Self-induced morbidity and mortality in the general hospital. *Rambam Maimonides Medical Journal, 6*(2), 1–6.

Bourgois, P., & Schonberg, J. (2009). *Righteous dopefiend.* Berkley: University of California Press.

Boyer, E. W., Babu, K. M., Adkins, J. E., McCurdy, C. R., & Halpern, J. H. (2008). Self-treatment of opioid withdrawal using kratom (*Mitragynia speciosa korth*). *Addiction, 103*(6). doi: 10.1111/j.1360-0443.2008.02209.x

Brady, M. C., Scher, L. M., & Newman, W. (2013). "I just saw big bird. He was 100 feet tall!" Malingering in the emergency department. *Current Psychiatry, 12*(10), 33–40.

Braithwaite, R. S., & Bryant, K. J. (2010). Influence of alcohol consumption on adherence to and toxicity of antiretroviral therapy and survival. *Alcohol Research and Health, 33*(3), 280–287.

Burgess, W. (2013). *Mental status examination: 52 challenging cases, DSM-5 & ICD-10 interviews, questionnaires & cognitive tests for diagnosis and treatment* (2nd ed.). Wes Burgess.

Caro, M. A., Shah, S. A., Jerry, J. M., Tesar, G. E., & Khawam, E. A. (2017). Loperamide abuse and life-threatening arrhythmias: A case report and literature review. *Psychosomatics, 58*(4), 441–445.

Cary, P. (2012). A review of court directed drug testing. Presentation to the Arkansas Drug Court. Retrieved from https://courts.arkansas.gov/drugcourt/2012_conference/Paul_Cary_Arkansas_Drug_Testing_4-15-12.pdf

Chesney, E., Goodwin, G. M., & Fazel, M. (2014). Risks of all-cause and suicide mortality in mental disorders: A meta-review. *World Psychiatry, 13*(2), 153–160.

Compton, M. T., & Broussard, B. (2009). *The first episode of psychosis: A guide for patients and their families.* New York: Oxford University Press.

Compton, W. M., Jones, C. M., & Baldwin, G. T. (2016). Relationship between nonmedical prescription-opioid use and heroin use. *The New England Journal of Medicine 374*(2), 154–163.

Corliss, J. (2010). *Alcohol use and abuse. Harvard Medical School special health report.* Boston: Harvard Health Publications.

Cowman, S. (2006). Safety and security in psychiatric clinical environments. In D. Richter & R. Whittington (Eds.), *Violence in mental health settings: Causes, consequences, management* (pp. 253–272). New York: Springer Science + Business Media, LLC.

Cullen, D. (2009). *Columbine.* New York: Twelve, Hachette Book Group.

Darke, S. (2011). *The life of the heroin user: Typical beginnings, trajectories and outcomes.* New York: Cambridge University Press.

Darke, S., Degenhardt, L., & Mattick, R. (2007). *Mortality amongst illicit drug users: Epidemiology, causes and interventions.* New York: Cambridge University Press.

Davenport-Hines, R. (2001). *The pursuit of oblivion: A global history of narcotics.* New York: W. W. Norton & Company.

Dhingra, K., Boduszek, D., & Klonsky, E.D. (2016). Empirically derived subgroups of self-injurious thoughts and behavior: Application of latent class analysis. *Suicide and Life-Threatening Behavior*, 1–14. doi: 10.1111/sltb.12232

Dickerson, F., Stallings, C. R., Origoni, A. E., Vaughan, C., Khushalani, S., Schroeder, J., & Yolken, R. H. (2013). Cigarette smoking among persons with schizophrenia or bipolar disorder in routine clinical settings, 1999–2011. *Psychiatric Services, 64*(1), 44–50.

Dimett, L. A., & Koerner, K. (2007). *Dialectical behavioral therapy in clinical practice: Applications across disorders and settings.* New York: Guilford Press.

Dugosh, K., Abraham, A., Seymour, B., McLoyd, K., Chalk, M., & Festinger, D. (2016). A systemic review on the use of psychosocial interventions in conjunction with medications for the treatment of opioid addiction. *Journal of Addiction Medicine, 10*(2), 93–103.

Erdogan, S. (2010). Quetiapine in substance use disorders, abuse and dependence possibility: A review. *Turkish Journal of Psychiatry, 2010*, 1–8.

Erickson, C. K. (2007). *The science of addiction: From neurobiology to treatment.* New York: W. W. Norton & Company.

Eriksen, K. A., Arman, M., Davidson, L., Sundfor, B., & Karlsson, B. (2014). Challenges in relating to mental health professionals: Perspectives of persons with severe mental illness. *International Journal of Mental Health Nursing, 23*, 110–117.

Flanagan, A. Y. (2013). *Violence in the healthcare workplace.* Sacramento, CA: CME Resource. NetCE continuing education series, Course #97451.

Frances, A. (2013a). *Essentials of psychiatric diagnosis: Responding to the challenges of DSM-5.* New York: Guilford Press.

Frances, A. (2013b). *Saving normal: An insider's revolt against out-of-control psychiatric diagnosis, DSM-5, Big Pharma, and the medicalization of ordinary life.* New York: HarperCollins Publishers.

Frances, R. J., Miller, S. I. & Mack, A. H. (Eds.). (2005). *Clinical textbook of addictive disorders* (3rd ed.). New York: Guilford Press.

Garvey, K. A., Penn, J. V., Campbell, A. L., Esposito-Smythers, C., & Spirito, A. (2009). Contracting for safety with patients: Clinical practice and forensic implications. *Journal of the American Academy of Psychiatry and the Law, 37*, 363–370.

Gelaye, B., Kajeepeta, S., & Williams, M. A. (2016). Suicidal ideation in pregnancy: An epidemiologic review. *Archive Women's Mental Health, 19*, 741–751. doi: 10.1007/s00737-016-0646-0

Gleason, B., West, A., Avula, D., Utah, O., Vogt, M., Cumpston, K., Kelly, M., Brasler, P., Wyatt, S., & Forlano, L. (2017). Collaborative public health investigation of clenbuterol-adulterated heroin outbreak—Richmond, Virginia, March–April 2015. *Journal of Public Health Management & Practice, 23*(2), 8–11.

Goode, E. (2007). *Drugs in American society* (7th ed.). New York: McGraw-Hill Publishing.

Hallgren. K. A., Ries, R. K., Atkins, D. C., Bumgardner, K., & Roy-Byrne, P. (2017). Prediction of suicide ideation and attempt among substance-using patients in primary care. *Journal of the American Board of Family Medicine, 30*(2), 150–160.

Hofmann, A. (2009). *LSD my problem child: Reflections on sacred drugs, mysticism and science* (4th English ed.). Sarasota, FL: Multidisciplinary Association for Psychedelic Studies.

Inaba, D. S., & Cohen, W. E. (2014). *Uppers, downers, all arounders: Physical and mental effects of psychoactive drugs* (8th ed.). Medford, OR: CNS Productions, Inc.

James, R. K., & Gilliland, B. E. (2013). *Crisis intervention strategies* (7th ed.). Belmont, CA: Brooks/Cole Cengage Learning.

Jansen, K. (2004). *Ketamine: Dreams and realities.* Sarasota, FL: Multidisciplinary Association for Psychedelic Studies.

Joiner, T. (2005). *Why people die by suicide.* Cambridge, MA: Harvard University Press.

Kanel, K. (2012). *A guide to crisis intervention* (4th ed.). Belmont, CA: Brooks/Cole Cengage Learning.

Katz, C., Bolton, J., & Sareen, J. (2016). The prevalence rates of suicide are likely underestimated worldwide: Why it matters. *Social Psychiatry Psychiatric Epidemiology, 51*, 125–127.

Kessler, R. C., Warner, C. H., & Ivany, C. (2015). Predicting suicides after psychiatric hospitalization in U.S. army soldiers. *Journal of the American Medical Association—Psychiatry, 72*(1), 49–57.

Kübler-Ross, E. (1969). *On death and dying: What the dying have to teach doctors, nurses, clergy & their own families.* New York: Scribner.

Kuhn, C., Swartzwelder, S., & Wilson, W. (2008). *Buzzed: The straight facts about the most used and abused drugs from alcohol to ecstasy.* New York: W. W. Norton & Company.

Lee, M. A. (2012). *Smoke signals: A social history of marijuana: Medical, recreational and scientific.* New York: Scribner.

Lee, M. A., & Shlain, B. (1985). *Acid dreams: The complete social history of LSD—The CIA, the sixties, and beyond.* New York: Grove Press.

Leneham, P. (2003). *Anabolic steroids and other performance enhancing drugs.* New York: Taylor & Francis.

Levine, P. A. (2015). *Trauma and memory: Brain and body in a search for the living past—A practical guide for understanding and working with traumatic memory.* Berkeley, CA: North American Books.

Lewis, S. J. (2016). *Legal and ethical issues for mental health clinicians: Best practices for avoiding litigation, complaints and malpractice.* Eau Claire, WI: PESI Publishing & Media.

Li, X., Shorter, D., & Kosten, T. R. (2016). Buprenorphine prescribing: To expand or not to expand. *Journal of Psychiatric Practice, 22*(3), 183–192.

Lipsky, L. V., & Burk, C. (2009). *Trauma stewardship: An everyday guide to caring for self while caring for others.* San Francisco: Berrett-Koehler Publishers.

Long, N. J., Wood, M. M., & Fecser, F. A. (2001). *Life space crisis intervention: Talking with students in conflict.* Austin, TX: Pro-Ed.

Lynch, M. J., Rabin, R. A., & George, T. P. (2012). The cannabis-psychosis link. *Psychiatric Times,* January 12.

Malekshahi, T., Tioleco, N., Ahmed, N., Campbell, A., & Haller, D. (2015). Misuse of atypical antipsychotics in conjunction with alcohol and other drugs of abuse. *Journal of Substance Abuse Treatment, 48*(1), 8–12.

Marich, J. (2012). *Fundamentals of trauma processing.* Sacramento, CA: CME Resource. NetCE continuing education series, Course #7623.

Marich, J. (2015). *Trauma made simple: Competencies in assessment, treatment and working with survivors.* Eau Claire, WI: PESI Publishing and Media.

Markel, H. (2011). *An anatomy of addiction: Sigmund Freud, William Halsted and the miracle drug cocaine.* New York: Pantheon Books.

Mate, G. (2010). *In the realm of hungry ghosts: Close encounters with addiction.* Berkley, CA: North Atlantic Books.

McKay, M., Wood, J. C., & Brantley, J. (2007). *The dialectical behavioral treatment skills workbook: Practical DBT exercises for learning mindfulness, interpersonal effectiveness, emotion regulation and distress tolerance.* Oakland, CA: New Harbinger Publications.

McKenna, K., & Paterson, B. (2006). Locating training within a strategic organizational response to aggression and violence. In D. Richter & R. Whittington (Eds.), *Violence in mental health settings: Causes, consequences, management.* New York: Springer Science + Business Media, LLC.

Mee-Lee, D., McLellan, A. T., & Miller, S. D. (2010). What works in substance abuse and dependence treatment. In B. L. Duncan, S. D. Miller, B. E., Wampold, & M. A. Hubble (Eds.), *The heart & soul of change: Delivering what works in therapy* (2nd ed.). Washington, DC: American Psychiatric Association.

Miotto, K., Darakjian, J., Basch, J., Murray, S., Zogg, J., & Rawson, R. (2001). Gamma-hydroxybutyric acid: Patterns of use, effects and withdrawal. *The American Journal on Addictions, 10*, 232–241.

Morgan, C. J., & Curran, H. V. (2011). Ketamine use: A review. *Addiction, 107*, 27–38.

Morrison, J. (2014). *The first interview* (4th ed.). New York: Guilford Press.

Morrison, J. (2015). *When psychological problems mask medical disorders: A guide for psychotherapists* (2nd ed.). New York: Guilford Press.

National Academies of Sciences, Engineering, and Medicine. (2017). *The health effects of cannabis and cannabinoids: The current state of evidence and recommendations for research.* Washington, DC: The National Academies Press.

National Institute on Drug Abuse. (1992). *Inhalant abuse: A volatile research agenda, Research monograph series 129.* Rockville, MD: National Institute on Drug Abuse.

Needham, I. (2006). Psychological responses following exposure to violence. In D. Richter & R. Whittington (Eds.), *Violence in mental health settings: Causes, consequences, management.* New York: Springer Science + Business Media, LLC.

Norcross, J. C. (2010). The therapeutic relationship. In B. L. Duncan, S. D. Miller, B. E. Wampold,

& M.A. Hubble (Eds.), *The heart & soul of change: Delivering what works in therapy* (2nd ed.). Washington, DC: American Psychiatric Association.

O'Hare, T., Shen, C., & Sherrer, M. (2014). Lifetime trauma and suicide attempts in people with severe mental illness. *Community Mental Health Journal, 50*, 673–680. doi: 10.1007/s10597-013-9658-7

Olfson, M., Marcus, S. C., & Bridge, J. A. (2014). Focusing suicide prevention on periods of high risk. *Journal of the American Medical Association, 311*(11), 1107–1108.

Ott, J. (1993). *Pharmacotheon: Entheogenic drugs, their plant sources and history.* Kennewick, WA: Natural Products Co.

Paris, J. (2015). *The intelligent clinician's guide to the DSM-5* (2nd ed.). New York: Oxford University Press.

Peck, M. S. (1978). *The road less traveled: A new psychology of love, traditional values and spiritual growth.* New York: Touchstone.

Porrata, T. (2005). GHB recognition, treatment and risk management. Presentation at the Sixth National Conference on Addiction and Criminal Behavior, September 2005.

Preston, J. D., O'Neal, J. H., & Talaga, M. C. (2013). *Handbook of clinical psychopharmacology for therapists* (7th ed.). Oakland, CA: New Harbinger Publications.

Prins, A., Ouimette, P., Kimerling, R., Cameron, R., Hugelshofer, D., Shaw-Hegwer, J., Thrailkill, A., Gusman, F., & Sheikh, J. (2003). The primary care PTSD screen (PC-PTSD): Development and operating characteristics. *Primary Care Psychiatry, 9*(1), 9–14.

Prozialeck, W. C., Jivan, J. K., & Andurkar, S. V. (2012). Pharmacology of kratom: An emerging botanical agent with stimulant, analgesic and opioid-like effects. *The Journal of the American Osteopathic Association, 112*(12), 792–799.

Quinones, S. (2015). *Dreamland: The true tale of America's opioid epidemic.* New York: Bloomsbury Press.

Ramsey, J. (2016). More menace than miracle: In southwest Virginia, drug touted for helping addicts now seen as part of the problem. *Richmond Times-Dispatch.* August 7, A1.

Ribeiro, J. D., Franklin, J. C., Fox, K. R., Bentley, K. H., Kleiman, E. M., Chang, B. P., & Nock, M. K. (2016). Self-injurious thoughts and behaviors as risk factors for future suicide ideation, attempts, and death: A meta-analysis of longitudinal studies. *Psychological Medicine, 46*(2), 225–236.

Richter, D. (2006). Nonphysical conflict management and de-escalation. In D. Richter & R. Whittington (Eds.), *Violence in mental health settings: Causes, consequences, management.* New York: Springer Science + Business Media, LLC.

Richter, D., & Whittington, R. (Eds.). (2006). *Violence in mental health settings: Causes, consequences, management.* New York: Springer Science + Business Media, LLC.

Roffman, R. A., & Stephens R. S. (Eds.). (2006). *Cannabis dependence: Its nature, consequences and treatment.* Cambridge, UK: Cambridge University Press.

Rose, M. (2012). *Opioid abuse and dependence.* Sacramento, CA: CME Resource. NetCE continuing education series, Course #9696.

Rose, M. (2013). *Club drugs.* Sacramento, CA: CME Resource. NetCE continuing education series, Course #9699.

Rose, M. (2016). *Novel psychoactive substances: Spice, bath salts and beyond.* Sacramento, CA: CME Resource. NetCE continuing education series, Course #96910.

Ross, E., Reisfield, G., Watson, M., Chronister, C., & Goldberger B. (2012). Psychoactive "bath salts" intoxication with methylenedioxypyrovalerone. *The American Journal of Medicine, 125*, 854–858.

Sadock, B. J., Sadock, V. A., & Ruiz, P. (2015). *Kaplan & Sadock's synopsis of psychiatry: Behavioral sciences/clinical psychiatry* (11th ed.). Philadelphia, PA: Wolters Kluwer.

Sansone, R., & Sansone, L. (2010). Is seroquel developing an illicit reputation for misuse/abuse? *Psychiatry, 7*(1), 13–16.

Sawyer, C., Peters, M. L., & Willis, J. (2013). Self-efficacy of beginning counselors to counsel clients in crisis. *Journal of Counselor Preparation and Supervision, 5*(2), 30–43.

Schiller, L., & Bennett, A. (1994). *The quiet room: A journey out of the torment of madness.* New York: Warner Books.

Schultes, R. E., Hormann, A., & Ratsch, C. (2001). *Plants of the gods: Their sacred, healing, and hallucinogenic powers.* Rochester, VT: Healing Arts Press.

Seppala, M. D., & Rose, M. E. (2010). *Prescription painkillers: History, pharmacology, and treatment.* Center City, MN: Hazelden.

Shah, A., Bhat, R., Zarate-Escudero, S., DeLeo, D., & Erlangson, A. (2016). Suicide rates in five-year age-bands after the age of 60 years: The international landscape. *Aging and Mental Health, 20*(2), 131–138.

Shulgin, A., & Shulgin, A. (2011). *PiHKAL: A chemical love story.* Berkeley, CA: Transform Press.

Shulgin, A., & Shulgin, A. (2014). *PiHKAL: The continuation*. Berkeley, CA: Transform Press.

Siegel, R. K. (2005). *Intoxication: The universal drive for mind-altering substances*. Rochester, VT: Park Street Press.

Steinert, T. (2006). Prediction of violence in inpatient settings. In D. Richter & R. Whittington (Eds.), *Violence in mental health settings: Causes, consequences, management*. New York: Springer Science + Business Media, LLC.

Strassman, R. (2001). *DMT: The spirit molecule: A doctor's revolutionary research into the biology of near-death and mystical experiences*. Rochester, VT: Park Street Press.

Streatfield, D. (2001). *Cocaine: An unauthorized biography*. New York: Picador.

Thies, T. A. (2009). *Legally stoned: 14 mind-altering substances you can obtain and use without breaking the law*. New York: Citadel Press.

Thompson, A. D., Nelson, B., Yuen, H. P., Lin, A., Amminger, G. P., McGorry, P. D., Wood, S. J., & Yung, A. R. (2014). Sexual trauma increases the risk of developing psychosis in an ultra-high-risk "prodromal" population. *Schizophrenia Bulletin, 40*(3), 697–706.

Trent, J. (2014). *A review of psychiatric emergencies*. Sacramento, CA: CME Resource. NetCE continuing education series, Course #96771.

Vakkalanda, J. P., Charlto, N. P., & Holstege, C. P. (2017). Epidemiologic trends in loperamide abuse and misuse. *Annals of Emergency Medicine, 69*(1), 73–78. doi: 10.1016/j.annemergmed.2016.08.444

van der Kolk, B. A. (2014). *The body keeps the score: Brain, mind, and body in the healing of trauma*. New York: Penguin Books.

VanderWeele, T. J., Li, S., Tsai, A. C., & Kawachi, I. (2016). Association between religious service attendance and lower suicide rates among U.S. women. *Journal of the American Medical Association—Psychiatry, 73*(8), 845–851.

Wainwright, T. (2016). *Narconomics: How to run a drug cartel*. New York: Public Affairs.

Wakefield, J. C. (2013). *DSM–5*: An overview of changes and controversies. *Clinical Social Work Journal, 41*, 139–154.

Webb, J. (2011). Gabapentin: Another drug of misuse? *British Columbia Drug and Poison Information Center Tablet, 17*(3), 12–13.

Weisheit, R., & White, W. L. (2009). *Methamphetamine: Its history, pharmacology, and treatment*. Center City, MN: Hazelden.

Whittington, R., & Richter, D. (2006). From the individual to the interpersonal: Environment and interaction in the escalation of violence in mental health settings. In D. Richter & R. Whittington (Eds.), *Violence in mental health settings: Causes, consequences, management*. New York: Springer Science + Business Media, LLC.

Williams, J. F., & Storck, M. (2007). Inhalant abuse. *Pediatrics, 119*(5), 1009–1017.

Winstock, A., Mitchenson, L., Ramsey, J., Davies, S., Puchnarewicz, M., & Marsden, J. (2011). Mephedrone: Use, subjective effects and health risks. *Addiction, 106*, 1991–1996.

Ziednosis, D. M, Guydish, J., Williams, J., Steinberg, M., & Fould, J. (2006). Barriers and solutions to addressing tobacco dependence in addiction treatment programs. *Alcohol Research & Health, 29*(3), 228–235.

Made in the USA
Monee, IL
18 January 2021